Just Enough **Scandinavian**

Danish • Norwegian • Swedish

£ 1- 50

Printed on recyclable paper

PASSPORT BOOKS
a division of *NTC Publishing Group*
Lincolnwood, Illinois USA

1995 Printing

This edition first published in 1985 by Passport Books,
a division of NTC Publishing Group, 4255 West Touhy
Avenue, Lincolnwood (Chicago), Illinois 60646-1975 U.S.A.
Originally published by Pan Books, © L. Bernadotte, D.L.
Ellis, M. Hoddevik, B. Stokvis 1984. All rights reserved.
No part of this book may be reproduced, stored in a retrieval
system, or transmitted in any form or by any means,
electronic, mechanical, photocopying or otherwise, without
the prior written permission of National Textbook Company.
Manufactured in the United States of America.

5 6 7 8 9 0 QB 9 8 7 6

Contents

Using the phrase book and a note on the pronunciation system

- This phrase book is designed to help you get by in Denmark, Norway and Sweden, to get what you want or need. It concentrates on the simplest but most effective way you can express these needs in an unfamiliar language.
- The CONTENTS for each different language section gives you a good idea of which pages to consult for the phrase you need.
- The INDEX at the end of each language section gives more detailed information about where to look for your phrase. When you have found the right page you will be given:

  either   – the exact phrase

  or   – help in making up a suitable sentence

  and   – help in getting the pronunciation right

- The English sentences in **bold type** will be useful for you in a variety of different situations, so they are worth learning by heart.
- In some cases you will find help in understanding what people say to *you*, in reply to your questions.
- Note especially these two sections:

  Everyday expressions

  Shop talk

  You are sure to want to refer to them most frequently.
- When you arrive in the foreign country make good use of the tourist information offices.

- The pronunciation system in this book is founded on three assumptions: firstly, that it is not possible to describe in print the sounds of a foreign language in such a way that the English speaker with no phonetic training will produce them accurately, or even intelligibly; secondly, that perfect pronunciation is not essential for communication; and lastly that the average visitor abroad is more interested in achieving successful communication than in learning how to pronounce new speech sounds. Observation and experience have shown these assumptions to be justified. The most important characteristic of the present system, therefore, is that it makes no attempt whatsoever to teach the sounds of the other language, but uses instead the nearest English sounds to them. The sentences transcribed for pronunciation are designed to be read as naturally as possible, as if they were ordinary English and with no attempt to make the words sound 'foreign.' In this way you will still sound quite American, but you will at the same time be understood. Practice always helps performance and it is a good idea to rehearse out loud any of the sentences you know you are going to need. When you come to the point of using them, say them with conviction.

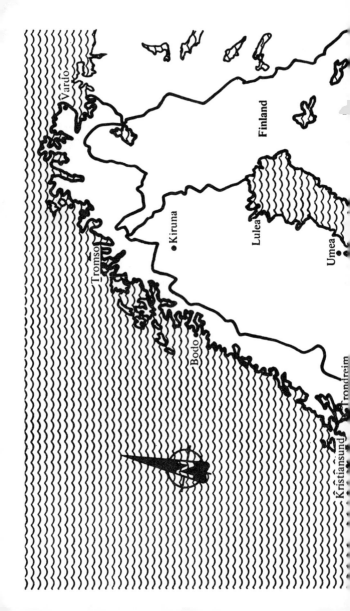

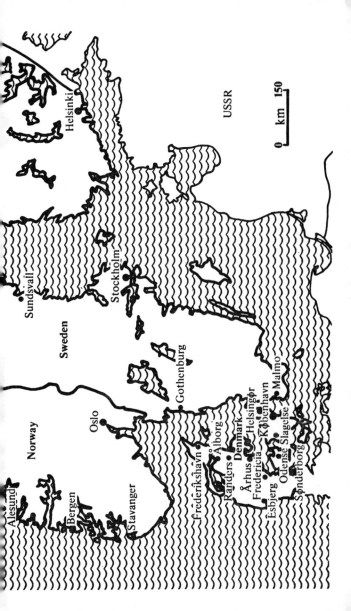

Danish

Danish

D. L. Ellis, B. Stokvis

Pronunciation **Dr J. Baldwin**

Useful address
75 Rockefeller Plaza
New York, NY 10019
(212) 582-2802

Contents

Everyday expressions

[See also 'Shop talk', p. 50]

- Although you will find the correct greetings listed below, the Danes commonly use the informal **dav** (dow) to express all of these.

Hello	**Dav/hej** dow/hi
Good morning	**Godmorgen** go-morn
Good day	**Goddag** go-day
Good evening	**Godaften** go-aften
Good night	**Godnat** go-nat
Goodbye	**Farvel** far-vel
Yes	**Ja** ya
Thank you	**Tak** tuck
Thank you very much	**Mange tak** mung-er tuck
That's right	**Det er rigtigt** day air regtit
No	**Nej** nigh
No thank you	**Nej tak** nigh tuck
I disagree	**Det er ikke rigtigt** day air igger regtit
Excuse me	**Undskyld** on-skool
That's good	**Det er godt** day air got
That's no good	**Det er ikke godt** day air igger got
I know	**Det ved jeg** day vethe yigh

It doesn't matter	**Det gør ikke noget**
	day gur igger no-et
Where's the toilet please?	**Hvor er toilettet?**
	vor air toilet-tet
Do you speak English?	**Taler De engelsk?**
	tayler dee eng-elsk
I'm sorry . . .	**Desværre . . .**
	desvair . . .
I don't speak Danish	**Jeg taler ikke dansk**
	yigh tayler igger dansk
I only speak a little Danish	**Jeg taler kun lidt dansk**
	yigh tayler kon lit dansk
I don't understand	**Jeg forstår det ikke**
	yigh forstor day igger
Please can you . . .	**Vil De være så venlig at . . .**
	vil dee vair saw venlee at . . .
repeat that?	**gentage det?**
	ghen-tay day
speak more slowly?	**tale langsommere?**
	tayler lung-sommer-er
write it down?	**skrive det ned?**
	skreever day nethe
What is this called in Danish?	**Hvad hedder det på dansk?**
[*point*]	va hither day paw dansk

Crossing the border

ESSENTIAL INFORMATION

- Don't waste time before you leave rehearsing what you are going to say to the border officials – the chances are that you won't have to say anything at all, especially if you travel by air. It is more useful to check that you have all your documents handy for the journey: passports, tickets, money, travelers' checks, insurance documents, driver's license and car registration documents.
  Look out for these signs: **TOLD** (customs)
  GRÆNSE (border) **GRÆNSEPOLITI** (frontier police)

● You may be asked routine questions by the customs officials [*see below*]. If you have to give personal details see 'Meeting people' p. 16. The other important answer to know is 'Nothing': **Ingenting** (ing-on-ting).

ROUTINE QUESTIONS

Passport?	**Pas?**
	p*a*s
Insurance?	**Forsikring?**
	for-s*ee*k-ring
Registration document? (logbook)	**Indregistreringsattest?**
	in-reggee-stray-rings-att*e*st
Ticket, please?	**Deres billet?**
	d*ai*r-es bill*e*t
Have you anything to declare?	**Har De noget at fortolde?**
	har dee no-et at for-t*o*ller
Where are you going?	**Hvor skal De hen?**
	vor skal dee h*e*n
How long are you staying?	**Hvor længe bliver De?**
	vor leng-er bl*ee*r dee
Where have you come from?	**Hvor Kommer De fra?**
	vor k*o*mmer dee fra

Meeting people

[*See also 'Everyday expressions', p. 14*]

Breaking the ice

How are you?	**Hvordan har De det?**
	vor-d*a*n har dee day
I am here . . .	**Jeg er her . . .**
	y*igh* air hair . . .
on vacation	**på ferie**
	paw f*ai*ree
on business	**på forretningsrejse**
	paw forr*e*tnings-rye-ser

Can I offer you . . .	**Må jeg tilbyde Dem . . .** maw yigh til-b*oo*ther dem . . .
a drink?	**en drink?** ain drink
a cigarette?	**en cigaret?** ain cigar*e*t
a cigar?	**en cigar?** ain cig*a*r
Are you staying long?	**Bliver De her længe?** bl*ee*r dee hair leng-er

Name

What's your name?	**Hvad hedder De?** v*a* hither dee
My name is . . .	**Jeg hedder . . .** yigh hither . . .

Family

Are you married?	**Er De gift?** air dee gift
I am . . .	**Jeg er . . .** yigh air . . .
married	**gift** gift
single	**ugift** *oo*-gift
This is . . .	**Det er . . .** day air . . .
my wife	**min kone** mean k*o*ner
my husband	**min mand** mean man
my son	**min søn** mean sern
my daughter	**min datter** mean d*a*tter
my boyfriend	**min ven** mean ven
my girlfriend	**min veninde** mean ven-*een*-ner
my colleague (male or female)	**min kollega** mean koll*ay*-ga
Do you have any children?	**Har De børn?** har dee burn

Danish

I have . . .	**Jeg har . . .**
	yigh har . . .
one daughter	**en datter**
	ain datter
one son	**en søn**
	ain sern
two daughters	**to døtre**
	toe der-trer
three sons	**tre sønner**
	tray sern-er
No, I haven't any children	**Nej, jeg har ingen børn**
	nigh yigh har eeng-en burn

Where you live

Are you . . .	**Er De . . .**
	air dee . . .
Danish?	**dansker?**
	dan-sker
German?	**tysker?**
	too-sker
Swedish?	**svensker?**
	sven-sker
I am . . .	**Jeg er . . .**
	yigh air . . .
American	**amerikaner**
	amair-ee-kayner
English	**englænder**
	eng-len-ner

[For other nationalities see p. 104]

I live . . .	**Jeg bor . . .**
	yigh bore . . .
in London	**i London**
	ee lon-don
in England	**i England**
	ee eng-lan
in America	**i Amerika**
	ee amair-ee-ka
in Canada	**i Canada**
	ee canada
in the west	**i Vest**
	ee vest
in the east	**i Øst**
	ee urst

[*For other countries, p. 102*]

For the businessman and woman

I'm from . . . (firm's name)	**Jeg er fra . . .** yigh air fra . . .
I have an appointment with . . .	**Jeg har en aftale med . . .** yigh har ain *ow*-tayler methe . . .
This is my card	**Her er mit visitkort** hair air meet vee-*seet*-kort
I'm sorry, I'm late	**Undskyld jeg kommer for sent** *on*-skool yigh kommer for sent
Can I make another appointment?	**Kan jeg få en anden aftale?** kan yigh faw ain *an*-on *ow*-tayler
I'm staying at the hotel . . .	**Jeg bor på hotel . . .** yigh bore paw hot*el* . . .

Asking the way

ESSENTIAL INFORMATION

• Keep a lookout for all these place names as you will find them on shops, maps, and signs.

WHAT TO SAY

Excuse me, please	**Undskyld** *on*-skool
How do I get . . .	**Hvordan kommer jeg . . .** vor-d*an* kommer yigh . . .
to the airport?	**til lufthavnen?** til *looft*-how-nen
to Copenhagen?	**til København?** til ker-ben-*hown*
to the beach?	**til stranden?** til str*un*-nen

Danish

20/Asking the way

How do I get . . .	Hvordan kommer jeg . . .
	vor-d*a*n k*o*mmer yigh . . .
to the bus station?	**til busterminalen?**
	til b*oo*s-tair-mee-nay-len
to the hotel (Ritz)?	**til hotel (Ritz)?**
	til hotel (reets)
to the market?	**til markedet?**
	til m*a*r-kethet
to the police station?	**til politistationen?**
	til poli-*tee*-stash-yonen
to the port?	**til havnen?**
	til h*ow*-nen
to the post office?	**til posthuset?**
	til posst-h*oo*-set
to the railway station?	**til banegården?**
	til b*a*ner-gaw-en
to the sports stadium?	**til stadion?**
	til st*a*y-dee-on
to the Tivoli?	**til Tivoli?**
	til *tee*-vo-lee
to the tourist information office?	**til turistkontoret?**
	til tour*i*st-kon-toe-ret
to the town center?	**til byens centrum?**
	til b*oo*-ens c*e*n-trum
to the town hall?	**til rådhuset?**
	til rothe-h*oo*-set
Excuse me, please	**Undskyld**
	*o*n-skool
Is there . . . near by?	**Er der . . . i nærheden?**
	air dair . . . ee n*ai*r-hethen
an art gallery	**et kunstgalleri**
	it konst-galler*ee*
a bakery	**en bager**
	ain bay-er
a bank	**en bank**
	ain bunk
a bar	**en bar**
	ain bar
a botanical garden	**en botanisk have**
	ain bo-*tay*-nisk h*a*ver
a bus stop	**et busstoppested**
	it b*oo*s-stop-per-stethe

a butcher's	**en slagter** ain sl*a*gter
a café	**en café** ain caf*é*
a cake shop	**et konditori** it con-dee-toe-r*ee*
a campsite	**en campingplads** ain *c*ampingplas
a car park	**en parkeringsplads** ain par-k*ai*r-ringsplas
a chemist's/drugstore	**et apotek** it uppo-t*a*ke
a church	**en kirke** ain k*ee*r-ker
a cinema/movie theater	**en biograf** ain bee-o-gr*a*hf
a delicatessen	**en viktualieforretning** ain vic-too-*a*y-lee-er-forr*e*tning
a dentist's	**en tandlæge** ain t*a*n-layer
a department store	**et stormagasin** it store-ma-ga-s*ee*n
a disco	**et diskotek** it disco-t*a*ke
a doctor's office	**en læge/doktor** ain l*a*yer/d*o*ctor
a dry cleaner's	**et renseri** it ren-ser-r*ee*
a fishmonger's	**en fiskehandler** ain f*i*sker-hanler
a garage (for repairs)	**et autoværksted** it *ow*-toe-v*ai*rk-stethe
a greengrocer's	**en grønthandler** ain gr*u*nt-hanler
a grocery store	**en købmand** ain k*u*r-man
a hairdresser's	**en frisør** ain free-s*er*
a hardware shop	**en isenkram** ain *ee*-sern-krum
a hospital	**et hospital/sygehus** it h*o*e-speet*a*l/s*oo*-yer-h*oo*s

Danish

Is there . . . near by?	Er der . . . i nærheden?
	air dair . . . ee nair-hethen
a hotel	**et hotel**
	it hotel
an ice-cream shop	**en iskiosk**
	ain *ees*-kiosk
a laundry	**et vaskeri**
	it vasker-*ree*
a local sickness insurance office	**et sygesikringskontor**
	it *soo*-yer-*seek*-rings-kon-*tor*
a museum	**et museum**
	it moo-s*ay*-oom
a night club	**en natklub**
	ain n*a*t-kloob
a park	**en park**
	ain park
a petrol/gas station	**en tankstation**
	ain t*u*nk-stash-yon
a post box/mailbox	**en postkasse**
	ain p*o*sst-kasser
a public toilet	**et offentligt toilet**
	it *o*ffent-lit toil*et*
a restaurant	**en restaurant**
	ain restor*u*ng
a (snack) bar	**en (snack) bar**
	ain (sn*a*ck) bar
a sports ground	**en sportsplads**
	ain sp*o*rtsplas
a supermarket	**et supermarked**
	it s*u*per-markethe
a sweet shop	**en chokoladeforretning**
	ain shoko-l*ai*ther-forretning
an (indoor) swimming pool	**en svømmehal**
	ain sv*e*r-mer-hal
a telephone (booth)	**en telefonboks**
	ain teleph*o*ne-box
a theater	**et teater**
	it tee-*air*-ter
a tobacco shop	**en tobakshandler**
	ain toe-b*u*ks-hanler
a travel agent's	**et rejsebureau**
	it r*y*e-ser-bee-r*o*

a youth hostel	**et vandrerhjem**
	it v*u*n-drer-yem
a zoo	**en zoologisk have**
	ain so-o-*lo*-gisk haver

DIRECTIONS

- Asking where a place is, or if a place is near by, is one thing; making sense of the answer is another.
- Here are some of the most important key directions and replies.

Left	**Venstre**
	v*e*n-strer
Right	**Højre**
	h*oy*-rer
Straight on	**Lige ud**
	lee-er *oo*the
There	**Der**
	dair
First left/right	**Første vej til venstre/højre**
	f*i*rst-er vy til v*e*n-strer/h*oy*-rer
Second left/right	**Anden vej til venstre/højre**
	*a*n-on vy til v*e*n-strer/h*oy*-rer
At the crossroads	**Ved krydset**
	vethe k*roo*-set
At the traffic lights	**Ved trafiklyset**
	vethe traf-f*i*k-*loo*-set
At the traffic rotary	**Ved rundkørslen**
	vethe r*o*n-kerslen
At the level crossing	**Ved jernbaneoverskæringen**
	vethe y*air*baner-*o*-er-skair-ing-en
It's near/far	**Det er nær ved/langt væk**
	day air n*air* vethe/l*a*ngt vek
One kilometre	**En kilometer**
	ain kilom*ai*t-ter
Two kilometres	**To kilometer**
	t*oe* kilom*ai*t-ter
Five minutes . . .	**Fem minutters . . .**
	fem mee-n*oo*ters . . .
on foot	**gang**
	gung
by car	**kørsel**
	k*e*r-sel

Take . . .	**Tag . . .**
	tay . . .
the bus	**bussen**
	b*oo*ssen
the train	**toget**
	t*oe*-et

[*For public transport, see p. 90*]

The tourist information office

ESSENTIAL INFORMATION

- Most towns in Denmark have a tourist information office; in smaller towns the local travel agent (**REJSEBUREAU**) provides the same information and services.
- Key word to look for: **TURISTINFORMATION** and this sign
- If your main concern is to find and book accommodation, **VÆRELSEANVISNING** is the best place to go to.
- Tourist offices offer you free information in the form of printed leaflets, fold-outs, brochures, lists and plans.
- For finding a tourist office, see p. 24.

WHAT TO SAY

Please, have you got . . .	**Har De . . .**
	har dee . . .
a plan of the town?	**et bykort?**
	it b*oo*-kort
a list of hotels?	**en liste over hoteller?**
	ain l*ee*-ster o-er hotel-ler
a list of campsites?	**en liste over campingpladser?**
	ain l*ee*-ster o-er c*a*mping-plasser

a list of restaurants?	**en liste over restauranter?**
	ain *lee*-ster o-er restor*u*ng-er
a list of events?	**en liste over begivenheder?**
	ain *lee*-ster o-er beg*ee*ven-hether
a leaflet on the town?	**en brochure om byen?**
	ain broch*u*re om b*oo*-en
a leaflet on the region?	**en brochure om egnen?**
	ain broch*u*re om *eye*-nen
a railway/bus timetable?	**en tog/buskøreplan?**
	ain t*oe*/b*oo*s-ker-er-pl*a*n
In English, please	**På engelsk**
	paw *eng*-elsk
How much do I owe you?	**Hvor meget bliver det?**
	vor *my*-et bl*ee*r day

LIKELY ANSWERS

You need to understand when the answer is 'No'. You should be able to tell by the assistant's expression, tone of voice and gesture but there are some language clues, such as:

No	**Nej**
	nigh
I'm sorry	**Desværre**
	desv*air*
I don't have a list of hotels	**Jeg har ikke en liste over hoteller**
	yigh h*ar* igger ain *lee*-ster o-er hotel-ler
I haven't got any left	**Jeg har ikke flere**
	yigh h*ar* igger fl*ee*-er
It's free	**Det er gratis**
	day air gr*a*tis

Accommodation

Hotel

ESSENTIAL INFORMATION

- If you want hotel-type
  accommodation, all the following
  words in capital letters are worth
  looking for on signs:
  HOTEL
  MISSIONSHOTEL (comfortable
  accommodation at a reasonable
  price – no alcohol served)
  PENSIONAT (boarding house)
  MOTEL
  KRO (country inn)
  VÆRELSE (room to let in private home – bed and breakfast)
- A list of hotels in the town or district can usually be obtained at
  the local tourist office (see p. 24).
- Hotels in Denmark are not graded by stars but the price level is
  a fair guide to the standard.
- Not all hotels provide meals apart from breakfast; inquire about
  this, on arrival, at the reception.
- The price quoted for the room is for the room itself, per night
  and not per person. It usually includes service charges and taxes,
  but quite often does not include breakfast.
- Breakfast is continental style with coffee or tea and rolls, butter
  and jam and mild Danish cheese. Some larger hotels also offer a
  MORGENBUFFET where you can help yourself to cereal,
  yoghurt, juice and the Danish breakfast pastry **WIENERBRØD**.
- Upon arrival you may be asked to fill in a registration form which
  most often bears an English translation.
- Finding a hotel, see p. 26.

WHAT TO SAY

I have a reservation	**Jeg har reserveret et værelse** yigh har reser-*vai*rt it *v*air-el-ser

Have you any vacancies, please?	**Har De et ledigt værelse?**
	h*a*r dee it l*a*y-theet v*ai*r-el-ser
Can I book a room?	**Har De et værelse?**
	h*a*r dee it v*ai*r-el-ser
It's for . . .	**Det er til . . .**
	day air til . . .
one person	**en person**
	*ai*n pair-*so*ne
two people	**to personer**
	t*oe* pair-s*o*-ner
[*For numbers, see p. 96*]	
It's for . . .	**Det er . . .**
	day air . . .
one night	**en overnatning**
	*ai*n o-er-natning
two nights	**to overnatninger**
	t*oe* o-er-natning-er
one week	**en uges overnatning**
	ain *oo*-ers o-er-natning
two weeks	**to ugers overnatning**
	t*oe* *oo*-ers o-er-natning
I would like . . .	**Jeg vil gerne have . . .**
	yigh vil g*ai*r-ner h*a* . . .
a room	**et værelse**
	it v*ai*r-el-ser
two rooms	**to værelser**
	t*oe* v*ai*r-el-ser
a room with a single bed	**et enkeltværelse**
	it *ai*n-kelt-v*ai*r-el-ser
a room with two single beds	**et værelse med to senge**
	it v*ai*r-el-ser methe t*oe* s*e*ng-er
a room with a double bed	**et dobbeltværelse**
	it d*o*bbelt-v*ai*r-el-ser
I would like a room . . .	**Jeg vil gerne have et værelse . . .**
	yigh vil g*ai*r-ner h*a* it v*ai*r-el-ser. . .
with a toilet	**med toilet**
	methe toil*e*t
with a bathroom	**med bad**
	methe b*a*the
with a shower	**med brusebad**
	methe br*oo*-ser-b*a*the
with a cot	**med en barneseng**
	methe ain b*a*rner-seng

Danish

I'd like . . . | **Jeg vil gerne have . . .**
yigh vil gair-ner ha . . .

full board | **fuld pension**
full pungs-yon

half board | **halv pension**
hal pungs-yon

Do you serve meals? | **Er her restaurant?**
air hair restorung

At what time is . . . | **Hvornår serveres der . . .**
vornor sevvairs dair . . .

breakfast? | **morgenmad?**
morn-mathe

lunch? | **frokost?**
fraw-kost

dinner? | **middag?**
medda

How much is it? | **Hvor meget koster det?**
vor my-et koster day

Can I look at the room? | **Må jeg se værelset?**
maw yigh say vair-el-set

I'd prefer a room . . . | **Jeg foretrækker et værelse . . .**
yigh fortrekker it vair-el-ser . . .

at the front/back | **mod gaden/gården**
mothe gathen/gaw-en

OK, I'll take it | **Det tager jeg**
day tar yigh

No thanks, I won't take it | **Nej tak, jeg vil ikke have det**
nigh tuck yigh vil igger ha day

The key to number (10) please | **Nøglen til nummer (ti)**
noy-len til noom-mer (tee)

Please, may I have . . . | **Jeg vil gerne have . . .**
yigh vil gair-ner ha . . .

a coat hanger? | **en bøjle?**
ain boiler

a glass? | **et glas?**
it glas

a towel? | **et håndklæde?**
it hon-klerthe

some soap? | **et stykke sæbe**
it stookker say-ber

an ashtray? | **et askebæger?**
it asker-bayer

another pillow?	**en hovedpude til** ain ho-ethe-*poo*-ther til
Come in!	**Kom ind!** kom in
One moment, please!	**Et øjeblik!** it *oy*-er-blik
Please can you . . .	**Vil De være så venlig at . . .** vil dee v*air* saw v*en*lee at . . .
do this laundry/dry-cleaning?	**sende dette til vask/rensning?** s*en*ner d*et*ter til v*ask*/r*ens*-ning
help me with my luggage?	**hjælpe mig med bagagen?** y*el*per my methe bag*ay*she
call me a taxi for . . .?	**bestille en taxa til klokken . . .?** best*il*ler ain t*ax*a til cl*ock*en . . .
call me at . . .?	**vække mig klokken . . .?** v*ek*ker my cl*ock*en . . .
[*For times, see p. 98*] The bill, please	**Må jeg få regningen?** maw yigh faw r*ye*-ningen
Is service included?	**Er det med betjening?** air day methe bech*ai*ning
I think this is wrong	**Jeg tror, der er en fejl** yigh tror dair air ain f*i*le
May I have a receipt?	**Må jeg få en kvittering?** maw yigh f*aw* ain kveett*ai*ring

At breakfast

Some more . . ., please	**Jeg vil gerne have mere . . .** yigh vil g*air*-ner ha m*e*re . . .
coffee	**kaffe** k*u*ffer
tea	**the** tay
bread	**brød** br*er*the
butter	**smør** smer
jam	**syltetøj** s*i*lter-toy
May I have a boiled egg?	**Må jeg få et blødkogt æg?** maw yigh f*aw* it bl*er*the-kogt aig

Danish

LIKELY REACTIONS

Have you an identity document?	**Har Det ID-kort eller pas?** har day *ee-day*-kort eller p*a*s
What is your name? [*see p. 17*]	**Hvad er Deres navn?** v*a* air dair-es n*ou*n
Sorry, we're full	**Desværre, alt er optaget** desv*ai*r alt air *o*p-tay-et
I haven't any rooms left	**Jeg har ingen ledige værelser** yigh har *ee*ng-en l*a*y-thee-er v*ai*r-el-ser
Do you want to have a look?	**Vil De se det?** vil dee s*a*y day
How many people is it for?	**Hvor mange personer er det til?** vor m*u*ng-er pair-soner air day til
From (7 o'clock) onwards	**Fra (klokken syv)** fra (clocken s*oo*)
From (midday) onwards	**Fra (klokken tolv middag)** fra (clocken tol m*e*dda)
[*For times, see p. 98*]	
It's (30) kroner	**Det koster (tredive) kroner** day koster (tr*e*the-ver) kr*o*ner

[*For numbers, see p. 96*]

Camping and youth hostelling

ESSENTIAL INFORMATION

Camping

- Look for the words: **CAMPINGPLADS** and **TELTPLADS**.
- Danish campsites are divided into 1, 2 and 3 star categories. 3 star sites have every facility; about a hundred are so well equipped that they stay open all year.
- An international camping carnet, obtainable from motoring organizations, national camping clubs etc., is obligatory but the campsite manager is also authorized to issue temporary passes for those who have left home without one.
- If you cannot find a campsite and wish to use private land be sure to get the landowner's permission.

Youth hostels

- Look for the word:
  VANDRERHJEM or this sign
- You must have a YHA card.
  You can buy a guest card, however,
  if you have not obtained one
  but these are comparatively
  expensive.
- Danish youth hostels are also open
  to tourists with cars. Many have
  family rooms to take 4 to 8 people;
  these are very popular and
  should be booked in advance.

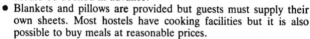

- Blankets and pillows are provided but guests must supply their own sheets. Most hostels have cooking facilities but it is also possible to buy meals at reasonable prices.
- For buying and replacing camping equipment, see p. 48.

WHAT TO SAY

Have you any vacancies?	**Har De ledige pladser?**
	har dee *lay*-thee-er pl*a*sser
It's for . . .	**Det er til . . .**
	day air til . . .
one adult/person	**en voksen/person**
	ain v*o*ksen/pair-s*o*ne
two adults/people	**to voksne/personer**
	t*oe* voksner/pair-s*o*-ner
and one child	**og et barn**
	o *i*t barn
and two children	**og to børn**
	o t*oe* burn
It's for . . .	**Det er for . . .**
	day air for . . .
one night	**en nat**
	*ai*n nat
one week	**en uge**
	*ai*n *oo*-er
How much is it . . .	**Hvor meget koster det . . .**
	vor my-et k*o*ster day . . .
for the tent?	**for teltet?**
	for t*e*ltet

Danish

How much is it . . .
Hvor meget koster det . . .
vor my-et koster day . . .

for the camper?
for campingvognen?
for camping-vonen

for the car?
for bilen?
for beelen

for the electricity?
for elektricitet?
for elektree-seetate

per person?
per person?
pair pair-sone

per day/night?
per dag/nat?
pair day/nat

May I look around?
Må jeg se mig omkring?
maw yigh say my omkreng

Do you provide anything . . .
Kan man få noget . . .
kan man faw no-et . . .

to eat?
at spise?
at spee-ser

to drink?
at drikke?
at dregger

Do you have . . .
Er her . . .
air hair . . .

a bar?
en bar?
ain bar

hot showers?
brusebad?
broo-ser-bathe

a kitchen?
et køkken?
it kerg-en

a laundry?
et vaskeri?
it vasker-ree

a restaurant?
en restaurant?
ain restorung

a shop?
en forretning?
ain forretning

a swimming pool?
et svømmebassin?
it svermer-basseng

[For food shopping, see p. 54, and for eating and drinking out, see p. 66]

Where are . . .
Hvor er . . .
vor air . . .

the wastebaskets?
affaldsspandene?
ow-fels-spanner-ner

the showers?	**brusebadet?**
	br*oo*-ser-bathet
the toilets?	**toiletterne?**
	toiletter-ner
At what time must one . . .	**Hvornår skal man . . .**
	vorn*o*r skal man . . .
go to bed?	**gå i seng?**
	gaw ee s*e*ng
get up?	**stå op?**
	staw op
Please, have you got . . .	**De har vel ikke . . .**
	dee h*a*r vel *i*gger . . .
a broom?	**en kost?**
	ain k*o*ast
a corkscrew?	**en proptrækker?**
	ain prop-trekker
a drying-up cloth?	**et viskestykke?**
	it v*ee*sker-st*oo*kker
a fork?	**en gaffel?**
	ain g*a*ffel
a fridge?	**et køleskab?**
	it c*u*rler-sk*a*b
a frying pan?	**en stegepande?**
	ain st*y*-er-panner
an iron?	**et strygejern?**
	it str*oo*-yer-yairn
a knife?	**en kniv?**
	ain k-n*ee*v
a plate?	**en tallerken?**
	ain tall*air*-ken
a saucepan?	**en gryde?**
	ain gr*oo*-the
a teaspoon?	**en teske?**
	ain tay-skay
a can opener?	**en dåseåbner?**
	ain d*a*wser-awbner
a bottle opener?	**en samfundshjælper?**
	ain s*a*mfoons-yelper
any liquid detergent?	**noget opvaskemiddel?**
	no-et opvasker-m*ee*thel
any laundry powder?	**noget vaskepulver?**
	no-et vasker-p*oo*lver

Danish

Problems

The toilet	**Toilettet** toilet-tet
The shower	**Bruseren** broo-ser-ren
The tap	**Hanen** hay-nen
The razor outlet	**Stikkontakten til barbermaskinen** stick-kon-tuckten til barbeer-maskeenen
The light	**Lyset** loo-set
. . . is not working	**. . . virker ikke** . . . veerker igger
My camping gas has run out	**Jeg har ikke mere campinggas** yigh har igger mere camping-gas

LIKELY REACTIONS

Have you an identity document?	**Har De legitimation?** har dee lay-gheet-ee-mashown
Your membership card, please	**Deres medlemskort** dair-es methe-lems-kort
What's your name? [see p. 17]	**Hvad er Deres navn?** va air dair-es noun
Sorry, we are full	**Desværre, alt er optaget** desvair alt air optay-et
How many people is it for?	**Hvor mange personer er det til?** vor mung-er pair-son-er air day til
How many nights is it for?	**Hvor mange nætter bliver De?** vor mung-er netter bleer dee
It's (20) kroner . . .	**Det koster (tyve) kroner . . .** day koster (too-ver) kroner . . .
per day/night	**per dag/nat** pair day/nat

[For numbers, see p. 96]

Rented accommodation: problem solving

ESSENTIAL INFORMATION

- If you are looking for accommodation to rent, look out for:
  TIL LEJE (to let)
  LEJLIGHED (flat)
  VÆRELSE (room)
  HUS (house)
  SOMMERHUS (summer house)
- For arranging details of your let, see 'Hotel' p. 26.
- Key words you will need if renting on the spot:
  depositum (deposit)
  nøgle (key)
- Having arranged your own accommodation and arrived with the key, check the obvious basics that you take for granted at home.
  Electricity: The electric current is 220V AC (50 Hz). Sockets are the standard 2-pin continental type.
  Gas: Town gas or bottled gas? Butane gas must be kept indoors, propane gas must be kept outdoors.
  Cooker: Don't be surprised to find the grill inside the oven, or no grill at all.
  Toilet: Mains drainage or septic tank? Don't flush disposable diapers or anything else down the toilet if you are on a septic tank.
  Water: Find the stopcock. Check taps and plugs – they may not operate in the way you are used to. Check how to turn on (or off) the hot water.
  Windows: Check the method of opening and closing windows and shutters.
  Insects: Is an insecticide spray provided? If not, get one locally.
  Equipment: For buying or replacing equipment, see p. 48.
- You will probably have an official agent, but be clear in your own mind whom to contact in an emergency, even if it is only a neighbor in the first instance.

WHAT TO SAY

My name is . . .   **Jeg hedder . . .**
                                    yigh hither . . .

Danish

I'm staying at . . .	**Jeg bor . . .** yigh bore . . .
They've cut off . . .	**Der er lukket for . . .** dair air look-ket for . . .
the electricity	**elektriciteten** elektree-see-taten
the gas	**gassen** gassen
the water	**vandet** vannet
Is there . . . in the area?	**Er der . . . i nærheden?** air dair . . . ee nair-hethen
an electrician	**en elektriker** ain elektree-ker
a plumber	**en VVS mand** ain VVS man
a gas fitter	**en gasarbejder** ain gas-ar-byder
Where is . . .	**Hvor er . . .** vor air . . .
the fuse box?	**elmåleren?** el-maw-lern
the tap?	**hovedhanen?** ho-ethe-hay-nen
the boiler?	**fyret?** foo-ret
the water heater?	**varmtvandsbeholderen?** varmt-vans-beholleren
Is there . . .	**Er der . . .** air dair . . .
bottled gas?	**flaskegas?** flasker-gas
a septic tank?	**septisk tank?** septisk tunk
central heating?	**centralvarme?** centrahl-varmer
The cooker	**Komfuret** komfooret
The hairdryer	**Hårtørreren** hor-tern
The heating	**Varmeanlægget** varmer-an-lay-get

The iron	**Strygejernet**
	str*oo*-yer-yairnet
The pilot light	**Vågeblusset**
	v*o*-er-bl*oo*sset
The refrigerator	**Køleskabet**
	c*u*rler-skabet
The telephone	**Telefonen**
	telef*o*nen
The toilet	**Toilettet**
	toil*e*t-tet
The washing machine	**Vaskemaskinen**
	v*a*sker-mask*ee*nen
. . . is not working	**. . . virker ikke**
	. . . v*ee*rker igger
Where can I get . . .	**Hvor kan jeg få . . .**
	vor kan yigh faw . . .
a bottle of butane gas?	**noget flaskegas?**
	no-et fl*a*skergas
a fuse?	**en sikring?**
	ain s*i*kring
an insecticide spray?	**en insektspray?**
	ain ins*e*ktspray
a light bulb?	**en pære?**
	ain p*air*
The drain	**Afløbet**
	ow-l*e*rbet
The sink	**Vasken**
	v*a*sken
The toilet	**Toilettet**
	toil*e*t-tet
. . . is blocked	**. . . er stoppet**
	. . . air st*o*ppet
The gas is leaking	**Gasledningen er utæt**
	gas-lethe-ningen air *oo*-tet
Can you mend it straightaway?	**Kan De reparere det nu?**
	kan dee repar*air* day *noo*
When can you mend it?	**Hvornår kan De reparere det?**
	vorn*o*r kan dee repar*air* day
How much do I owe you?	**Hvor meget bliver det?**
	vor my-et bl*ee*r day
When is the rubbish collected?	**Hvornår hentes affaldet?**
	vorn*o*r hen-tes *ow*-fallet

Danish

LIKELY REACTIONS

What's your name?	**Hvad er Deres navn?**
	va air dair-es noun
What's your address?	**Hvad er Deres adresse?**
	va air dair-es adresser
There's a shop . . .	**Der er en forretning . . .**
	dair air ain forretning . . .
in town	**i byen**
	ee boo-en
in the village	**i landsbyen**
	ee lans-boo-en
I can't come . . .	**Jeg kan ikke komme . . .**
	yigh kan igger kommer . . .
today	**i dag**
	ee day
this week	**i denne uge**
	ee denner oo-er
until Monday	**før mandag**
	fur manda
I can come . . .	**Jeg kan komme . . .**
	yigh kan kommer . . .
on Tuesday	**på tirsdag**
	paw teers-da
when you want	**når De ønsker det**
	nor dee ernsker day
Every day	**Hver dag**
	vair day
Every other day	**Hveranden dag**
	vair-annen day
On Wednesdays	**Om onsdagen**
	om ons-day-en

[*For days of the week, see p. 99*]

General shopping

The drugstore/The chemist's

ESSENTIAL INFORMATION

- Look for the word
  APOTEK (drugstore/chemist's)
  or this sign:
- There are two kinds of drugstore in
  Denmark. The **APOTEK** (dispensing
  pharmacy) is the place to go for
  prescriptions, medicines, etc; toilet and
  household articles as well as patent
  medicines are sold at the **MATERIALIST**
  (drugstore) as well as at department stores and supermarkets.
- The **APOTEK** is open Monday to Thursday 9.00 a.m. – 5.30 p.m.,
  Friday 9.00 a.m. – 7.00 p.m. and Saturday 9.00 a.m. – 1.00 p.m.
- Pharmacists take it in turn to stay open over the weekend and all
  night. If the drugstore is shut, a notice on the door will give the
  address of the nearest pharmacist on duty (**APOTEKERVAGT**).
- Finding a drugstore, see p. 21.

WHAT TO SAY

I'd like . . .	**Jeg vil gerne have . . .**
	yigh vil g*air*-ner h*a* . . .
a box of aspirin	**en æske aspirin**
	ain esker aspir*in*
some Alka Seltzer	**nogle Alka Seltzer**
	no-ler *a*lka seltzer
some antiseptic	**et antiseptisk middel**
	it antiseptisk meethel
some bandage	**en bandage**
	ain band*air*-sher
some cotton wool	**noget vat**
	no-et v*a*t
some eye drops	**nogle øjendråber**
	no-ler *o*yen-draw-ber

Danish

I'd like . . .	**Jeg vil gerne have . . .** yigh vil g*air*-ner h*a* . . .
some inhalant	**et indhaleringsmiddel** it *i*n-ha-l*ai*rings-meethel
some insect repellent	**en myggebalsam** ain m*oo*gger-b*a*l-sam
some lip salve/chapstick	**en læbepomade** ain l*ay*-ber-pom*ay*-ther
some sticking plaster	**noget hæfteplaster** n*o*-et hefter-pluster
some throat lozenges	**nogle halspastiller** n*o*-ler h*a*lss-past*i*ll-er
some Vaseline	**noget Vaseline** n*o*-et vaselee*ner*
I'd like something for . . .	**Jeg vil gerne have noget mod . . .** yigh vil g*air*-ner h*a* n*o*-et mothe . . .
bites (dog)	**bid** b*ee*the
burns	**forbrændinger** forbrenning-er
a cold	**forkølelse** fork*er*-lel-ser
constipation	**forstoppelse** forstoppel-ser
a cough	**hoste** h*o*-ster
diarrhea	**diarré** dee-ar*ay*
earache	**ørepine** *e*rr-er-p*ee*-ner
flu	**influenza** influenza
sore gums	**ømme gummer** *e*rr-mer g*o*mmer
stings (mosquitoes, bees)	**stik** stick
sunburn	**solskoldning** s*o*le-skol-ning
travel sickness	**køresyge** k*e*r-er-s*oo*-yer
I need . . .	**Jeg skal bruge . . .** yigh skal br*oo*-er . . .

some baby food	**noget baby mad**
	no-et baby mathe
some contraceptives	**noget prævention**
	no-et pray-venshown
a deodorant	**en deodorant**
	ain day-o-dorunt
some disposable diapers	**nogle papirbleer**
	no-ler papeer-blee-er
some handcream	**en håndcreme**
	ain hon-craim
some lipstick	**en læbestift**
	ain lay-berstift
some make-up remover	**en rensecreme**
	ain ren-ser-craim
some paper tissues	**papirlommetørklæder**
	papeer-lommer-ter-klether
some razor blades	**barberblade**
	barbeer-blather
some safety pins	**sikkerhedsnåle**
	sikker-hethes-naw-ler
some sanitary napkins	**en pakke bind**
	ain pukker bin
some soap	**et stykke sæbe**
	it stookker say-ber
some suntan oil/lotion	**en sololie/lotion**
	ain sole-oo-lee-er/lo-shown
some talcum powder	**noget talkum**
	no-et talkum
some Tampax	**en pakke Tampax**
	ain pukker tampax
some (soft) toilet paper	**(blødt) toiletpapir**
	(blert) toilet-papeer
some toothpaste	**en tube tandpasta**
	ain toober tann-pasta

[*For other essential expressions, see 'Shop talk', p. 50*]

Holiday items

ESSENTIAL INFORMATION

- Places to shop at and signs to look for:
  BOGHANDEL (bookshop, stationer)
  FOTO (films)   **GAVEARTIKLER** (gift shop)
- In Copenhagen there are three major department stores:
  MAGASIN DU NORD, ILLUM and **DAELLS VAREHUS**

WHAT TO SAY

I'd like . . .	**Jeg vil gerne have . . .** yigh vil g*air*-ner ha . . .
a bag	**en taske** ain t*a*ssker
a beach ball	**en badebold** ain b*a*ther-bolld
a bucket	**en spand** ain sp*a*n
an English newspaper	**en engelsk avis** ain *e*ng-elsk av*ee*s
some envelopes	**nogle konvolutter** n*o*-ler konvo-l*oo*tter
a guide book	**en rejsehåndbog** ain r*ye*-ser-hon-bo
a map (of the area)	**et kort (over egnen)** it kort (o-er *eye*-nen)
some postcards	**nogle postkort** n*o*-ler p*o*sskort
a spade	**en spade** ain sp*ay*-ther
a sun hat	**en solhat** ain s*o*le-hat
some sunglasses	**et par solbriller** it par s*o*le-breller
an umbrella	**en paraply** ain parapl*oo*
some writing paper	**noget skrivepapir** n*o*-et skr*ee*ver-pap*ee*r

I'd like . . . [*show the camera*]	**Jeg vil gerne have . . .**
	yigh vil *g*air-ner h*a* . . .
a roll of color film	**en farvefilm**
	ain f*a*rver-film
a roll of black and	**en sort-hvid film**
white film	ain sort-v*ee*the film
for prints	**til papirbilleder**
	til pap*ee*r-b*ee*llether
for slides	**til lysbilleder**
	til l*oo*s-b*ee*llether
Please can you . . .	**Vil De være så venlig at . . .**
	vil d*ee* v*a*ir saw venlee at . . .
develop/print this?	**fremkalde/lave aftryk?**
	fremk*a*ller/l*a*y-ver *ow*-trook
load the camera for me?	**sætte filmen i for mig?**
	s*e*tter filmen *ee* for my

[*For other essential expressions, see 'Shop talk' p. 50*]

The tobacco shop

ESSENTIAL INFORMATION

- Tobacco is sold where you see the signs:
  CIGARHANDLER and **TOBAKSHANDEL**
- To ask if there is one near by, see p. 22.
- Most usual brands of tobacco, cigars and cigarettes may be bought
  at supermarkets, kiosks and station restaurants.

WHAT TO SAY

A pack of cigarettes . . .	**En pakke cigaretter . . .**
	ain p*u*kker cigar-r*e*tter . . .
with filters	**med filter**
	m*e*the filter
without filters	**uden filter**
	oo-then filter

Danish

A pack of cigarettes . . .	**En pakke cigaretter . . .** ain pukker cigar-retter . . .
king size	**king size** king size
menthol	**med menthol** methe mentol
Those up there . . .	**De der . . .** dee dair . . .
on the right	**til højre** til hoy-rer
on the left	**til venstre** til venstrer
These [*point*]	**De her** dee hair
Have you got . . .	**Har De . . .** har dee . . .
English cigarettes?	**engelske cigaretter?** eng-elsker cigar-retter
rolling tobacco?	**rulletobak?** rooller-tobuk
A packet of pipe tobacco	**En pakke pibetobak** ain pukker peeber-tobuk
This one [*point*]	**Den her** den hair
A cigar, please	**En cigar** ain cigar
Some cigars, please	**Nogle cigarer** no-ler cigar-er
Those [*point*]	**De der** dee dair
A box of matches	**En æske tændstikker** ain esker ten-sticker
A packet of pipe cleaners	**En pakke piberensere** ain pukker peeber-ren-ser
A packet of flints [*show lighter*]	**Nogle sten** no-ler sten
Lighter fluid	**Noget tændvæske** no-et ten-vesker
Lighter gas	**En gaspatron** ain gas-patroone

[*For other essential expressions, see 'Shop talk' p. 50*]

Buying clothes

ESSENTIAL INFORMATION

- Look for:
  DAMETØJ (women's clothes)
  HERRETØJ (men's clothes)
  BØRNETØJ (children's clothes)
  SKOTØJSFORRETNING (shoe shop)
- Don't buy without being measured first or without trying things on.
- Don't rely on conversion charts of clothing sizes (see p. 335).
- If you are buying for someone else, take their measurements with you.

WHAT TO SAY

I'd like . . .	**Jeg vil gerne have . . .**
	yigh vil *g*air-ner h*a* . . .
an anorak/parka	**en anorak**
	ain anor*u*ck
a belt	**et bælte**
	it b*e*lter
a bikini	**en bikini**
	ain bik*i*ni
a bra	**en BH**
	ain beh*aw*
a pair of briefs	**et par trusser**
	it par tr*oo*sser
a swimming cap	**en badehætte**
	ain b*a*ther-hetter
a cardigan	**en cardigan**
	ain c*a*rdigan
a coat	**en frakke**
	ain fr*a*kker
a dress	**en kjole**
	ain k-y*o*ler
a hat	**en hat**
	ain h*a*t
a jacket	**en jakke**
	ain y*a*kker

Danish

I'd like . . .	**Jeg vil gerne have . . .**
	yigh vil gair-ner ha . . .
a pair of jeans	**et par cowboybukser**
	it par cowboy-bawkser
a jumper	**en strikket bluse**
	ain strikket bloo-ser
a nightgown	**en natkjole**
	ain nat-k-yoler
a pullover	**en pullover**
	ain pullo-er
a pair of pajamas	**et pyjamas**
	it pee-ya-mas
a raincoat	**en regnfrakke**
	ain rine-frakker
a blouse	**en bluse**
	ain bloo-ser
a shirt (men)	**en skjorte**
	ain sk-yorter
a suit (women)	**en dragt**
	ain drukt
a suit (men)	**en habit**
	ain habeet
a swimsuit	**en badedragt**
	ain bather-drukt
a T-shirt	**en T-shirt**
	ain T-shirt
a pair of tights	**et par strømpebukser**
	it par stroom-per-bawkser
a pair of trousers	**et par bukser**
	it par bawkser
I'd like a pair of . . .	**Jeg vil gerne have et par . . .**
	yigh vil gair-ner ha it par . . .
gloves	**handsker**
	hansker
socks (short/long)	**sokker (korte/lange)**
	sokker (korter/lun-ger)
stockings	**strømper**
	stroomper
shoes	**sko**
	sko
canvas shoes	**lærredssko**
	laireths-sko

sandals	**sandaler**
	sand*ay*-ler
beach shoes	**strandsko**
	str*u*n-sko
smart shoes	**elegante sko**
	eleg*a*nter sk*o*
moccasins	**mokkasiner**
	mokkas*ee*ner
My size is . . .	**Jeg bruger størrelse . . .**
	yigh br*oo*-er st*i*rl-ser . . .
[*For numbers, see p. 96*]	
Can you measure me, please?	**Vil De tage mine mål?**
	vil d*ee* t*ay* m*ee*ner m*a*wl
Can I try it on?	**Må jeg prøve den?**
	m*a*w yigh pr*oo*ver den
It's for a present	**Det er til en gave**
	day air til ain g*ay*-ver
These are the measurements. . .	**Her er målene . . .**
[*show written*]	hair air m*a*wler-ner . . .
bust/chest	**brystmål**
	br*oo*st-m*a*wl
collar	**halsvidde**
	h*a*lss-veeder
hip	**hoftemål**
	h*o*fter-m*a*wl
leg	**benlængde**
	b*ee*n-leng-der
waist	**taljemål**
	t*a*l-yer-mawl
Have you got something . . .	**Har De noget . . .**
	har d*ee* n*o*-et . . .
in black?	**i sort?**
	ee sort
in white?	**i hvidt?**
	ee v*ee*t
in gray?	**i gråt?**
	ee grot
in blue?	**i blåt?**
	ee blot
in brown?	**i brunt?**
	ee br*oo*nt
in pink?	**i lyserødt?**
	ee l*oo*-ser-r*oo*t

Danish

Have you got something . . .	**Har De noget . . .**
	har dee no-et . . .
. in green?	**i grønt?**
	ee grernt
in red?	**i rødt?**
	ee root
in yellow?	**i gult?**
	ee goolt
in this color? [point]	**i den farve?**
	ee den farver
in cotton?	**i bomuld?**
	ee bom-ool
in denim?	**i cowboystof?**
	ee cowboy-stof
in leather?	**i skind?**
	ee skin
in nylon?	**i nylon?**
	ee nylon
in suede?	**i ruskind?**
	ee roo-skin
in wool?	**i uld?**
	ee ool
in this material? [point]	**i det stof her?**
[For other essential expressions, see 'Shop talk', p. 50]	ee day stof hair

Replacing equipment

ESSENTIAL INFORMATION

- Look for these shop signs:
  ISENKRAM (hardware)
  EL-INSTALLATØREN (electrical goods)
- In a supermarket look for this display:
  HUSHOLDNINGSARTIKLER (household cleaning materials)
- To ask the way to a shop, see p. 19.
- At a campsite try their shop first.

WHAT TO SAY

Have you got . . .	**Har De . . .**
	har dee. . .
an adaptor?	**et mellemstik?**
[*show appliance*]	it mellemstick
a bottle of butane gas?	**flaskegas/butan?**
	flasker-gas/bootan
a bottle of propane gas?	**flaskegas/propan?**
	flasker-gas/propan
a bottle opener?	**en samfundshjælper?**
	ain samfoons-yelper
a corkscrew?	**en proptrækker?**
	ain prop-trekker
any disinfectant?	**et disinfektionsmiddel?**
	it disinfek-shown-smeethel
any disposable cups?	**engangskrus?**
	ain-gungs-kroos
a drying-up cloth?	**et viskestykke?**
	it veesker-stookker
any forks?	**nogle gafler?**
	no-ler gafler
a fuse? [*show old one*]	**en sikring?**
	ain sik-ring
insecticide spray?	**en insektspray?**
	ain insektspray
paper kitchen towels?	**en køkkenrulle?**
	ain kerg-en-rooller
any knives?	**nogle knive?**
	no-ler k-neever
a light bulb? [*show old one*]	**en pære?**
	ain pair
a plastic bucket?	**en plast spand?**
	ain plast-span
a scouring pad?	**en grydesvamp?**
	ain groo-the-svump
a wrench?	**en skruenøgle?**
	ain skroo-er-noy-ler
a sponge?	**en svamp?**
	ain svump
any string?	**noget snor?**
	no-et snor

Danish

Have you got . . .	**Har De . . .** har dee. . .
any tent pegs?	**nogle teltpløkke?** no-ler telt-plookker
a can opener?	**en dåseåbner?** ain daw-ser-awbner
a flashlight?	**en lommelygte?** ain lommer-loog-ter
any flashlight batteries?	**lommelygtebatterier?** lommer-loog-ter-batteree-er
a universal plug (for the sink)?	**en bundprop?** ain boonprop
a washing line?	**en tøjsnor?** ain toy-snor
any laundry powder?	**vaskepulver?** vasker-poolver
a scrub brush?	**en opvaskebørste?** ain opvasker-burster
any liquid detergent?	**et opvaskemiddel?** it opvasker-meethel
[*For other essential expressions, see 'Shop talk', p. 50*]	

Shop talk

ESSENTIAL INFORMATION

- Danish coins: see illustration
  Danish notes: 20, 50, 100, 500 and 1,000 kroner.
- Know how to say the important weights and measures.
  You will hear grams, kilos and pounds in shops and markets.
  [*For numbers, see p. 96*]

50 grams	**halvtreds gram** hal-tress grum
100 grams	**hundrede gram** hoonrer-ther grum
200 grams	**to hundrede gram** toe hoonrer-ther grum

½ lb (250 grams)	**et halvt pund**
	it h*u*lt p*oo*n
1 lb	**et pund**
	it p*oo*n
1 kilo	**et kilo**
	it k*i*lo
2 kilos	**to kilo**
	t*oe* k*i*lo
½ litre	**en halv liter**
	ain hal l*ee*ter
1 litre	**en liter**
	ain l*ee*ter
2 litres	**to liter**
	t*oe* l*ee*ter

- In small shops don't be surprised if customers, as well as the shop assistant, say 'hello' and 'goodbye' to you.

CUSTOMER

I'm just looking	**Jeg kigger bare**
	yigh k*i*gger b*a*r-er
Excuse me	**Undskyld**
	on-skool
How much is this/that?	**Hvor meget koster den her/den der?**
	vor my-et k*o*ster den h*ai*r/den d*ai*r
What's that/those?	**Hvad er det?**
	v*a* air day
Is there a discount?	**Er der rabat?**
	air dair ra-b*a*t
I'd like that, please	**Jeg vil gerne have den/det**
	yigh vil g*ai*r-ner ha den/d*a*y
Not that	**Ikke den/det**
	*i*gger den/d*a*y
Like that	**Ligesom den/det**
	l*ee*-er-som den/d*a*y
That's enough, thank you	**Det er nok**
	day air nok
More, please	**Lidt mere**
	lit m*e*re
Less, please	**Lidt mindre**
	lit m*i*ndrer

That's fine	**Det er fint**
	day air f*ee*nt
OK	**Godt**
	got
I won't take it, thank you	**Jeg vil ikke have den/det**
	yigh vil igger h*a* den/day
It's not right	**Det er ikke det rigtige**
	day air *i*gger day r*e*gtee-er
Have you got something . . .	**Har De noget . . .**
	har dee n*o*-et . . .
better?	**bedre?**
	b*e*the-rer
cheaper?	**billigere?**
	b*i*llee-er
different?	**andet?**
	*a*nnet
larger?	**større?**
	st*i*rrer
smaller?	**mindre?**
	m*i*ndrer
At what time do you . . .	**Hvornår . . .**
	vorn*o*r . . .
open?	**åbner De?**
	*aw*bner dee
close?	**lukker De?**
	l*oo*kker dee
Can I have a bag, please?	**Jeg vil gerne have en bærepose**
	yigh vil g*ai*r-ner h*a* ain b*a*re-po-ser
Can I have a receipt?	**Jeg vil gerne have en kvittering**
	yigh vil g*ai*r-ner h*a* ain kveett*ai*ring
Do you take . . .	**Tager De . . .**
	tar dee . . .
English/American money?	**engelske/amerikanske penge?**
	eng-elsker/amerik*a*nsker p*e*ng-er
travelers' checks?	**rejsechecks?**
	rye-ser-shecks
credit cards?	**kreditkort?**
	kred*i*tkort
I'd like . . .	**Jeg vil gerne have . . .**
	yigh vil g*ai*r-ner h*a* . . .
one like that	**sådan en**
	s*u*dden ain

Danish

SHOP ASSISTANT

Can I help you?	**Kan jeg hjælpe Dem?**
	kan yigh yelper dem
What would you like?	**Hvad skulle det være?**
	va skooller day vair
Will that be all?	**Var der ellers andet?**
	var dair ellers annet
Anything else?	**Ellers andet?**
	ellers annet
Would you like it wrapped?	**Skal det pakkes ind?**
	skal day pukkes in
Sorry, none left	**Jeg beklager, der er ikke flere**
	yigh beklay-er dair air igger flee-er
I haven't got any	**Jeg har ingen**
	yigh har ing-en
I haven't got any more	**Jeg har ikke flere**
	yigh har igger flee-er
How many do you want?	**Hvor mange ønsker De?**
	vor mung-er ern-sker dee
How much do you want?	**Hvor meget ønsker De?**
	vor my-et ern-sker dee
Is this enough?	**Er det nok?**
	air day nok

Shopping for food

Bread

ESSENTIAL INFORMATION

- Finding a bakery, see p. 20.
- Key words to look out for:
  BAGERI (bakery)
  BAGER (baker)
  BRØD OG KAGER (bread and cakes)

- Supermarkets of any size and general stores nearly always sell bread.
- Bakeries are open from 7.00 a.m. to 5.30 p.m. weekdays, 7.00 a.m. to 2.00 p.m. on Saturdays. Bakers in a given area take it in turn to open very early on Sundays when many people buy **MORGENBRØD** – special rolls and Danish pastries.

WHAT TO SAY

A loaf (like that)	**(Sådan) et brød** (su*dd*en) it br*e*rthe
A white loaf	**Et franskbrød** it fru*n*sk-br*e*rthe
a large one	**et stort** it st*o*rt
a small one	**et lille** it l*i*ller
A loaf of rye bread	**Et rugbrød** it r*oo*-br*e*rthe
a whole one	**et helt** it h*e*lt
half a one	**et halvt** it h*u*lt
A bread roll	**Et rundstykke** it r*oo*n-st*oo*kker
A bun	**En bolle** ain b*o*ller
Four buns	**Fire boller** f*ee*rer b*o*ller
A French stick	**En flute** ain fl*oo*ter
A wholemeal loaf	**Et grovbrød** it gr*ow*-br*e*rthe

[*For other essential expressions, see 'Shop talk' p. 50*]

Danish

Cakes

ESSENTIAL INFORMATION

- Key words to look for:
  BAGERI (bakery)
  BAGER (baker)
  KONDITORI (cake shop, often with tea/coffee shop attached)
- To find a cake shop, see p. 21.

WHAT TO SAY

The type of cakes you find in the shops may vary from region to region but the following are the most common; cake is *not* bought per slice but gâteau is.

wienerbrød	Danish pastry
veener-brerthe	
kringle	yeast pastry
krengler	
en smørkage	butter cake/pastry
ain smer-kayer	
en tærte	tart
ain tairter	
en formkage	plain/fruit cake (to slice)
ain form-kayer	
en lagkage	layercake/gâteau
ain la-oo-kayer	
et stykke kransekage	almond cake
it stookker kran-ser-kayer	
en flødekage	cream cake
ain flerther-kayer	
småkager	biscuits
smokkayer	

Ice cream and sweets

ESSENTIAL INFORMATION

- Key words to look for:
  IS (ice cream)
  ISKIOSK (ice cream shop)
  CHOKOLADEFORRETNING (candy store)
  BAGERI (bakery)
- Best known ice-cream brands are:
  FRISKO
  PREMIERE
- When buying ice cream, specify what price cone or tub you want.
- Pre-packed candies are available in general stores and supermarkets.

WHAT TO SAY

A . . . ice, please	**En . . . is** ain . . . ees
caramel	**nougat** nooga
chocolate	**chokolade** shoko-laither
lemon	**citron** citrone
mocha	**mokka** mokka
strawberry	**jordbær** yor-bear
vanilla	**vanille** vanilla
One (5 kr) cone	**En vaffel til fem kroner** ain vuffel til fem kroner
Two (7 kr) tubs	**To bægre til syv kroner** toe bare til soo kroner
A lollipop	**En slikkepind** ain slikker-pin
A packet of . . .	**En pakke . . .** ain pukker . . .

Danish

100 grams of . . .	**Hundrede gram . . .**
	hoonrer-ther grum . . .

[*For further details of Danish weights, see 'Shop talk' p. 50*]

chewing gum	**tyggegummi**
	toogger-goommee
chocolates	**chokolade**
	shoko-laither
licorice	**lakrids**
	lakris
mints	**pebermynte**
	pev-er-moonter
candy	**bolsjer**
	boll-sher
toffee	**karameller**
	karameller

[*For other essential expressions, see 'Shop talk' p. 50*]

Picnic food

ESSENTIAL INFORMATION

● Key words to look out for:
  DELIKATESSEN
  PÅLÆG   delicatessen
  SLAGTER (butcher)

WHAT TO SAY

Two slices of . . .	**To skiver . . .**
	toe skeever . . .
roast beef	**roast beef**
	roast beef
roast pork	**flæskesteg**
	flesker-sty
ham (cooked)	**skinke**
	skinker
ham (smoked)	**røget skinke**
	rer-yet skinker

saveloy sausage	**cervelatpølse**
	ser-verlat-pullser
salami	**spegepølse**
	spy-er-pullser
150 grams of . . .	**Hundredeoghalvtreds gram . . .**
	hoonrer-ther-o-hal-tress grum. . .
potato salad	**kartoffelsalat**
	kartoffel-salat
herring salad	**sildesalat**
	siller-salat
Russian salad	**italiensk salat**
	ee-tay-lee-ensk salat
mackerel salad	**makrelsalat**
	makrel-salat

You might also like to try some of these:

en røget makrel	a smoked mackerel
ain rer-yet makrel	
en røget ål	a smoked eel
ain rer-yet awl	
en røget sild	a smoked herring
ain rer-yet sill	
en frikadelle	tasty pork and veal meatball
ain frikka-deller	
en fiskefrikadelle	as above, made with fish
ain fisker-frikka-deller	
et stykke medisterpølse	piece of pork sausage
it stookker medister-pullser	
en rødspættefilet med remoulade	fried plaice fillet with tangy mayonnaise dressing
ain rerthe-spetter-fee-lay methe rem-o-laither	
rullepølse	rolled pork
rooller-pullser	
leverpostej	liver pâté, often sold warm
laverpo-sty	
Havarti ost	Havarti cheese (mild and mature)
havarti oast	
Samsø ost	Samsø cheese
samser oast	
Castello ost	Castello, soft blue-veined cheese
castello oast	

Fruit and vegetables

ESSENTIAL INFORMATION

● Key words to look out for:
  FRUGT (fruit)
  GRØNTHANDLER (greengrocer)
  GRØNTSAGER (vegetables)
[*For details of Danish weights, see 'Shop talk' p. 50*]

WHAT TO SAY

1 kilo (2 lbs) of . . .	**Et kilo . . .**
	it kilo . . .
apples	**æbler**
	*e*b-ler
bananas	**bananer**
	ba-n*ai*ner
cherries	**kirsebær**
	k*eer*-ser-bear
grapes	**vindruer**
	v*ee*n-droo-er
oranges	**appelsiner**
	appel-s*ee*ner
pears	**pærer**
	p*ear*
peaches	**ferskner**
	f*ai*rsk-ner
plums	**blommer**
	bl*o*mmer
raspberries	**hindbær**
	h*i*n-bear
strawberries	**jordbær**
	y*or*-bear
A pineapple, please	**En ananas**
	ain *a*nnanas
A grapefruit	**En grapefrugt**
	ain gr*a*pe-frookt
A melon	**En melon**
	ain mel*o*ne

A watermelon	**En vandmelon**
	ain v*a*n-melone
½ kilo of . . .	**Et halvt kilo . . .**
	it h*u*lt k*i*lo . . .
carrots	**gulerødder**
	g*oo*ller-r*e*rther
green beans	**grønne bønner**
	gr*e*rner b*u*rnner
leeks	**porrer**
	pore
mushrooms	**champignoner**
	sham-peen-y*o*ng-er
onions	**løg**
	l*o*y
peas	**ærter**
	*a*ir-ter
potatoes	**kartofler**
	kart*o*fler
red cabbage	**rødkål**
	r*e*rthe-kawl
spinach	**spinat**
	spee-n*a*t
tomatoes	**tomater**
	toe-m*a*ter
A bunch of . . .	**Et bundt . . .**
	it b*oo*nt . . .
chives	**purløg**
	p*oo*r-loy
radishes	**radiser**
	ra-d*i*sser
garlic	**Et hvidløg**
	it v*ee*the-loy
A head of lettuce	**Et salathoved**
	it sal*a*t-h*o*-ethe
cauliflower	**Et blomkål**
	it bl*o*m-kawl
cabbage	**Et hvidkål**
	it v*ee*the-kawl
cucumber	**En agurk**
	ain ag*oo*rk
Like that, please	**Sådan en/et**
	s*u*dden *ai*n/it

[For other essential expressions, see 'Shop talk' p. 50]

Danish

Meat

ESSENTIAL INFORMATION

- Key words to look out for:
  SLAGTER (butcher)
- The diagrams opposite are to help you make sense of labels on counters and supermarket displays and decide which cut or joint to have. Translations do not help and you don't need to say the Danish word involved.
- You will find that lamb and especially mutton are much less popular in Denmark. The butcher's display will tell you what is available.

WHAT TO SAY

For a joint, choose the type of meat and then say how many people it is for:

I'd like . . .	**Jeg vil gerne have . . .**
	yigh vil gair-ner ha . . .
some beef	**noget oksekød**
	no-et okser-kethe
some lamb	**noget lammekød**
	no-et lummer-kethe
some pork	**noget flæskekød**
	no-et flesker-kethe
some veal	**noget kalvekød**
	no-et kal-ver-kethe
A joint . . .	**En steg . . .**
	ain sty . . .
for four people	**til fire personer**
	til feerer pair-so-ner
I'd like . . .	**Jeg vil gerne have . . .**
	yigh vil gair-ner ha . . .
some steak	**noget oksesmåkød**
	no-et okser-smaw-kerthe
some liver	**noget lever**
	no-et laver
some kidneys	**nogle nyrer**
	no-ler noo-rer
some sausages	**nogle pølser**
	no-ler pullser

Beef Oksekød

1 Mellemskært	6 Bov
2 Tykkam	7 Tværreb
3 Højreb	8 Bryst
4 Tyndsteg	9 Låret
5 Tyksteg	10 Skank

Veal Kaluekød

1 Mellemskært	8 Skank
2 Mellemkam	9 Bryst
3 Tyndbov	10 Slaget
4 Kam	11 Skank
5 Nyresteg	
6 Mellemkølle	
7 Skankekølle	

Pork Flæskekød

1 Nakkekam	6 Stegeflæsk
2 Koteletstykket	7 Kogeflæsk
3 Kam	8 Skinke
4 Halssnitte	9 Skank
5 Bov	

Lamb Lammekød

1 Hals med nakke
2 Kam (koteletter)
3 Sadel (nyrestykke)
4 Bov
5 Bryst
6 Kølle

Danish

Two veal scallops	**To kalveschnitzler** toe kal-ver-sneets-ler
Three pork chops	**Tre svinekoteletter** tray sveener kotter-letter
Four lamb chops	**Fire lammekoteletter** feerer lummer-kotter-letter
You may also want:	
A chicken	**En kylling** ain koo-ling
A duck	**En and** ain an
A tongue	**En tunge** ain toong-er
Please can you . . .	**Vil De være venlig at . . .** vil dee vair venlee at . . .
mince it?	**hakke det?** hukker day
dice it?	**skære det i småstykker?** skair day ee smaw-stookker
trim the fat?	**skære fedtet fra?** skair fit-tet fra

[*For other essential expressions see 'Shop talk' p. 50*]

Fish

ESSENTIAL INFORMATION

● The word to look out for: **FISKEHANDLER** (fishmonger's)
● Some supermarkets have a fresh fish counter.

WHAT TO SAY

Purchase large fish and small shellfish by weight:

½ kilo of . . .	**Et halvt kilo . . .** it hult kilo . . .
cod	**torsk** torsk

eel	**ål**
	awl
haddock	**kuller**
	koo*l*ler
herring	**sild**
	sill
plaice	**rødspætte**
	r*e*rthe-sp*e*tter
turbot	**pighvarre**
	p*i*g-var
mussels	**muslinger**
	m*oo*sling-er
prawns	**Nordsørejer**
	n*o*r-sir-r*y*e-er
shrimps	**rejer**
	r*y*e-er
A piece of . . .	**Et stykke . . .**
	it st*oo*kker . . .
salmon	**laks**
	luks

For some shellfish and pan fish, specify the number you want:

A crab, please	**En krabbe**
	ain kr*u*bber
A lobster	**En hummer**
	ain h*oo*mmer
A trout	**En ørred**
	ain *e*rthe
A sole	**En søtunge**
	ain s*i*r-toong-er
A mackerel	**En makrel**
	ain makr*e*l

Other essential expressions [*see also p. 50*]

Please can you . . .	**Vil De være venlig at . . .**
	vil dee v*ai*r venlee at . . .
take the head off?	**skære hovedet af?**
	sk*ai*r ho-er-thet *ay*
clean them?	**rense dem?**
	ren-ser dem
fillet them?	**filere dem?**
	feel*ai*r dem

[*For other essential expressions, see 'Shop talk' p. 50*]

Danish

Eating and drinking out

Ordering a drink

ESSENTIAL INFORMATION

- The places to ask for:
  EN BAR/PUB/CAFÉ/KRO (in the country)
  EN BODEGA/VINSTUE (wine bar)
  ET KONDITORI (coffee/pastry shop)
- There is waiter service in all pubs, cafés and wine bars. In many places you can also drink at the bar if you wish.
- When the bill is presented the amount will be inclusive of service and **VAT (MOMS)**.
- Pubs, cafés and bars serve drinks and cold food and are open all day and often until the early hours of the morning.
- Wine bars serve non-alcoholic and alcoholic drinks and a choice of simple meals.
- Coffee shops serve coffee/tea and very good Danish pastries. Cream/milk is always served separately with coffee or tea.
- Children are allowed into bars.

WHAT TO SAY

I'll have . . ., please	**Jeg vil gerne have . . .** yigh vil gair-ner ha . . .
a black coffee	**en kop kaffe** ain kop kuffer
a tea	**en kop te** ain kop tay
with milk	**med mælk** methe melk
with lemon	**med citron** methe citrone
a glass of milk	**et glas mælk** it glas melk
a hot chocolate	**en kop (varm) chokolade** ain kop (varm) shoko-laither
a mineral water	**en mineralvand** ain mineral-van

a lemonade	**en limonade**
	ain leemo-n*ai*ther
a Coca-Cola	**en Coca Cola**
	ain coca c*o*la
an orangeade	**en appelsinvand**
	ain appels*ee*nvan
an orange juice	**en appelsinjuice**
	ain appel-s*ee*njuice
a grape juice	**en druesaft**
	ain dr*oo*er-saft
an apple juice	**en æblemost**
	ain *e*bler-mosst
a beer	**en øl**
	ain *e*rl
a draught beer	**en fadøl**
	ain f*a*the-*e*rl
a half	**en lille**
	ain l*i*ller
an alcohol-free beer	**en lys øl**
	ain l*oo*s *e*rl
a lager	**en pilsner**
	ain p*i*lsner
A glass of . . .	**Et glas . . .**
	it glas . . .
Two glasses of . . .	**To glas . . .**
	t*oe* glas . . .
red wine	**rødvin**
	rerthe-v*ee*n
white wine	**hvidvin**
	veethe-v*ee*n
rosé wine	**rosévin**
	rosé-v*ee*n
dry	**tør**
	ter
sweet	**sød**
	serthe
A bottle of . . .	**En flaske . . .**
	ain fl*a*sker . . .
sparkling wine	**mousserende vin**
	moos-s*ai*ren-ner veen
champagne	**champagne**
	shamp*a*n-yer

Danish

A whisky	**En whisky**
	ain whisky
with ice	**med is**
	methe *ees*
with water	**med vand**
	methe *van*
with soda	**med dansk vand**
	methe dansk *van*
A gin	**En gin**
	ain gin
with tonic	**med tonic**
	methe tonic
with bitter lemon	**med bitter lemon**
	methe bitter lemon
A brandy/cognac	**en cognac**
	ain cognac

The following are local drinks you may like to try:

snaps/akvavit snaps/akva-*veet*	a strong spirit distilled from potatoes and almost always enjoyed with food. There are many different kinds of snaps, flavoured with various herbs and spices
Cherry Heering cherry h*eering*	a famous cherry liqueur named after the Heering family.
Kirsebærvin K*eer*ser-bear-v*een*	a cherry-based dessert wine
Solbærrom s*o*lbear-rom	a blackcurrant-based dessert wine: both these wines are often served with ice as an apéritif
Malt øl m*a*l-terl	a dark, sweet malt beer
Carlsberg Elefant øl c*a*rlsbear elef*a*nt *e*rl	
Tuborg Guld Export t*oo*bore g*oo*l export	extra strong beers
Påskebryg p*aw*-sker-br*oo*k	a strong beer brewed only at Easter
Julebryg y*oo*le-br*oo*k	a strong beer brewed only at Christmas

Other essential expressions:

Miss! [*this does not sound abrupt in Danish*]	**Frøken!** frer-ken
Waiter!	**Tjener!** chainer
The bill, please	**Må jeg betale?** maw yigh betaler
How much does that come to?	**Hvor meget bliver det?** vor my-et bleer day
Is service included?	**Er det med betjening?** air day methe bechaining
Where is the toilet, please?	**Hvor er toilettet?** vor air toilet-tet

Ordering a snack

ESSENTIAL INFORMATION

- Look for any of these places:
  PØLSEVOGN (a street kiosk selling warm snacks)
  CAFETERIA
  GRILLBAR
- Apart from snacks, the cafeterias and grill bars also sell soft drinks, bottled beer, coffee and tea.
- If you want a 'take-away' sandwich lunch look out for **SMØRRE-BRØDSFORRETNING**. Here you can buy an assortment of Danish open sandwiches from the display.
- For cakes, see p. 56; for ice-cream, see p. 57; for picnic-type snacks, see p. 58.

WHAT TO SAY

I'll have . . . please	**Jeg vil gerne have . . .** yigh vil gair-ner ha . . .
a cheese sandwich	**et stykke brød med ost** it stookker brerthe methe oast
a ham sandwich	**et stykke smørrebrød med skinke** it stookker smerrer-brerthe methe skinker

I'll have . . . please	**Jeg vil gerne have . . .**
	yigh vil gair-ner ha . . .
toasted cheese and ham	**toast med skinke og ost**
sandwich	toast methe skinker aw oast
an omelet	**en omelet**
	ain omelet
with mushrooms	**med champignoner**
	methe shampeen-yong-er

These are some other snacks you might like to try:

en rød pølse	red pork sausage
ain rerthe pullser	
en stegt pølse	fried pork sausage
ain stegt pullser	
en frikadelle	pork meatball
ain frikka-deller	
en rødspætte filet	fried plaice fillet
ain rerthe-spetter fillay	
en halv kylling	half a (roast) chicken
ain hal koo-ling	
en dansk bøf med løg	large hamburger with fried onions
ain dansk berf methe loy	
et spejlæg	a fried egg
it spy-leg	
pommes frites	french fries
pom frits	
kartoffelsalat	potato salad
kartoffel-salat	

[*For other essential expressions see 'Ordering a drink', p. 66*]

In a restaurant

ESSENTIAL INFORMATION

● The place to ask for: **EN RESTAURANT** [*see p. 22*]
● You can eat at the following places:

RESTAURANT
HOTEL-RESTAURANT
BANEGÅRDSRESTAURANT (railway station restaurant)
MOTEL
CAFE-RESTAURANT (limited choice here)

- Most restaurants display the menu in the window and that is the only way to judge if a place is right for your needs.
- A service charge of 12–15% is always added to the bill.
- Most restaurants have children's portions.
- Many restaurants offer a set dinner **DAGENS RET** at a reasonable price.
- Restaurants displaying the sign **DAN MENU** serve a 2-course traditional Danish meal - often some local specialty – at a fixed price throughout the country. A brochure with names and addresses of restaurants participating in the plan is available from the Danish Tourist Board in New York City.

- Hot meals are served from 12.00 p.m. – 2.00 p.m. at lunchtime and from 6.00 p.m. – 9/10.00 p.m. at night. After that many restaurants offer snacks for latecomers.

WHAT TO SAY

May I reserve a table?	**Jeg vil gerne bestille et bord**
	yigh vil g*air*-ner best*i*ller it b*o*r
I've reserved a table	**Jeg har bestilt et bord**
	yigh har best*i*lt it b*o*r
A table . . .	**Et bord . . .**
	it b*o*r . . .
for one	**til en person**
	til ain pair-s*o*ne
for three	**til tre personer**
	til tr*a*y pairso-ner
The à la carte menu, please	**A la carte menuen**
	a la carte men*oo*-en
Today's special menu, please	**Dagens ret**
	d*a*y-ens ret

Danish

What's this, please? [point to menu]	**Hvad er det?** va air day
The wine list	**Vinkortet** veenkortet
A glass of wine	**Et glas vin** it glas veen
A half bottle	**En halv flaske** ain hal flasker
A bottle	**En flaske** ain flasker
A litre	**En liter** ain leeter
Red/white/rosé/house wine	**Rødvin/hvidvin/rosévin/husets vin** rerthe-veen/veethe-veen/rosé-veen/ hoo-sets veen
Some more bread, please	**Noget mere brød** no-et mere brerthe
Some more wine	**Noget mere vin** no-et mere veen
Some dressing	**Noget dressing** no-et dressing
Some salt	**Noget salt** no-et selt
Some pepper	**Noget peber** no-et paver
With/without garlic	**Med/uden hvidløg** methe/oothen veethe-loy
Some water	**Noget vand** no-et van
How much does that come to?	**Hvor meget bliver det?** vor my-et bleer day
Is service included?	**Er det med betjening?** air day methe bechaining
Miss! [this does not sound abrupt in Danish]	**Frøken!** frer-ken
Waiter!	**Tjener!** chainer
The bill, please	**Må jeg betale?** maw yigh betailer

Key words for courses, as seen on some menus. [*Only ask this question if you want the waiter to remind you of the choice*]

What have you got in the way of . . .	Hvilke . . . har De?
	veelker . . . har dee
STARTERS?	**FORRETTER?**
	for-retter
SOUP?	**SUPPER?**
	soopper
EGG DISHES?	**ÆGGERETTER?**
	egger-retter
FISH?	**FISKERETTER?**
	fisker-retter
MEAT?	**KØDRETTER?**
	kerthe-retter
GAME?	**VILDTRETTER?**
	vilt-retter
FOWL?	**FJERKRÆRETTER?**
	f-yair-kray-retter
VEGETABLES?	**GRØNTSAGER?**
	grernt-sayer
CHEESE?	**OSTE?**
	oaster
FRUIT?	**FRUGT?**
	frookt
ICE CREAM?	**IS?**
	ees
DESSERT?	**DESSERTER?**
	dessairter

UNDERSTANDING THE MENU

- You will find the names of the principal ingredients of most dishes on these pages:

  Starters p. 58
  Meat p. 62
  Fish p. 64
  Vegetables p. 61

  Fruit p. 60
  Cheese p. 59
  Ice cream p. 57
  Dessert p. 56

- Used together with the following lists of cooking and menu terms, they should help you to decode the menu.
- These cooking and menu terms are for understanding – not for speaking aloud.

Danish

Cooking and menu terms

bagt	baked
blandet	mixed
bouillon	broth, clear soup
brunet i smør	sautéed
dampet	steamed
filet	fillet
fløde	cream
flødeskum	whipped cream
fyldt	stuffed
garneret	garnished
gennemstegt (steak)	well done
glaseret	glazed
gratineret	au gratin
grydestegt	braised
hjemmelavet	homemade
jævnet	thickened
kogt	boiled
marineret	marinated
paneret	breaded
pikant	spicy
puré	purée
ragout	stew
revet	grated
ristet	toasted
rød	rare (steak)
røget	smoked
rå	raw
sovs	sauce
stegt	fried
sur	sour
sød	sweet

Further words to help you understand the menu

æggekage	Danish omelette garnished with tomatoes, bacon and chives
agurkesalat	cucumber in sweet/sour dressing
and	duck
aspargessuppe	asparagus soup
boller i karry	pork meatballs in curry sauce served with rice

bøf med løg	beef hamburger with fried onions and sauce
engelsk bøf	fillet of beef
flæskesteg med svær	roast pork with crackling
flæskesteg med rødkål	roast pork with red cabbage, traditional Sunday dish
frikadeller	pork and veal meatballs
gemyse	vegetables
gule ærter	split pea soup with pork
hachis	minced steak with onions, spices and vinegar
hamburgerryg	smoked, glazed pork
hindbær	raspberries
hofdessert	meringue, whipped cream and chocolate sauce
hønsekødssuppe	clear chicken soup with meatballs and vegetables
jordbærgrød	strawberry dessert served with fresh cream
kalvefrikasse	veal stew with vegetables
karamelbudding	crème caramel
kærnemælkskoldskål	buttermilk dessert served with biscuits
lagkage	layer cake
laks	salmon
lever, stegt med løg	fried liver with onions
medisterpølse	spiced, fried pork sausage
muslinger	mussels
mørbradbøf	fillet of pork
oksefilet	fillet of beef
ørred	trout
pandekager	pancakes
peberrodssovs	horseradish sauce
rejer	shrimps
remoulade	creamy dressing with mustard and herbs
rødbeder, syltede	beetroot in sweet/sour dressing
rødgrød med fløde	dessert made from raspberries, redcurrants and blackcurrants and served with fresh cream
rødkål	red cabbage cooked with sugar and vinegar

Danish

stegt/kogt rødspætte	fried or boiled plaice – sometimes served with shrimp sauce
svinekotelet	pork chop
sylte	brawn
torsk med sennepssovs	cod with mustard sauce
æbleflæsk	fried apples and onions with bacon
æblekage	stewed apples with toasted breadcrumbs and whipped cream
ål, stegt	fried eel

Health

ESSENTIAL INFORMATION

- It is preferable to purchase a medical insurance policy through a travel agent, a broker or a motoring organization.
- Take your own first aid kit with you.
- For finding your own way to a doctor, dentist, or pharmacist see p. 21.
- If staying in the country, the name of the medical practitioner on duty at weekends and at nights can be found in the local papers. In Copenhagen, ring **LÆGEVAGTEN** on 0041 if you require medical assistance at weekends or weekdays after 4.00 p.m.

WHAT'S THE MATTER?

I have a pain in my . . .	Jeg har ondt i . . .
	yigh har *o*nt ee . . .
ankle	**anklen**
	*a*nk-len
arm	**armen**
	*a*rmen
back	**ryggen**
	r*oo*ggen
bowels	**tarmene**
	t*a*rmerner
breast/chest	**brystet**
	brer-stet
ear	**øret**
	*e*rert
eyes	**øjnene**
	oy-nerner
foot	**foden**
	f*oe*-then
head	**hovedet**
	h*o*-erthet
heel	**hælen**
	h*ay*-len
jaw	**kæben**
	k*ay*-ben
leg	**benet**
	b*ee*net
lung	**lungen**
	l*oo*ng-en
neck	**nakken**
	n*u*kken
penis	**min penis**
	mean penis
shoulder	**skulderen**
	sk*oo*llern
stomach/abdomen	**maven**
	m*ay*-ven
testicle	**testiklerne**
	test*ee*k-ler-ner
throat	**halsen**
	h*a*l-sen

Danish

I have a pain in my . . .	**Jeg har ondt i . . .** yigh har *o*nt ee . . .
vagina	**skeden** sk*ai*then
wrist	**håndledet** h*o*n-lethet
I have a pain here [*point*]	**Jeg har ondt her** yigh har *o*nt h*ai*r
I have a toothache	**Jeg har tandpine** yigh har t*a*nn-p*ee*ner
I have broken my dentures	**Min protese er gået i stykker** mean prot*ay*-ser air gaw-et ee st*oo*kker
I have broken my glasses	**Mine briller er gået i stykker** m*ea*ner br*i*ller air gaw-et ee st*oo*kker
I have lost . . .	**Jeg har tabt . . .** yigh har tubt . . .
my contact lenses	**mine kontaktlinser** m*ea*ner kont*a*kt-*lee*n-ser
a filling	**en plombe** ain pl*o*m-ber
My child is ill	**Mit barn er sygt** meet b*a*rn air s*oo*-oot
He/she has a pain in his/her . . .	**Han/hun har ondt i . . .** h*a*n/h*oo*n har *o*nt ee . . .
stomach [*see list above*]	**maven** m*ay*-ven
How bad is it?	
I'm ill	**Jeg er syg** yigh air s*oo*-oo
It's serious	**Det er alvorligt** day air al-v*o*r-lit
It's not serious	**Det er ikke alvorligt** day air igger al-v*o*r-lit
It hurts (a lot)	**Det gør meget ondt** day gher my-et *o*nt
I have been in pain for . . .	**Jeg har haft ondt i . . .** yigh har haft *o*nt ee . . .
one hour/one day	**en time/en dag** ain t*ee*mer/ain d*ay*

It's a . . . **Det er en . . .**
day air ain . . .

sharp pain **stikkende smerte**
st*i*kkener sm*ai*rter

dull ache **dump smerte**
d*oo*mp sm*ai*rter

nagging pain **vedvarende smerte**
v*e*the-var-en-er sm*ai*rter

I feel dizzy **Jeg er svimmel**
y*i*gh air sv*i*mmel

I feel sick **Jeg har kvalme**
y*i*gh har k-v*a*lmer

I have a temperature **Jeg har feber**
y*i*gh har f*a*ber

Already under treatment for something else?

I take . . . regularly [*show*] **Jeg tager regelmæssigt . . .**
y*i*gh tar r*ay*-el-messit . . .

this medicine **denne medicin**
denner medic*i*n

these pills **disse tabletter**
d*i*sser tabl*e*tter

I have . . . **Jeg har . . .**
y*i*gh har . . .

a heart condition **dårligt hjerte**
d*o*r-lit y*ai*r-ter

hemorrhoids **haemorroider**
hemmo-r*ee*ther

rheumatism **gigt**
gh*ee*gt

I think I have . . . **Jeg tror, jeg har . . .**
y*i*gh tr*o*r y*i*gh har . . .

food poisoning **madforgiftning**
m*a*the-for-gh*i*ft-ning

sunstroke **hedeslag**
h*ai*ther-sl*a*y

I'm . . . **Jeg er . . .**
y*i*gh air . . .

diabetic/pregnant **diabetiker/gravid**
dee-ab*ai*tiker/gra-v*ee*the

allergic to penicillin **allergisk over for penicillin**
al-air-gisk o-er for penicill*ee*n

Danish

I'm asthmatic

Jeg har astma
yigh har ast-ma

Other essential expressions

Please can you help?

Kan De hjælpe mig?
kan dee yelper my

A doctor, please

En læge/doktor
ain layer/doktor

A dentist

En tandlæge
ain tann-layer

I don't speak Danish

Jeg taler ikke dansk
yigh tayler igger dansk

What time does . . . arrive?

Hvornår kommer . . .?
vornor kommer . . .

  the doctor

lægen/doktoren
layen/doktoren

  the dentist

tandlægen
tann-layen

From the doctor: key sentences to understand

Take this . . .

De skal tage dette . . .
dee skal ta detter . . .

  every day/hour

hver dag/time
vair day/teemer

  four times a day

fire gange daglig
feerer gung-er dowlee

Stay in bed

Bliv i sengen
bleev ee seng-en

Don't travel . . .

De må ikke rejse . . .
dee maw igger rye-ser . . .

  for . . . days/weeks

i de næste . . . dage/uger
ee dee nester . . . day-er/oo-er

You must go to the hospital

De skal på hospitalet
dee skal paw ho-speetay-let

Problems: complaints, loss, theft

ESSENTIAL INFORMATION

- Problems with:
  camping facilities, see p. 30.
  household appliances, see p. 48.
  health, see p. 76.
  the car, see p. 87.
- If the worst comes to the worst, find a police station.
  To ask the way, see p. 20.
- Look for:
  POLITI
- If you lose your passport report the loss to the nearest police station
  and go to the American embassy.
- In an emergency dial 0-0-0 and state which service you require.
  Emergency calls from public telephone boxes are free.

COMPLAINTS

I bought this . . .	**Jeg købte det/den . . .**
	yigh kerbter day/den . . .
today	**i dag**
	ee day
yesterday	**i går**
	ee gor
on Monday [see p. 99]	**i mandags**
	ee mandas
It's no good	**Det/den duer ikke**
	day/den doo-er igger
Look	**Se**
	say
Here [point]	**Her**
	hair
Can you . . .	**Kan De . . .**
	kan dee . . .
change it?	**bytte det/den?**
	bootter day/den
mend it?	**reparere det/den?**
	reparair day/den

Danish

Here's the receipt	**Her er kvitteringen** hair air kveett*ai*ring-en
Can I have a refund?	**Kan jeg få pengene tilbage?** kan yigh faw peng-en-er tilb*ay*-er

LOSS
[*See also 'Theft' below: the lists are interchangeable*]

I have lost . . .	**Jeg har mistet . . .** yigh har m*i*stet . . .
my bag	**min taske** mean t*a*ssker
my bracelet	**mit armbånd** meet *a*rmbon
my camera	**mit kamera** meet k*a*mera
my car keys	**mine bilnøgler** me*a*ner beel-n*oy*-ler
my logbook	**min indregistreringsattest** mean *i*n-reggee-stray-rings-attest
my driver's license	**mit kørekort** meet k*er*-kort
my insurance certificate	**mit forsikringsbevis** meet fors*eek*-rings-bev*ee*s

THEFT
[*See also 'Loss' above: the lists are interchangeable*]

Someone has stolen . . .	**Der er en, der har stjålet . . .** dair air *ai*n dair har st-y*aw*-let . . .
my car	**min bil** mean b*ee*l
my money	**mine penge** me*a*ner peng-er
my purse	**min pung** mean p*oo*ng
my tickets	**mine billetter** me*a*ner bill*e*tter
my travelers' checks	**mine rejsechecks** me*a*ner r*ye*-ser-shecks
my wallet	**min tegnebog** mean t*ie*-ner-bo

my watch	**mit ur**
	meet oor
my luggage	**min bagage**
	mean bagaysher

LIKELY REACTIONS: key words to understand

Wait	**Vent**
	vent
When?	**Hvornår?**
	vornor
Where?	**Hvor?**
	vor
Name?	**Navn?**
	noun
Address?	**Adresse?**
	adresser
I can't help you	**Jeg kan ikke hjælpe Dem**
	yigh kan igger yelper dem

The post office

ESSENTIAL INFORMATION

- To find a post office, see p. 20.
- Key words to look for:
  POSTHUS
  POSTKONTOR
- Look for this sign:
- For stamps look for the word
  FRIMÆRKER on a machine, or at
  a post office counter.
- Many stationers and kiosks selling
  postcards also sell stamps.
- Letter boxes are red.

Danish

WHAT TO SAY

To England, please	**Til England** til *eng*-lan
[*Hand letters, cards or parcels over the counter*]	
To Australia	**Til Australien** til ow-*straw*-lee-en
To the United States	**Til Amerika** til am*air*-ee-ka
[*For other countries, see p. 102*]	
Airmail	**Luftpost** *loo*ft-posst
Surface mail	**Overfladepost** *o*-er-*flay*-ther-posst
I'd like to send a telegram	**Jeg vil gerne sende et telegram** yigh vil *gair*-ner *se*nner it telegr*u*m

Telephoning

ESSENTIAL INFORMATION

- Instructions on how to use the phone are printed inside the directory in several languages.
- The code for the UK is 00944 and for the USA 01144.
- For calls to countries which cannot be dialled direct go to a post office and write the country, town and number on a piece of paper. Add **PERSONLIG SAMTALE** if you want a person-to-person call and **MODTAGEREN BETALER** if you want to reverse the charges. Get them to put the call through for you.
- If you need a number abroad or to reverse the charges ring inquiries (**OPLYSNINGEN**). They speak English.

WHAT TO SAY

I'd like this number . . . [*show number*]	**Vil De give mig dette nummer?** vil dee ghee my detter *noo*m-mer

in England	**i England** ee eng-lan
in Canada	**i Canada** ee canada
[*For other countries see p. 102*]	
Can you dial it for me, please?	**Vil De dreje det for mig?** vil dee dry-er day for my
May I speak to . . .?	**Jeg vil gerne tale med . . .** yigh vil gair-ner tayler methe . . .
Extension . . .	**Lokal . . .** lokal . . .
Do you speak English?	**Taler De engelsk?** tayler dee eng-elsk
Thank you, I'll phone back	**Tak, jeg ringer senere** tuck yigh ring-er say-nor

LIKELY REACTIONS

That's (15 kroner)	**Det bliver (femten kroner)** day bleer (femten kroner)
Cabin number (3)	**Kiosk nummer (tre)** kiosk noom-mer (tray)
[*For numbers, see p. 96*]	
Don't hang up	**Læg ikke røret på** leg igger rer-ret paw
I'm trying to connect you	**Jeg prøver at få forbindelsen** yigh proover at faw for-binnelsen
You're through	**Forbindelsen er klar** for-binnelsen air klar
There's a delay	**Der er ventetid** dair air venter-teethe
I'll try again	**Jeg prøver igen** yigh proover ee-ghen

Cashing checks and changing money

ESSENTIAL INFORMATION

- Finding your way to a bank, see p. 20.
- Look for these words on buildings:
  BANK (bank)
  SPAREKASSE (savings bank)
- Banks are open weekdays from 9.30 a.m. – 4.00 p.m. On Thursdays or Fridays they stay open until 6.00 p.m. They are closed Saturday and Sunday.
- Small currency exchange offices **VEKSELKONTOR** operate in many tourist centers.
- Have your passport handy.

WHAT TO SAY

I'd like to cash . . .	**Jeg vil gerne indløse . . .**
	yigh vil *g*air-ner *in*-ler-ser . . .
this travelers' check	**denne rejsecheck**
	de*nn*er r*ye*-ser-sheck
these travelers' checks	**disse rejsechecks**
	d*i*sser r*ye*-ser-shecks
this check	**denne check**
	de*nn*er sheck

For excursions into neighboring countries

I'd like to change this . . .	**Jeg vil gerne have vekslet . . .**
[*show banknotes*]	yigh vil *g*air-ner h*a* veks-let . . .
into German marks	**til D-mark**
	til d*ee*-mark
into Norwegian kroner	**til norske kroner**
	til n*o*rsker kr*o*ner
into Swedish kroner	**til svenske kroner**
	til sv*e*nsker kr*o*ner

LIKELY REACTIONS

Passport, please	**Må jeg se Deres pas**
	maw yigh say dair-es pas
Sign here	**Vil De skrive under her**
	vil dee skreever on-ner hair
Your banker's card, please	**Må jeg se Deres checkkort**
	maw yigh say dair-es sheck-kort
Go to the cash desk	**Gå til 'Kassen'**
	gaw til kassen

Car travel

ESSENTIAL INFORMATION

- Finding a filling station or garage, see p. 22.
  Is it a self-service station? Look out for
  SELVBETJENING
- Grades of gasoline:
  NORMAL (standard/regular)
  SUPER (premium)
  DIESEL
- 1 gallon is about 4½ litres (accurate enough up to 6 gallons).
- The minimum sale is 5 litres.
- Filling stations are usually able to help with minor mechanical problems. For major repairs you have to find a garage:
  REPARATIONSVÆRKSTED.

WHAT TO SAY

[*For numbers, see p. 96*]

(20) litres of . . .	**(Tyve) liter . . .**
	(toover) leeter . . .
(120) kroners of . . .	**For (hundrede og tyve) kroner . . .**
	for (hoonrer-ther aw toover) kroner . . .

standard/regular	**normal** norm*a*l
premium	**super** s*u*per
diesel	**diesel** d*ie*sel
Fill it up, please	**Fyld tanken op** f*oo*l t*a*nken op
Will you check . . .	**Vil De checke . . .** vil dee ch*e*cker . . .
the oil?	**olien?** *o*l-yen
the battery?	**batteriet?** batter*ee*-et
the radiator?	**køleren?** k*e*r-ler-ren
the tires?	**dækkene?** d*e*kker-ner
I've run out of gas	**Jeg er løbet tør for benzin** y*igh* air l*e*rbet t*e*r for ben-s*ee*n
Can I borrow a can, please?	**Kan jeg låne en dunk?** kan y*igh* l*aw*ner ain d*oo*nk
My car has broken down	**Min bil er brudt sammen** m*ea*n b*ee*l air br*u*te s*a*mmen
Can you help me, please?	**Kan De hjælpe mig?** kan dee y*e*lper my
Do you do repairs?	**Laver De reparationer?** l*a*ver dee repar*a*-sh*ow*ner
I have a puncture	**Jeg er punkteret** y*igh* air p*oo*nk-t*ai*rt
I have a broken windscreen	**Min forrude er gået i stykker** m*ea*n f*or*-r*oo*the air g*aw*-et ee st*oo*kker
I think the problem is here . . . [point]	**Jeg tror, problemet er her . . .** y*igh* tror probl*ee*-met air h*air* . .
Can you . . .	**Kan De . . .** kan dee . . .
repair the fault?	**reparere fejlen?** repar*air* f*y*len
come and look?	**komme og se på den?** k*o*mmer aw say p*aw* den
estimate the cost?	**give mig en pris?** gh*ee* my ain pr*ee*s

write it down?	**skrive det ned?**
	skreever day nethe
How long will the repair take?	**Hvor lang tid vil det tage?**
	vor lang teethe vil day tay
This is my insurance document	**Her er mit forsikringsbevis**
	hair air meet forseek-rings-bevees.

RENTING A CAR

Can I rent a car?	**Kan jeg leje en bil?**
	kan yigh lie-er ain beel
I need a car . . .	**Jeg skal bruge en bil . . .**
	yigh skal broo-er ain beel . . .
for five people	**til fem personer**
	til fem pairsoner
for a week	**i en uge**
	ee ain oo-er
Can you write down . . .	**Vil De skrive . . . ned?**
	vil dee skreever . . . nethe
the deposit to pay?	**depositum**
	depo-see-toom
the charge per kilometre?	**kilometer prisen**
	kilomait-ter pree-sen
the daily charge?	**dagsprisen**
	dows-pree-sen
the cost of insurance?	**forsikringsomkostningerne**
	forseek-rings-om-kostning-erner
Can I leave it in (Esbjerg)?	**Kan jeg aflevere den i (Esbjerg)?**
	kan yigh ow-levair den ee (esbyer)?
What documents do I need?	**Hvilke papirer behøver jeg?**
	veel-ker papee-er behoover yigh

LIKELY REACTIONS

I don't do repairs	**Jeg foretager ikke reparationer**
	yigh fortayer igger reparas-showner
Where is your car?	**Hvor er Deres bil?**
	vor air dair-es beel
What make is it?	**Hvilket bilmærke er det?**
	veel-ket beel-mairker air day
Come back tomorrow/on Wednesday [For days of the week, see p. 99]	**Kom igen i morgen/på onsdag**
	kom ee-ghen ee morn/paw onsda

Danish

We don't rent cars	**Vi lejer ikke biler ud** vee *lie*-er igger b*eel*er *oo*the
Your driver's license, please	**Deres kørekort** dair-es k*er*-erkort
The mileage is unlimited	**Ubegrænset kilometerantal** *oo*-begren-set kilom*ai*t-ter-*a*ntal

Public transport

ESSENTIAL INFORMATION

- Finding the way to the bus station, a bus, the railway station, see p. 20.
- Remember that waiting in line for buses is unheard of!
- To get a taxi you usually have to telephone the local firm or go to a taxi stand. Hailing a taxi is less common and does not always work. work.
- Types of trains:
  INTERCITY (long-distance express train, stopping only at principal stations)
  LYNTOG (high-speed train)
  REGIONALTOG (stops at all stations along the route)
  S-TOG (short distance train, suburbs of Copenhagen only)
- Key words on signs:
  BILLETTER (tickets)
  INDGANG (entrance)
  UDGANG (exit)
  FORBUDT (forbidden)
  SPOR (lit. track)
  PERRON (platform)
  OPLYSNINGEN (information)
  DSB (initials of Danish railways)
  GARDEROBESKABE (left luggage)
  BUSSTOPPESTED (bus stop)
  AFGANG (departures)
  ANKOMST (arrivals)

KØREPLAN (timetable)
REJSEGODSKONTOR (forwarding office)

- Buying a ticket?
  Buy your train ticket at the ticket office inside the station.
- When travelling on the S-train, Copenhagen only, you can purchase a ticket for use on both the S-train and the ordinary trains.
- When travelling by bus you usually pay as you enter. Most ticket machines give change.
- In some larger cities a **KLIPPEKORT** can be purchased. This entitles the buyer to a specific number of journeys at reduced cost and is obtainable from tobacconists and kiosks.
- Further reductions can be obtained by buying a weekly (**UGEKORT**) ticket or a monthly (**MÅNEDSKORT**) ticket.

WHAT TO SAY

Where does the train for (Odense) leave from?	**Hvor går toget til (Odense) fra?** vor gor *toe*-et til (*o*-then-ser) fra
At what time does the train for (Odense) leave?	**Hvornår går toget til (Odense)?** vornor gor *toe*-et til (*o*-then-ser)
At what time does the train arrive in (Odense)?	**Hvornår er toget i (Odense)?** vornor air *toe*-et ee (*o*-then-ser)
Is this the train for (Odense)?	**Er det toget til (Odense)?** air d*ay toe*-et til (*o*-then-ser)
Where does the bus for (Virum) leave from?	**Hvor går bussen til (Virum) fra?** vor gor b*oo*ssen til (*vee*-rom) fra
Is this the bus for (Virum)?	**Er det bussen til (Virum)?** air d*ay* b*oo*ssen til (*vee*-rom)
Do I have to change?	**Skal jeg skifte?** skal yigh sk*i*fter
Can you put me off at the right stop, please?	**Vil De sige mig, hvornår jeg skal af?** vil dee *see*-yer my vornor yigh skal *a*
Where can I get a taxi?	**Hvor kan jeg få en taxa?** vor kan yigh f*aw* ain t*axa*
Can I book a seat?	**Kan jeg reservere en plads?** kan yigh reser-v*air* ain pl*a*s
A single	**En enkelt** ain *enk*-elt
A return	**En retur** ain rer-*tour*
First class	**Første klasse** f*i*rster klasser

Danish

Second class	**Fællesklasse** fel-les-klasser
One adult	**En voksen** ain voksen
Two adults	**To voksne** toe voksner
and one child	**og et barn** o it barn
and two children	**og to børn** o toe burn
How much is it?	**Hvor meget bliver det?** vor my-et bleer day

LIKELY REACTIONS

Over there	**Derovre** dair-o-er
Here	**Her** hair
Platform (1) [*For times, see p. 99*]	**Perron (et)** pairrong (it)
Change at (Roskilde)	**Skift i (Roskilde)** skift ee (ros-killer)
Change at (the town hall)	**Skift ved (rådhuset)** skift vethe (roothe-hoo-set)
This is your stop	**De skal af her** dee skal a hair
There's only first class	**Der er kun første klasse** dair air kon firster klasser
There's a supplement	**Der er et tillæg** dair air it tilleg

Leisure

ESSENTIAL INFORMATION

- Finding the way to a place of entertainment, see p. 21.
- For times of day, see p. 98.
- Important signs, see p. 19.
- No smoking in cinemas, theatres or concert halls and in some restaurants.
- It is customary to leave one's coat in the cloakroom in theatres.

WHAT TO SAY

At what time does . . . open?	**Hvornår åbner . . .**
	vornor *aw*b-ner . . .
the museum	**museet?**
	moo-s*ay*-et
At what time does . . . close?	**Hvornår lukker . . .**
	vornor lookker . . .
the skating rink	**skøjtebanen?**
	sk*oy*-ter-baynen
At what time does . . . start?	**Hvornår begynder . . .**
	vornor begern-ner . . .
the cabaret	**kabareten?**
	kaba-r*ay*en
the concert	**koncerten?**
	kons*air*-ten
the film	**filmen?**
	f*i*lmen
the match	**kampen?**
	k*u*mpen
the play	**skuespillet?**
	sk*oo*-er-spillet
the race	**væddeløbet?**
	vether-lerbet
How much is it . . .	**Hvor meget koster det . . .**
	vor my-et koster day . . .
for an adult?	**for en voksen?**
	for *ai*n voksen
for a child?	**for et barn?**
	for *i*t barn

Do you have . . .   **Har De . . .**
har dee . . .

  a program?   **et program?**
it progr*u*m

  a guidebook?   **en vejledning?**
ain v*y*-lethe-ning

I'd like a lesson in . . .   **Jeg vil gerne have undervisning i at . . .**
yigh vil g*air*-ner h*a oo*nner-vees-ning ee at . . .

  sailing   **sejle**
s*i*gh-ler

  skating   **løbe på skøjter**
l*e*rber paw sk*oy*-ter

  waterskiing   **stå på vandski**
st*aw* paw v*a*n-skee

Can I rent . . .   **Kan jeg leje . . .**
kan yigh l*ie*-er . . .

  a bicycle?   **en cykel**
ain s*oo*kel

  a boat?   **en båd?**
ain b*aw*the

  a fishing rod?   **en fiskestang?**
ain f*i*sker-stung

  the necessary equipment?   **det nødvendige udstyr?**
day nerthe-ven-dee-er *oo*the-st*oo*r

How much is it?   **Hvor meget koster det?**
vor my-et k*o*ster day

  per day/per hour?   **per dag/per time?**
pair d*a*y/pair t*ee*mer

Do I need a license?   **Behøver jeg en tilladelse?**
beh*oo*ver yigh ain t*i*l-lay-thel-ser

Asking if things are allowed

ESSENTIAL INFORMATION

- May one smoke here?
  May we smoke here?
  May I smoke here?
  Can one smoke here?
  Can I smoke here?
  Is it possible to smoke here?

  Må man ryge her?
  maw man *roo*-yer hair

- All these English variations can be expressed in one way in Danish. To save space only the first English version: May one . . .? is shown below.

WHAT TO SAY

Excuse me, please	**Undskyld**
	on-skool
May one . . .	**Må man . . .**
	m*a*w man . . .
camp here?	**campere her?**
	cam-p*air* hair
dance here?	**danse her?**
	d*a*nser hair
fish here?	**fiske her?**
	f*i*sker hair
leave one's things here?	**efterlade sine ting her?**
	*e*fter-layther s*ee*ner t*ee*ng hair
look around?	**se sig omkring?**
	s*ay* sigh omkr*e*ng
park here?	**parkere her?**
	park*air* hair
picnic here?	**spise her?**
	sp*ee*-ser hair
sit here?	**sidde her?**
	s*i*ther hair
smoke here?	**ryge her?**
	r*oo*-yer hair
swim here?	**svømme her?**
	sv*er*-mer hair

May one . . .	**Må man . . .** m*aw* man . . .
telephone here?	**telefonere her?** telefon*air* hair
wait here?	**vente her?** v*en*ter hair

LIKELY REACTIONS

Yes, certainly	**Ja, gerne** y*a* g*air*-ner
Help yourself	**De må gerne selv tage** dee maw g*air*-ner s*el* t*ay*
I think so	**Det tror jeg** day tror yigh
Of course	**Naturligvis** nat*oo*r-lee-v*ee*s
Yes, but be careful	**Ja, men pas på** y*a* men p*as* paw
No, certainly not	**Nej, bestemt ikke** nigh bestemt igger
I don't think so	**Det tror jeg ikke** day tror yigh igger
Not normally	**Normalt ikke** norm*a*lt igger
Sorry	**Desværre** desv*air*

Reference

NUMBERS
Cardinal numbers

0	**nul**	n*oo*l
1	**en**	*ai*n
2	**to**	t*oe*
3	**tre**	tray
4	**fire**	f*ee*rer

5	**fem**	f*em*
6	**seks**	s*e*x
7	**syv**	s*oo*
8	**otte**	*aw*-der
9	**ni**	n*ee*
10	**ti**	t*ee*
11	**elleve**	*e*lver
12	**tolv**	tɔll
13	**tretten**	tr*e*tten
14	**fjorten**	f-y*o*rten
15	**femten**	f*e*mten
16	**seksten**	sigh-sten
17	**sytten**	s*oo*tten
18	**atten**	*a*tten
19	**nitten**	n*i*tten
20	**tyve**	t*oo*ver
21	**enogtyve**	*ai*n-o-t*oo*ver
22	**toogtyve**	t*oe*-o-t*oo*ver
23	**treogtyve**	tr*a*y-o-t*oo*ver
24	**fireogtyve**	f*ee*rer-o-t*oo*ver
25	**femogtyve**	f*e*m-o-t*oo*ver
30	**tredive**	tr*ai*the-ver
36	**seksogtredive**	s*e*x-o-tr*ai*the-ver
37	**syvogtredive**	s*oo*-o-tr*ai*the-ver
38	**otteogtredive**	*aw*-der-o-tr*ai*the-ver
39	**niogtredive**	n*ee*-o-tr*ai*the-ver
40	**fyrre**	f*u*r-er
41	**enogfyrre**	*ai*n-o-f*u*r-er
50	**halvtreds**	hal-tr*e*ss
51	**enoghalvtreds**	*ai*n-o-hal-tr*e*ss
60	**tres**	tr*e*ss
61	**enogtres**	*ai*n-o-tr*e*ss
70	**halvfjerds**	hal-f-y*e*rs
71	**enoghalvfjerds**	*ai*n-o-hal-f-y*e*rs
80	**firs**	f*ee*rs
81	**enogfirs**	*ai*n-o-f*ee*rs
90	**halvfems**	hal-f*e*ms
91	**enoghalvfems**	*ai*n-o-hal-f*e*ms
100	**hundrede**	h*oo*nrer-ther
101	**hundrede og en**	h*oo*nrer-ther o *ai*n
102	**hundrede og to**	h*oo*nrer-ther o t*oe*
125	**hundrede og femogtyve**	h*oo*nrer-ther o f*e*m-aw-t*oo*ver

150	**hundrede og halvtreds**	*h*oonrer-ther o hal-tress
175	**hundrede og femoghalvfjerds**	*h*oonrer-ther o fem-ao-hal-f-yers
200	**to hundrede**	*t*oe hoonrer-ther
250	**to hundrede og halvtreds**	*t*oe hoonrer-ther o hal-tress
300	**tre hundrede**	tray hoonrer-ther
400	**fire hundrede**	feerer hoonrer-ther
500	**fem hundrede**	fem hoonrer-ther
700	**syv hundrede**	soo hoonrer-ther
1,000	**tusinde**	*t*oo-sinner
1,100	**et tusinde et hundrede**	*it* too-sinner-*it*-hoonrer-ther
2,000	**to tusinde**	*t*oe too-sinner
5,000	**fem tusinde**	fem *t*oo-sinner
10,000	**ti tusinde**	tee *t*oo-sinner
100,000	**hundrede tusinde**	hoonrer-ther *t*oo-sinner
1,000,000	**en million**	*a*in mil-yoan

Ordinal numbers

1st	**første**	f*i*rster
2nd	**anden**	*a*nnen
3rd	**tredje**	tray-ther
4th	**fjerde**	f-y*air*
5th	**femte**	fem-ter
6th	**sjette**	s-y*e*tter
7th	**syvende**	soovenner
8th	**ottende**	*o*t-tenner
9th	**niende**	n*ee*-enner
10th	**tiende**	tee-enner
11th	**ellevte**	elv-ter
12th	**tolvte**	tol-ter

TIME

What time is it? — **Hvad er klokken?** / v*a* air cl*o*cken

It's . . . — **Den er . . .** / den air . . .

one o'clock — **et** / *it*

two o'clock	**to**	
	t*o*e	
three o'clock	**tre**	
	tr*ay*	
It's . . .	**Det er . . .**	
	day air . . .	
noon	**middag**	
	me*dd*a	
midnight	**midnat**	
	m*ee*the-nat	
It's . . .	**Den er . . .**	
	den air . . .	
five past five	**fem minutter over fem**	
	fem mee-n*oo*tter o-er fem	
twenty past five	**tyve minutter over fem**	
	t*oo*ver-mee-n*oo*tter o-er fem	
twenty to six	**tyve minutter i seks**	
	t*oo*ver mee-n*oo*tter ee s*e*x	
ten to six	**ti minutter i seks**	
	t*ee* mee-n*oo*tter ee s*e*x	
At what time . . . (does the train leave)?	**Hvornår . . . (går toget)?**	
	vorn*o*r . . . (gor t*o*e-et)	
At . . .	**Klokken . . .**	
	cl*o*cken . . .	
13.00	**tretten**	
	tretten	
18.25	**attenfemogtyve**	
	*a*tten-fem-o-t*oo*ver	
23.50	**treogtyvehalvtreds**	
	tr*ay*-o-t*oo*ver-hal-tress	

DAYS

Monday	**mandag**	
	m*a*nda	
Tuesday	**tirsdag**	
	t*ee*rs-da	
Wednesday	**onsdag**	
	*o*ns-da	
Thursday	**torsdag**	
	t*o*rs-da	
Friday	**fredag**	
	fr*ay*-da	

Danish

Saturday	**lørdag** ler-da
Sunday	**søndag** sern-da
last Monday	**i mandags** ee mandas
next Tuesday	**næste tirsdag** nerster teers-da
on Wednesday	**på onsdag** paw ons-da
on Thursdays	**om torsdagen** om tors-day-en
until Friday	**indtil fredag** in-til fray-da
before Saturday	**før lørdag** fer ler-da
after Sunday	**efter søndag** efter sern-da
the day before yesterday	**i forgårs** ee for-gors
two days ago	**for to dage siden** for toe dayer seethen
yesterday	**i går** ee gor
yesterday morning	**i går morges** ee gor mors
yesterday afternoon	**i går eftermiddags** ee gor efter-meddas
last night	**i aftes** ee aftes
today	**i dag** ee day
this morning	**i formiddag** ee for-medda
this afternoon	**i eftermiddag** ee efter-medda
tonight	**i aften** ee aften
tomorrow	**i morgen** ee morn
tomorrow morning	**i morgen formiddag** ee morn for-medda

tomorrow afternoon	**i morgen eftermiddag**
	ee morn *e*fter-medda
tomorrow evening	**i morgen aften**
	ee morn *a*ften
the day after tomorrow	**i overmorgen**
	ee *o*-er-morn

MONTHS AND DATES

January	**januar**
	y*a*-noo-ar
February	**februar**
	f*ay*-broo-ar
March	**marts**
	marts
April	**april**
	ah-pr*eel*
May	**maj**
	m*y*
June	**juni**
	y*oo*-nee
July	**juli**
	y*oo*-lee
August	**august**
	ow-g*oo*st
September	**september**
	sept*e*mber
October	**oktober**
	okt*o*ber
November	**november**
	nov*e*mber
December	**december**
	dec*e*mber
last month	**sidste måned**
	s*ee*ster m*a*w-nethe
this month	**denne måned**
	denner m*a*w-nethe
next month	**næste måned**
	n*e*ster m*a*w-nethe
in spring	**om foråret**
	om f*o*r-aw-ret
in summer	**om sommeren**
	om s*o*mmer-ren

Danish

in autumn	**om efteråret** om *ef*ter-aw-ret
in winter	**om vinteren** om *vin*-ter-ren
this year	**i år** ee or
last year	**sidste år** *see*ster or
next year	**næste år** *nes*ter or
in 1985	**i nitten hundrede og femogfirs** ee *nit*ten-*hoon*rer-ther o fem-o- *fee*rs
What's the date today?	**Hvad dato er det i dag?** va *day*-toe air *day* ee *day*
It's the 6th of March	**Det er den sjette marts** *day* air den s-*yet*ter m*arts*

Public holidays

● Shops, schools and offices are closed on the following dates:

January 1	**Nytårsdag**	New Year
. . .	**Skærtorsdag**	Maundy Thursday
. . .	**Langfredag**	Good Friday
. . .	**2. påskedag**	Easter Monday
. . .	**Store Bededag**	Common Prayer Day
. . .	**Kr. Himmelfartsdag**	Ascension Day
. . .	**2. pinsedag**	Whit Monday
. . .	**Grundlovsdag**	Constitution Day
December 25	**Juledag**	Christmas Day
December 26	**2. juledag**	Boxing Day

COUNTRIES AND NATIONALITIES

Countries

America	**Amerika** am*air*-ee-ka
Australia	**Australien** ow-str*aw*-lee-en
Austria	**Østrig** *er*-stree

Belgium	**Belgien** bel-ghee-en
Britain	**Storbritannien** stor-brittan-nee-an
Canada	**Canada** canada
East Germany	**Østtyskland** erst-toosk-lan
Eire/Ireland	**Irland** eer-lan
England	**England** eng-lan
Finland	**Finland** fin-lan
France	**Frankrig** frun-kree
Greece	**Grækenland** gray-ken-lan
India	**Indien** in-dee-en
Italy	**Italien** ee-tay-lee-en
New Zealand	**New Zealand** new sealand
Norway	**Norge** nor-yer
Pakistan	**Pakistan** pakistan
Poland	**Polen** po-len
Portugal	**Portugal** por-too-gal
Scotland	**Skotland** skot-lan
South Africa	**Sydafrika** soothe-ah-freeka
Spain	**Spanien** spay-nee-en
Sweden	**Sverige** svair-ee-er
Wales	**Wales** wales

Danish

West Germany	**Vesttyskland**
	vest-toosk-lan
Yugoslavia	**Jugoslavien**
	you-go-slay-vee-en

Nationalities

American	**amerikaner**
	amair-ee-kayner
Australian	**australier**
	ow-straw-lee-er
British	**britte**
	britter
Canadian	**canadier**
	ca-nay-dee-er
English	**englænder**
	eng-lenner
Finnish	**finne**
	finner
Irish	**irer**
	ee-er
Norwegian	**nordmand**
	nor-man
Scottish	**skotte**
	skotter
Swedish	**svensker**
	sven-sker
Welsh	**waliser**
	va-lee-ser

Do it yourself

Some notes on the language

This section does not deal with 'grammar' as such. The purpose here is to explain some of the most obvious and elementary nuts and bolts of the language, based on the principal phrases included in the book. This information should enable you to produce numerous sentences of your own making.

There is no pronunciation guide in most of this section partly because it would get in the way of the explanations and partly because you have to do it yourself at this stage if you are serious: work out the pronunciation from earlier examples in the book.

A/An

All nouns in Danish belong to one of two genders: common or neuter, irrespective of whether they refer to living beings or inanimate objects. A/an is expressed by **en** with common gender nouns and by **et** with neuter gender nouns.

A/an	common	neuter
an address	**en adresse**	
an apple		**et æble**
a bill	**en regning**	
a hotel		**et hotel**
a key	**en nøgle**	
a map		**et kort**
a menu	**en menu**	
a newspaper	**en avis**	
a suitcase	**en kuffert**	
a telephone directory	**en telefonbog**	
a ticket	**en billet**	
a timetable	**en køreplan**	

Important things to remember

- There is no way of telling a noun's gender. Although most nouns are of common gender you have to learn and remember the gender of each noun.

● Does it matter? Not unless you want to make a serious attempt to speak correctly and scratch beneath the surface of the language. You would be understood if you said **et adresse** or **en æble**, provided your pronunciation was good.

Practice saying and writing these sentences in Danish:

Have you got an apple?	**Har De . . .?**
Have you got a menu?	
I'd like a telephone directory	**Jeg vil gerne have . . .**
I'd like a timetable	
Where can I get a ticket?	**Hvor kan jeg få . . .?**
Where can I get a map?	
Is there a key?	**Er der . . .?**
Is there a newspaper?	
Is there an address?	

THE

Where we in English say 'the newspaper', the Danish equivalent is 'newspaper the'. In other words, 'the' is added on to the end of the noun. Common gender nouns add **-en** and neuter gender nouns add **-et**. If the noun already ends in **-e**, only **n** or **t** is added.

the	common (**n**)	neuter (**t**)
the address	**adressen**	
the apple		**æblet**
the bill	**regningen**	
the hotel		**hotellet**
the key	**nøglen**	
the map		**kortet**
the menu	**menuen**	
the newspaper	**avisen**	
the suitcase	**kufferten**	
the telephone directory	**telefonbogen**	
the ticket	**billetten**	
the timetable	**køreplanen**	

PLURALS
indefinite

addresses	**adresser**
apples	**æbler**
bills	**regninger**
hotels	**hoteller**
keys	**nøgler**
maps	**kort**
menus	**menuer**
newspapers	**aviser**
suitcases	**kufferter**
telephone directories	**telefonbøger**
tickets	**billetter**
timetables	**køreplaner**

definite

the addresses	**adresserne**
the apples	**æblerne**
the bills	**regningerne**
the hotels	**hotellerne**
the keys	**nøglerne**
the maps	**kortene**
the menus	**menuerne**
the newspapers	**aviserne**
the suitcases	**kufferterne**
the telephone directories	**telefonbøgerne**
the tickets	**billetterne**
the timetables	**køreplanerne**

- There are three plural forms for Danish nouns: **-(e)ne**, **(er)ne** or no ending at all. Often the third group of nouns will have a change of vowel, for example **et barn – to børn**.
- There is no easy way of knowing which plural ending a noun takes. You have to learn this along with the noun.

Practice saying and writing these sentences in Danish:

Have you got the key?	**Har De nøglen?**
Have you got the suitcases?	**Har De . . .?**
Have you got the telephone directory?	
Have you got the menu?	

Danish

I'd like the keys	**Jeg vil gerne have nøglerne**
I'd like the bill	**Jeg vil . . .**
I'd like the suitcase	
Where is the key?	**Hvor er nøglen?**
Where is the timetable?	**Hvor er . . .?**
Where is the address?	
Where are the suitcases?	**Hvor er . . .?**
Where are the keys?	
Where are the apples?	
Where are the newspapers?	
Where can I get the address?	**Hvor kan jeg få . . .?**
Where can I get the timetables?	
Where can I get the maps?	

Now make up more sentences along the same lines.

Important things to remember

- Danish has two forms for 'you'. The informal **du** is used when talking to relatives, friends and children and between young people. **De** is used in all other cases. Throughout this book the polite form of address **De** has been used. However, the informal **du** is being used more and more and if you find yourself being addressed as **du** you may like to use this informal word yourself in your response.
- In Danish there is no general word for 'please'. When asking for something it is polite to say **Jeg vil gerne have . . .** In other situations the tone of your voice and a pleasant way of speaking will see you through.

THIS AND THAT

	common gender	neuter gender
this	**den her**	**det her**
that	**den der**	**det der**

If you don't know the Danish word for an object you can point and say: **den her/det her** about something displayed close to you and **den der/det der** about something displayed further away from you. As you don't know the Danish word you will not know the correct gender either but you will still be understood.

Jeg vil gerne have den/det her	I'd like this
Jeg vil gerne have den/det der	I'd like that

HELPING OTHERS

You can help yourself with phrases such as:

I'd like . . . an open sandwich	**Jeg vil gerne have . . . et stykke smørrebrød**
Where can I get . . . a cup of tea?	**Hvor kan jeg få . . . en kop te?**
I'll have . . . a glass of wine	**Jeg vil have . . . et glas vin**
I need . . . a receipt	**Jeg skal bruge . . . en kvittering**

If you come across a compatriot having trouble making himself or herself understood, you should be able to speak to a Danish person on their behalf.

He'd like . . .	**Han vil gerne have . . . en kop te** han vil g*air*-ner h*a* . . . ain kop t*ay*
She'd like . . .	**Hun vil gerne have . . . en kop te** h*oo*n vil g*air*-ner h*a* . . . ain kop t*ay*
Where can he get . . .?	**Hvor kan han få et stykke smørrebrød?** vor kan han f*aw* it st*oo*kker smerrer-brerthe
Where can she get. . .?	**Hvor kan hun få et stykke smørrebrød?** vor kan h*oo*n f*aw* it st*oo*kker smerrer-brerthe
He'll have . . .	**Han vil have et glas vin** han vil h*a* it glas v*ee*n
She'll have . . .	**Hun vil have et glas vin** h*oo*n vil h*a* it glas v*ee*n
He needs . . .	**Han skal bruge en kvittering** han skal br*oo*-er ain kveett*a*iring
She needs . . .	**Hun skal bruge en kvittering** h*oo*n skal br*oo*-er ain kveett*a*iring

You can also help a couple or a group if they are having difficulties. The Danish word for *they* is **de**.

They'd like . . .	**De vil gerne have et værelse** dee vil g*air*-ner h*a* it v*air*-el-ser
Where can they get . . .?	**Hvor kan de få nøglen?** vor kan dee f*aw* n*oy*-len

They'll have . . .	**De vil have et dobbeltvaerelse**
	dee vil ha it dobbelt-vair-el-ser
They need . . .	**De skal bruge en kvittering**
	dee skal broo-er ain kveettairing

What about the two of you? No problem. The word for *we* is **vi**.

We'd like . . .	**Vi vil gerne have et glas vin**
	vee vil gair-ner ha it glas veen
Where can we get . . .?	**Hvor kan vi få en kop te?**
	vor kan ee faw ain kop tay
We'll have . . .	**Vi vil have en dessert**
	vee vil ha ain dessairt
We need . . .	**Vi skal bruge penge**
	vee skal broo-er peng-er

Try writing out your own checklist for these four useful phrase-starters like this:

Jeg vil gerne have . . .	**De vil gerne have . . .**
Han vil gerne have . . .	**Vi vil gerne have . . .**
Hun vil gerne have . . .	
Hvor kan jeg få . . .?	**Hvor kan de få . . .?**
Hvor kan han få . . .?	**Hvor kan vi få . . .?**
Hvor kan hun få . . .?	

MORE PRACTICE

Here are some useful Danish names of things. See how many different sentences you can make up, using the various points of information given earlier in this section.

	singular	plural
1 ashtray	**askebæger(t)**	**askebægre**
2 ball-point pen	**kuglepen(n)**	**kuglepenne**
3 bag	**taske(n)**	**tasker**
4 bottle	**flaske(n)**	**flasker**
5 car	**bil(n)**	**biler**
6 cigarette	**cigaret(n)**	**cigaretter**
7 corkscrew	**proptrækker(n)**	**proptrækkere**
8 egg	**æg(t)**	**æg**

		singular	plural
9	house	**hus(t)**	**huse**
10	knife	**kniv(n)**	**knive**
11	mountain	**bjerg(t)**	**bjerge**
12	plate	**tallerken(n)**	**tallerkener**
13	postcard	**postkort(t)**	**postkort**
14	room	**værelse(t)**	**værelser**
15	shoe	**sko(n)**	**sko**
16	stamp	**frimærke(t)**	**frimærker**
17	street	**gade(n)**	**gader**
18	ticket	**billet(n)**	**billetter**
19	train	**tog(t)**	**tog**
20	wallet	**tegnebog(n)**	**tegnebøger**

Danish Index

Norwegian

Norwegian

M. Hoddevik

Pronunciation **Dr J. Baldwin**

Useful address
Norwegian/Swedish
National Tourist Office
75 Rockefeller Plaza
New York, NY 10019
(212) 582-2802

Contents

Everyday expressions

[See also 'Shop talk', p. 158]

Hello	**Morn**
Good morning ⎤	morn
Good day ⎦	**God dag**
	goo dahg
Good afternoon	**God kveld**
	goo kvel
Good night	**God natt**
	goo natt
Goodbye	**Adjø**
	ad-yer
	Ha det bra
	ha-de bra
Yes	**Ja**
	ya
Please	**Vær så snild**
	var saw snil
Yes, please	**Ja, takk**
	ya takk
Thank you	**Takk**
	takk
Thank you very much	**Tusen takk**
	toossen takk
That's right	**Det er riktig**
	day ar riktee
No	**Nei**
	nay
No thanks	**Nei takk**
	nay takk
I disagree	**Jeg er ikke enig**
	yay ar ikker aynee
Excuse me ⎤	**Unnskyld meg**
Sorry ⎦	oonshil may
That's good ⎤	**Det er bra**
I like it ⎦	day ar bra
That's no good ⎤	**Jeg liker det ikke**
I don't like it ⎦	yay leeker day ikker
I know	**Jeg vet det**
	yay vait day

It doesn't matter	**Det gjør ikke noe** day yor *i*kker n*oo*-er
Where's the toilet, please?	**Hvor er toilettet?** vor ar twa-letter
Do you speak English?	**Snakker De engelsk?** sn*a*kker dee *e*ng-elsk
I'm sorry . . .	**Unnskyld meg men . . .** *oo*nshil may men . . .
I don't speak Norwegian	**Jeg snakker ikke norsk** yay sn*a*kker *i*kker noshk
I only speak a little Norwegian	**Jeg snakker bare litt norsk** yay sn*a*kker b*a*hrer litt noshk
I don't understand	**Jeg forstår ikke** yay forst*o*r *i*kker
Please can you . . .	**Kan de . . .** kan dee . . .
repeat that?	**gjenta det?** y*e*nta day
speak more slowly?	**snakke saktere?** sn*a*kker s*u*ckter-er
write it down?	**skrive det ned?** skr*ee*ver day ned
What is this called in Norwegian? [*point*]	**Hvordan sier man det på norsk?** v*o*rdun s*ee*-er mann day paw n*o*shk

Crossing the border

ESSENTIAL INFORMATION

- Don't waste time rehearsing what to say to border officials – the chances are you won't have to say anything at all.
- When entering Norway, have your documents ready: passport, tickets, money, travelers' checks, insurance documents, driver's license and car registration documents.
- Look for these signs:
  TOLL (customs)
  GRENSE (OVERGANG) (frontier)
  GRENSEPOLITI (frontier police)

Norwegian

● Random customs checks are frequent and fines for excess quantities of alcohol and tobacco high. You may be asked routine questions by customs officials [see below]. The other most important answer to know is 'Nothing': **Nei, ingen ting** (nay ing-en ting).

ROUTINE QUESTIONS

Passport?	**Pass?**
	pass
Insurance?	**Forsikring?**
	forsikring
Registration document?	**Vognkort?**
(logbook)	vogn-kort
Ticket, please	**Billetten Deres, takk**
	billet-en dayress, takk
Have you anything to declare?	**Har De noe å fortolle?**
	har dee noo-er aw for-toller
Where are you going?	**Hvor skal De?**
	vor skahl dee
How long are you staying?	**Hvor lenge skal De være her?**
	vor leng-er skahl dee varer har
Where have you come from?	**Hvor kommer De fra?**
	vor kommer dee fra

Meeting people

[See also 'Everyday expressions', p. 120]

Breaking the ice

How are you?	**God dag**
	goo dahg
Pleased to meet you	**Hyggelig å hilse på Dem**
	higge-lee aw hil-ser paw dem
I am here . . .	**Jeg er her . . .**
	yay ar har . . .
on vacation	**på ferie**
	paw fairee-er

on business	**på forretningsreise**
	paw forretning-sraysser
Can I offer you . . .	**Vil De ha . . .**
	vil dee ha . . .
a drink?	**en drink?**
	en drink
a cigarette?	**en sigarett?**
	en sigarett
a cigar?	**en sigar?**
	en sigar
Are you staying long?	**Skal De være her lenge?**
	skahl dee varer har leng-er

Name

What is your name?	**Hva heter De?**
	va hayter dee
My name is . . .	**Jeg heter . . .**
	yay hayter . . .

Family

Are you married?	**Er De gift?**
	ar dee yift
I am . . .	**Jeg er . . .**
	yay ar . . .
married	**gift**
	yift
single	**ugift**
	oo-yift
This is . . .	**Dette er . . .**
	detter ar . . .
my wife	**min kone**
	meen koner
my husband	**min mann**
	meen mann
my son	**min sønn**
	meen sirn
my daughter	**min datter**
	meen dot-ter
my boyfriend	**min venn**
	meen venn
my girlfriend	**min venninne**
	meen venn-*in*-er

Norwegian

This is . . .   **Dette er . . .**
detter ar . . .

  my fiancé(e)   **min forlovede**
meen forlaw-ved-er

  my colleague   **min kollega**
meen kolleg-ah

Do you have any children?   **Har De noen barn?**
har dee noo-en barn

I have . . .   **Jeg har . . .**
yay har . . .

  one daughter   **en datter**
ain dot-ter

  one son   **en sønn**
ain sirn

  two daughters   **to døtre**
too dirtrer

  three sons   **tre sønner**
tray sirnner

No, I haven't any children   **Nei, jeg har ingen barn**
nay yay har ing-en barn

Where you live

Are you . . .   **Er De . . .**
ar dee . . .

  Norwegian?   **norsk?**
noshk

  Swedish?   **svensk?**
svensk

I am . . .   **Jeg er . . .**
yay ar . . .

  American   **amerikansk**
ahmerikahnsk

  English   **engelsk**
eng-elsk

[*For other nationalities, see p. 211*]

I live . . .   **Jeg bor . . .**
yay boor . . .

  in London   **i London**
ee lon-don

  in England   **i England**
ee eng-lahn

in the United States	**i USA**
	ee oo-ess-ah
in Canada	**i Kanada**
	ee ka-na-da
in the south	**i Sør . . .**
	ee sir . . .
in the west	**i Vest . . .**
	ee vest . . .
in the center (of town)	**midt i (byen)**
	mitt ee (bee-en)

For the businessman and woman

I'm from . . . (firm's name)	**Jeg er fra . . .**
	yay ar fra . . .
I have an appointment with ...	**Jeg har en avtale med . . .**
	yay har en ahv-tahler may . . .
May I speak to . . .?	**Kan jeg snakke med . . .?**
	kan yay snakker may . . .?
This is my card	**Her er kortet mitt**
	har ar korter mitt
I'm sorry I'm late	**Unnskyld at jeg kommer for sent**
	oonshil aht yay kommer for saint
Can I make another appointment?	**Kan jeg avtale et nytt møte?**
	kan yay ahv-tahler et nitt mirter
I'm staying at the (Grand) hotel	**Jeg bor på (Grand) Hotell**
	yay boor paw (grang) hotel
I'm staying in the (Olavsgaten)	**Jeg bor i (Olavsgaten)**
	yay boor ee (olafs-gahten)

Asking the way

ESSENTIAL INFORMATION

● Keep a look out for street names, road signs, shops, cinemas etc.

WHAT TO SAY

Excuse me, please	**Unnskyld meg**
	*oo*nshil may
How do I get . . .	**Hvordan kommer jeg . . .**
	v*or*dun k*o*mmer yay . . .
to Oslo?	**til Oslo?**
	til *o*shlo
to Storgata?	**til Storgata?**
	til st*oor*-gahta
to the airport?	**til flyplassen?**
	til fl*ee*-pl*a*hssen
to the beach?	**til stranda?**
	til str*a*nda
to the bus station?	**til rutebilstasjonen?**
	til r*oo*ter-b*ee*l-stash*oo*nen
to the historic site?	**til det historiske området?**
	til day hist*oo*risker *o*mrawder
to the market?	**til torget?**
	til t*o*rg-er
to the police station?	**til politistasjonen?**
	til polit*ee*-stash*oo*nen
to the port?	**til havnen?**
	til h*a*vnen
to the post office?	**til postkontoret?**
	til p*o*sst-kont*oo*rer
to the railway station?	**til jernbanestasjonen?**
	til y*a*rn-bahner-stash*oo*nen
to the sports stadium?	**til idrettsplassen?**
	til *ee*drets-pl*a*hssen
to the tourist information office?	**turistinformasjonen?**
	tour*i*st-informa-sh*oo*nen
to the town center?	**til sentrum?**
	til s*e*ntrum
to the town hall?	**til rådhuset?**
	til r*a*wd-h*oo*sser
Excuse me, please	**Unnskyld meg**
	*oo*nshil may
Is there . . . near by?	**Er det . . . i nærheten?**
	ar day . . . ee n*ai*r-hayten
an art gallery	**et kunstgalleri**
	et k*oo*nst-galler*ee*

a bakery	**en bakerforretning**
	en ba hker-forretning
a bank	**en bank**
	en bank
a bar	**en bar**
	en bar
	et sjenkested
	et shenker-stayd
a botanical garden	**en botanisk hage**
	en bootahnisk hahg-er
a bus stop	**en bussholdeplass**
	en bus-holder-plahss
a butcher's	**en kjøttforretning**
	en shert-forretning
a café	**en kafé**
	en kafay
a cake shop	**et konditori**
	et konditoree
a campsite	**en kampingplass**
	en camping-plahss
a car park	**en parkeringsplass**
	en parkairingss-plahss
a currency exchange	**et vekslekontor**
	et veksler-kontoor
a chemist's/drugstore	**et apotek**
	et apottayk
	et parfymeri
	et parfeemer-ree
a church	**en kirke**
	en sheerker
a cinema/movie theater	**en kino**
	en sheeno
a delicatessen	**en delikatesseforretning**
	en dellika-tesser-forretning
a dentist's	**en tannlege**
	en tahnn-laygher
a department store	**et stormagasin**
	et stor-magasseen
a disco	**et diskotek**
	et diskotayk
a doctor's office	**en lege**
	en laygher

Norwegian

Is there . . . near by?	Er det . . . i nærheten?
	ar day . . . ee nair-hayten
a dry-cleaner's	**et renseri**
	et rain-seree
a fish store	**en fiskehandel**
	en fisker-handel
a garage (for repairs)	**et verksted**
	et vairk-sted
a greengrocer's	**en grønnsakhandel**
	en grern-sahk-handel
a grocer's	**en kolonialhandel**
	en kolonee-ahl-handel
a hairdresser's (ladies)	**en damefrisør**
	en dahmer-free-sir
a barber-hairdresser (men)	**en barberer**
	en barbairer
a hardware store	**en jernvarehandel**
	en yairn-va-rer-handel
a hospital	**et sykehus**
	et seeker-hooss
a hotel	**et hotell**
	et hotel
a laundry	**et selvbetjeningsvaskeri**
	et sel-bet-yainingss-vaskeree
a museum	**et museum**
	et moossay-oom
a newsstand	**en avisbutikk**
	en ahveess-bootick
a night club	**en nattklubb**
	en natt-kloobb
a park	**en park**
	en park
a petrol/gas station	**en bensinstasjon**
	en ben-seen-stashoon
a post box/mailbox	**en postkasse**
	en posst-kasser
a public garden	**en park**
	en park
a public toilet	**et offentlig toalett**
	et offentlee twa-let
a restaurant	**en restaurant**
	en restoo-rung

a snack bar	**en snackbar**
	en snackbar
a sports ground	**en idrettstadion**
	en eedrets-stahdee-on
a supermarket	**et supermarked**
	et sooper-mar-ked
a sweet/candy shop	**en godtebutikk**
	en gotter-bootikk
a swimming pool	**et svømmebasseng**
	et svermmer-basseng
a taxi stand	**en drosjeholdeplass**
	en drosher-holder-plahss
a theater	**et teater**
	et tay-ahter
a tobacco shop	**en tobakksforretning**
	en tobaks-forretning
a travel agent's	**et reisebyrå**
	et racer-beeraw
a youth hostel	**et ungdomsherberge**
	et oong-domss-hair-bairg-er
a zoo	**en zoologisk hage**
	en soo-law-ghisk-hahg-er

DIRECTIONS

- Asking where a place is, or if a place is near by, is one thing; making sense of the answer is another.
- Here are some of the most important key directions and replies.

Left/Right	**Venstre/Høyre**
	venstrer/hay-rer
Straight on	**Rett fram**
	rett frahm
There	**Der**
	dar
First on the left/right	**Første gate til venstre/høyre**
	firster gahter til venstrer/hay-rer
Second on the left/right	**Annen gate til venstre/høyre**
	annan gahter til venstrer/hay-rer
At the crossroads	**Ved veikrysset**
	vay vay-kreesser
At the traffic lights	**Ved trafikklyset**
	vay trafeekk-leesser

At the traffic rotary	**Ved rundkjøringen** vay roon-shir-ing-en
At the level crossing	**Ved jernbaneovergangen** vay yarn-bahner-awver-gahng-en
It's near/far	**Det er like i nærheten/langt unna** day ar leeker ee nair-hayten/ lahngt oonna
One kilometre	**En kilometer** en sheelo-mayter
Two kilometres	**To kilometer** too sheelo-mayter
Five minutes . . .	**Fem minutter . . .** fem minooter . . .
on foot/by car	**å gå/med bil** aw gaw/may beel
Take . . .	**Ta . . .** ta . . .
the bus	**bussen** boossen
the train	**toget** tawg-er
the tram/trolley	**trikken** trikken
the underground/subway	**undergrunden** oonner-groonnen

[*For public transport, see p. 199*]

The tourist information office

ESSENTIAL INFORMATION

- You will find a tourist information office in most major towns and resorts.
- Look for the word **TURISTINFORMASJON** or this sign:
- Tourist information offices are open all the

year round in major towns and resorts. In smaller towns they open for varying periods during the months of May, June, July, August and September.

- They will accept advance reservations for accommodation locally as well as assisting you on your arrival. They will also help you to make train, ferry, boat and bus reservations and give details on prices and road conditions.
- These offices give you free local information in the form of printed leaflets, fold-outs, brochures, lists and plans.
- For finding a tourist office, see p. 126, 130.

WHAT TO SAY

Please, have you got . . .	**Har De . . .** har dee . . .
a plan of the town?	**et kart over byen?** et kart awwer bee-en
a list of events?	**en liste over begivenheter** en lister awwer bay-yeeven-hayter
a list of hotels?	**en liste over hoteller** en lister awwer hoteller
a list of campsites?	**en liste over campingplasser?** en lister awwer camping-plahsser
a list of restaurants?	**en liste over restauranter?** en lister awwer restoo-runger
a leaflet on the town?	**en brosjyre om byen?** en brush-eerer om bee-en
a leaflet on the region?	**en brosjyre om distriktet?** en brush-eerer om districk-ter
a railway/bus timetable?	**en tog/buss tabell?** en tawg/bus ta-bell
In English, please	**På engelsk, takk** paw eng-elsk takk
How much do I owe you?	**Hvor mye skylder jeg Dem?** vor mee-er shiller yay dem

LIKELY ANSWERS

You need to understand when the answer is 'No'. You should be able to tell by the assistant's facial expression, tone of voice and gesture; but there are some language clues, such as:

No	**Nei** nay

Norwegian

I'm sorry	**Nei dessverre**
	nay dess-*vai*rrer
I don't have a list of campsites	**Jeg har ingen liste over campingplasser**
	yay har *ing*-en *li*ster *aw*ver camping-pla*hs*ser
I haven't got any left	**Jeg har ikke flere igjen**
	yay har *ik*ker *flay*rer ee-yen
It's free	**Det er gratis**
	day ar *gra*-tiss

Accommodation

Hotel

ESSENTIAL INFORMATION

- If you want hotel-type accommodation, look for this sign or the following words in capital letters on name boards:

HOTELL (usually high standard expensive establishment)
TURISTHOTELL (high standard, expensive resort establishment with wide range of facilities)
HØYFJELLSHOTELL (high mountain resort, expensive, high standard with wide range of facilities)
PENSJONAT (boarding house, standard varying from relatively high and expensive to modest and inexpensive)
GJESTGIVERI/VERTSHUS/TURISTHEIM (same as *pensjonat*)
TURISTHYTTE (tourist lodge, usually inexpensive and modest)
ROM (room in private house)
- A list of establishments may be obtained from the nearest Norwegian tourist office.
- Hotels are ungraded in Norway but strict legal requirements are made before establishments can use the term 'hotell'. 'Turisthotell'

and 'høfjellshotell' are of even higher standards and invariably hold a liquor license.

- Unlisted establishments can be slightly cheaper but are probably as good as the listed ones.
- Not all boarding houses etc. provide meals apart from breakfast. Inquire about this on arrival.
- On arrival also inquire about the cost of the room before accepting it.
- The cost is per person per night. It includes VAT and service charges but not always breakfast.
- Breakfast must be ordered when registering if not included in the price. In cities you'll be offered a choice of a cold table or an English or Continental breakfast. In the country, it'll be a cold table with the fare varying from the lavish to the simple according to the standard of the establishment.
- A cheaper full pension rate is available to guests staying at least 3–5 days. There are usually reductions of 75% for children under 3 and 50% for children 3–12(15) when sharing a room with adults.
- On arrival, you will be asked to show your passport and to fill in a special form for foreigners which usually carries an English translation.
- Leaving a tip will be appreciated but not expected.

WHAT TO SAY

I have a reservation	**Jeg har reservert** yay har resser-va*i*rt
Have you any vacancies?	**Har De noe ledig rom?** har dee n*oo*-er l*ay*dee room
Can I book a room?	**Kan jeg reservere et rom?** kan yay resser-va*i*rer et r*oo*m
It's for . . .	**Det er for . . .** day ar for . . .
one person	**en person** *ai*n pesh*oo*n
two persons	**to personer** t*oo* pesh*oo*ner

[*For numbers, see p. 205*]

[*For numbers, see p. 205*]

It's for . . .	**Det er for . . .** day ar for . . .
one night	**en natt** ain natt

It's for . . .	**Det er for . . .**
	day ar for . . .
two nights	**to netter**
	too netter
one week	**en uke**
	ain ooker
two weeks	**to uker**
	too ooker
I would like . . .	**Jeg vil ha . . .**
	yay vil ha . . .
a room	**et rom**
	et room
two rooms	**to rom**
	too room
with a single bed	**et enkeltrom**
	et enkelt room
with two single beds	**med to enkelsenger**
	may too enkel-seng-er
with a double bed	**med dobbelsenger**
	may dawbel-seng-er
with a toilet	**med toilett**
	may twa-let
with a bathroom	**med bad**
	may bahd
with a shower	**med dusj**
	may doosh
with a cot	**med barneseng**
	may barner-seng
with a balcony	**med balkong**
	may bal-kong
I would like . . .	**Jeg vil ha . . .**
	yay vil ha . . .
full board	**helpensjon**
	hail-pen-shoon
half board	**halvpensjon**
	hahl-pen-shoon
bed and breakfast	**overnatting med frokost**
	awver-natting may froo-kost
Is breakfast included?	**Er frokost inkludert?**
	ar froo-kost in-kloo-dairt
Do you serve meals?	**Serverer dere middag og lunsj?**
	servay-rer dayrer middag aw lunsh

At what time is . . . **Når serverer dere . . .**
nor serv*ay*-rer d*ay*rer . . .

  breakfast? **frokost?**
  fr*oo*-kost

  lunch? **lunsj?**
  lunsh

  dinner? **middag?**
  m*i*ddag

How much is it? **Hvor mye koster det?**
vor m*ee*-er k*o*st-er day

Can I look at the room? **Kan jeg se rommet?**
kan yay s*a*y r*o*ommer

I'd prefer a room . . . **Jeg foretrekker et rom . . .**
yay f*o*rer-trekker et room

  at the front/at the back **på forsiden/baksiden**
  paw f*o*r-seeden/b*ah*k-seeden

OK, I'll take it **Det er fint, jeg tar det**
day ar f*ee*nt yay tar day

No thanks, I won't take it **Nei takk, det passer ikke**
nay takk day p*ah*sser *i*kker

The key to room number (10), please **Kan jeg få nøkkelen til rom nummer (ti)?**
kan yay faw n*i*rk-ellen til room n*oo*mmer (*tee*)

Please may I have . . . **Kan jeg få . . .**
kan yay faw . . .

  a coat hanger? **en kleshenger?**
  en kl*ai*ss-heng-er

  a towel? **et håndkle?**
  et h*aw*n-kler

  a glass? **et glass?**
  et gl*ah*ss

  some soap? **et såpestykke?**
  et s*aw*per-st*i*cker

  an ashtray? **et askebeger?**
  et *a*sk-er-b*ay*gher

  another pillow? **en pute til?**
  en p*oo*ter til

  another blanket? **et teppe til?**
  et t*e*pper til

Come in! **Kom inn!**
kom *i*n

One moment, please!	**Et øyeblikk!** et er-yer-blick
Please can you . . .	**Kan De . . .** kan dee . . .
do this laundry/dry-cleaning?	**vaske/rense dette tøyet?** vasker/rainss-er detter ter-yer
call me at . . .?	**ringe meg klokken . . .?** ring-er may klokken . . .
help me with my luggage?	**hjelpe meg med bagasjen?** yelper may mer ba-ga-shen
call a taxi for . . .? [*For times, see p. 207*]	**skaffe en drosje til klokken . . .?** skaffer en drosher til klokken . . .
The bill, please	**Regningen, takk** raining-en takk
Is service included?	**Er service inkludert?** ar service inkloodairt
I think this is wrong	**Jeg tror dette er feil** yay troor detter ar fail
Can you give me a receipt?	**Kan De gi meg en kvittering?** kan dee yee may en kvittairing

At breakfast

Some more . . . please	**Kan jeg få litt mer . . .** kan yay faw litt mair . . .
coffee	**kaffe** kaffer
tea	**te** tay
bread	**brød** brer
butter	**smør** smer
jam	**syltetøy** seelter-tai
May I have a boiled egg?	**Kan jeg få et kokt egg?** kan yay faw et kokt egg

LIKELY REACTIONS

Have you an identity document, please?	**Har De legitimasjon?** har dee lay-ghee-tee-mashoon

What's your name?	**Hva er navnet?**
[see p. 123]	va ar nahvner
Sorry, we're full	**Det er dessverre fullt her**
	day ar dess-varrer fullt har
I haven't any rooms left	**Jeg har ikke flere ledige rom**
	yay har ikker flayrer laydee-yer
	room
Do you want to have a look?	**Vil De se rommet?**
	vil dee say roommer
How many people is it for?	**Hvor mange personer er det for?**
	vor mang-er peshooner ar day for
From (7 o'clock) onwards	**Fra klokken (sju)**
	fra klokken (shoo)
From (midday) onwards	**Fra klokken (tolv)**
[For times, see p. 207]	fra klokken (tawll)
It's (80 kroner)	**Det koster (åtti kroner)**
[For numbers, see p. 205]	day koster (awtti kroner)

Camping and youth hostelling

ESSENTIAL INFORMATION

- Look for the word: **CAMPING** or these signs

- You pay per car (if applicable), for the tent/camper and per person. Children under 5 go free.

- Be prepared to provide proof of identity.
- Campsites in Norway are classified as one, two and three-star camps. Charges vary according to number of stars awarded.
- You are allowed to camp on private, unused land with the landowner's permission, as well as on state owned land. You must, however, camp away from houses and cultivated areas and leave no litter behind.
- Roads in the North and West and in the mountain regions are often too narrow for a camper. Camper vacations are therefore recommended around Oslo, the southeastern part of the country and in the eastern valleys.
- Two and three-star sites have a watchman, flush toilets, shower, electric power points, laundry and ironing rooms. A notice of available amenities is posted up in each camp.
- Many sites have cabins/chalets to rent quite cheaply. These are popular and reservations should be made early in the afternoon. They are usually fitted with 4 bunk beds, an electric heater and a hot plate for cooking. Other equipment must be provided by the camper. Chalets must be left spotlessly clean.
- Picnic area have tables and bench seats and should be left clean.

Youth hostels

- Look for this sign or **UNGDOMSHERBERGE**.

- Youth hostels are located throughout the country. The standard is usually high. Not all are open during the winter.
- There is no age limit. Most accommodate families with children in family rooms with 4–6 beds.
- Most youth hostels have cooking facilities. A hot meal and breakfast can often be purchased.
- Sheet sleeping bags are obligatory. You can bring your own or rent one at the hostel.
- Groups must make advance bookings. All are welcome, but members of **NUH** (Norwegian Youth Hostel Association) or similar associations in other countries have priority. Non-members can purchase international membership cards at most youth hostels.

WHAT TO SAY

Have you any vacancies?	**Har De noen ledig plass?**
	har dee noo-en laydee plahss
It's for . . .	**Det er for . . .**
	day ar for . . .
one adult/one person	**en voksen/en person**
	ain vaksen/ain peshoon
two adults/two people	**to voksne/to personer**
	too vaksner/too peshooner
and one child	**og et barn**
	aw ait barn
and two children	**og to barn**
	aw too barn
It's for . . .	**Det er for . . .**
	day ar for . . .
one night	**en natt**
	ain natt
one week	**en uke**
	ain ooker
How much is it . . .	**Hvor mye koster det . . .**
	vor mee-er koster day . . .
for the tent?	**for teltet?**
	for telter
for the camper?	**for campingvogna?**
	for camping-vogna
for the car?	**for bilen?**
	for beelen
for the electricity?	**for strømmen?**
	for strermmen
per person?	**per person?**
	pair peshoon
per day/night?	**per dag/natt?**
	pair dahg/natt
Do you provide anything . . .	**Får man kjøpt noe . . .**
	for man shirpt noo-er . . .
to eat?	**å spise?**
	aw speesser
to drink?	**å drikke?**
	aw drikker

Norwegian

Do you have . . .	**Har dere . . .**
	har da*y*rer . . .
a bar?	**en bar?**
	en bar
hot showers?	**varme dusjer?**
	varmer d*oo*sher
a kitchen?	**et kjøkken?**
	et sh*e*rkken
a laundry?	**vaskemaskiner?**
	v*a*sker-mash*ee*ner
a restaurant?	**en restaurant?**
	en restoo-r*u*ng
a shop?	**en butikk?**
	en boo-t*i*ck
a swimming pool?	**et svømmebasseng?**
	et sv*e*rmmer-bass*e*ng
a takeaway?	**ferdigmat/takeaway mat?**
	f*ai*rdee-maht/takeaway maht

[*For food shopping, see p. 162 and for eating and drinking out, see p. 174*]

Where are . . .	**Hvor er . . .**
	vor ar . . .
the wastebaskets?	**søppelkassene?**
	s*i*rppel-k*a*hssener
the showers?	**dusjene?**
	d*oo*shener
the toilets?	**toalettene?**
	twa-l*e*tt-ener
At what time must one . . .	**Når må man . . .**
	nor maw mann . . .
go to bed?	**gå til sengs?**
	gaw til s*ai*ngss
get up?	**stå opp?**
	st*aw* opp
Please, have you got. . .?	**Har dere . . .**
	har d*a*yrer
a broom?	**en feiekost?**
	en f*a*yer-k*oo*st
a corkscrew?	**en korketrekker?**
	en k*o*rker-tr*e*kker
a drying-up cloth?	**et oppvaskhåndkle?**
	et *o*ppvask-h*aw*n-kler

a fork?	**en gaffel?**
	en ga-fel
a fridge?	**et kjøleskap?**
	et shirler-skahp
a frying pan?	**en stekepanne?**
	en stayker-pahnner
an iron?	**et strykejern?**
	et streeker-yarn
a knife?	**en kniv?**
	en k-neev
a plate?	**en tallerken?**
	en tal-lairken
a saucepan?	**en kjele?**
	en shayler
a teaspoon?	**en teskje?**
	en tay-shay
a can opener?	**en bokseåpner?**
	en boxer-awpner
any laundry powder?	**vaskepulver?**
	vasker-poolver
any liquid detergent?	**oppvaskmiddel?**
	oppvask-middel

Problems

The toilet	**Toilettet**
	twa-letter
The shower	**Dusjen**
	dooshen
The tap	**Vannkranen**
	vahnn-krahnen
The razor outlet	**Stikkontakten**
	stick-kontakten
The light	**Lyset**
	leesser
. . . is not working	**. . . virker ikke**
	. . . veerker ikker
My camping gas has run out	**Gassflasken min er tom**
	gahss-flask-en meen ar tom

LIKELY REACTIONS

Have you an identity document?	**Har De legitimasjon?**
	har dee lay-ghee-tee-mashoon

Norwegian

Your membership card, please	**Kan jeg få se medlemskortet deres**
	kan yay faw say maid-lemss-korter dayress
What's your name? [see p. 123]	**Hva er navnet?**
	va ar nahvner
Sorry, we're full	**Det er dessverre fullt her**
	day ar dess-varrer fullt har
How many people is it for?	**Hvor mange personer er det for?**
	vor mang-er peshooner ar day for
How many nights is it for?	**Hvor mange netter er det for?**
	vor mang-er netter ar day for
It's (40) kroner . . .	**Det blir (førti) kroner . . .**
	day bleer (firtee) kroner . . .
per day/per night	**per dag/per natt**
[For numbers, see p. 205]	pair dahg/pair natt

Rented accommodation: problem solving

ESSENTIAL INFORMATION

- **For short vacations:** Arrange your accommodations before leaving. Travel agents and the Norwegian Tourist Board at home will be able to help you.
- If you want to rent accommodation when already in Norway, look for **TIL LEIE** in local newspapers or put in an advert yourself.
- For vacations the following types of accommodation are popular and readily available when booked in advance.
- **BONDEGÅRD** (farmhouse vacation). Vacation on selected working farms; guests are not expected to do any work.
- **HYTTE** (chalet vacation). Inexpensive open air vacations. Chalets situated throughout Norway, sometimes near a city. Chalets are usually comfortable and equipped for 4–6 people. Inventory complete except for linen and towels.
- **Rental apartments**. Flat or chalet with high standard of amenities.

with total or partial self-service. Accommodation often around or near cafeteria, lounges, TV rooms, grocer's shop, sauna etc.

- **RORBU** vacations. A cabin on the seashore equipped with basic amenities. Mostly in the North of Norway.
- Having arranged your own accommodation and arrived with the key, check the obvious basics that you take for granted at home.
- **Electricity:** Appliances from home can be used, but may need an adaptor plug, as you will only find two-pin plugs. Electric heaters (rather like small radiators) are often attached to the wall. They get very hot and must not be covered. Fuses look like a round, white radio battery. Light bulbs screw on.
- **Gas:** Only bottled propane gas for cooking in remote chalets and *rorbus*. No gas fires. Fireplaces can be open or closed.
- **Cooker:** Always electric. Oven and plates for cooking, usually no grill. Plates sometimes slow.
- **Toilet:** Mains drainage or septic tank. Don't flush disposable diapers etc. down the toilet if you're on a septic tank.
- **Windows:** Check method of opening and shutting. Must not be left open after dark with light on because of insects.
- **Insects and snakes:** Mosquitoes bad in eastern and northern regions, particularly in June. Kept partly away by smoke spiral (**røkspiral**) which can be purchased in sports shops, general stores and 'apoteks'. In dry forest regions, look out for adders as in Norway their bites can kill. Buy antidote tablets **ormtabletter** from 'apotek' or general stores. If bitten, bleed wound and seek medical attention straightaway. Don't picnic on dry stony spots.
- **Equipment:** For buying and replacing equipment, see p. 156.
- Be clear in your mind who to contact in an emergency, even if only a Norwegian neighbor in the first instance.

WHAT TO SAY

My name is . . .	**Jeg heter . . .**
	yay hayter . . .
I'm staying at . . .	**Jeg bor i . . .**
	yay boor ee . . .
They've cut off . . .	**De har kuttet av . . .**
	dee har koottet ahv . . .
the electricity	**strømmen**
	strermmen
the water	**vannet**
	vahnner

Do you know of . . .
Vet De om . . .
vait dee om . . .

  an electrician?
  en elektriker?
  en ela*i*k-tricker

  a plumber?
  en rørlegger?
  en rer-legger

Where is . . .
Hvor er . . .
vor ar . . .

  the fuse box?
  sikringstavlen?
  s*i*ck-ringss-t*ah*vlen

  the tap?
  stopperkranen?
  st*o*pper-kr*ah*nen

  the boiler?
  fyren?
  f*ee*ren

  the water heater?
  varmtvannsbeholderen?
  v*a*rmt-vahnnss-bay-h*o*lderen

Is there . . .
Er det . . .
ar day . . .

  bottled gas?
  propangass?
  prop*ah*n-gahss

  mains drainage?
  kloakkutløp?
  kloo-*ah*k-ootlerp

  a septic tank?
  en septiktank?
  en s*e*ptik-tahnk

  central heating?
  sentralvarme?
  sentr*ah*l-varmer

The cooker
Komfyren
kom-f*ee*ren

The hairdryer
Hårtørkeren
h*o*r-terk-*ai*ren

The heating
Oppvarmingen
*o*pp-varming-en

The electric heater
Den elektriske ovnen
den ela*i*k-trissker *o*vnen

The iron
Strykejernet
str*ee*ker-*ya*rner

The refrigerator
Kjøleskapet
sh*i*rler-sk*ah*per

The telephone
Telefonen
telef*oo*nen

The toilet
Toalettet
twa-l*e*tter

The washing machine	**Vaskemaskinen** vasker-masheenen
. . . is not working	**. . . virker ikke** . . . veerker ikker
Where can I get . . .	**Hvor kan jeg få . . .** vor kan yay faw . . .
an adaptor for this?	**en overgangskontakt til denne?** en awver-gangss-kontahkt til denner
a bottle of propane gas?	**en flaske propangass?** en flask-er proopahn-gahss
a fuse?	**en sikring?** en sick-ring
insecticide spray?	**et insektmiddel?** et insekt-middel
a light bulb?	**en lyspære?** en leess-parer
The drain	**Avløpsrøret** ahv-lerps-rer-rer
The sink	**Vasken** vahsken
. . . is blocked	**. . . er tett** . . . ar tett
The toilet is blocked	**Toalettet er tett** twa-letter ar tett
The gas is leaking	**Gassen lekker** gahssen lekker
Can you mend it right away?	**Kan De reparere det med en gang?** kan dee reppa-rairer day med ain gahng
When can you mend it?	**Når kan De reparere den?** nor kan dee reppa-rairer den
How much do I owe you?	**Hvor mye skylder jeg Dem?** vor mee-er shiller yay dem
When is the rubbish collected?	**Når er det søppeltømming?** nor ar day sir-pel-termming

LIKELY REACTIONS

What's your name?	**Hva er navnet?** va ar nahvner
What's your address?	**Hva er adressen Deres?** va ar ah-dress-en dayress

Norwegian

There's a shop . . .	**Det er en butikk . . .**
	day ar en boot*i*kk
in town	**i byen**
	ee b*ee*-en
I can't come . . .	**Jeg kan ikke komme . . .**
	yay kan *i*kker k*o*mmer . . .
today	**i dag**
	ee dahg
this week	**denne uken**
	denner *oo*ken
until Monday	**før mandag**
	fir m*a*hn-dahg
I can come . . .	**Jeg kan komme . . .**
	yay kan k*o*mmer . . .
on Tuesday	**på tirsdag**
	paw t*ee*sh-dahg
when you want	**når De vil**
	nor dee v*i*l
Every day	**Hver dag**
	var dahg
Every other day	**Annen hver dag**
	*ah*nen var d*a*hg
On Wednesday	**På onsdag**
	paw *oo*nss-dahg

[*For days of the week, see p. 208*]

General shopping

The drugstore/The chemist's

ESSENTIAL INFORMATION

- Look for the word **APOTEK** in capital letters.
- Medicines (drugs) are available only at an *apotek*.
- Some non-drugs can be bought at supermarkets and groceries.
- Toiletries are bought in small shops called **PARFYMERI** and in supermarkets, department stores and groceries, never in an *apo-*

tek. A *parfymeri* sells toiletries only not photographic equipment, baby utensils etc.

- *Apoteks* are open 9–5 Monday to Friday and 9–1 or 3 on Saturdays. They are closed on Sundays and holidays.
- All-night drugstores are only found in major cities.
- In emergencies ask for a doctor or the medical emergency service **LEGEVAKT**.
- Prescriptions are needed for most drugs like antibiotics etc. There is a prescription charge.
- For minor injuries and ailments *apoteks* may be able to suggest treatment that does not need prescription.
- Finding the drugstore, see p. 127.

The following articles can normally only be bought at an *apotek*. Articles marked * can also be bought at supermarkets and department stores.

I'd like . . . please	**Kunne jeg få . . .**
	k*oo*n-ner yay faw . . .
*some Alka Seltzer	**noe nyco/samarin**
	n*oo*-er n*ee*co/s*a*mar*ee*n
some antiseptic	**et antiseptisk middel**
	et *a*nti-s*e*ptisk m*i*ddel
*some bandages	**noen bandasjer**
	n*oo*-en ban-d*a*-sher
some contraceptives	**et prevensjonsmiddel**
	et pray-vang-sh*oo*nss-m*i*ddel
*some cotton wool	**noe vatt**
	n*oo*-er v*a*htt
some eye drops	**noen øyendråper**
	n*oo*-en er-yen-dr*a*w-per
some inhalant	**et innåndingsmiddel**
	et *i*n-awn-dingss-m*i*ddel
*some insect repellent	**et insektmiddel**
	et *i*nsect-m*i*ddel
*some sticking plaster	**noe plaster**
	n*oo*-er pl*a*ster
*some throat lozenges	**noen halspastiller**
	n*oo*-en h*a*hlss-pa-st*i*ller
I'd like something for . . .	**Kunne jeg få noe for . . .**
	k*oo*n-ner yay faw n*oo*-er for . . .
bites/stings	**insektstikk**
	*i*nsect-st*i*ck

I'd like something for . . .	Kunne jeg få noe for . . .
	koon-ner yay faw noo-er for . . .
burns/scalds	**brannsår**
	brahn-sor
a cold	**forkjølelse**
	for-shirlel-ser
constipation	**forstoppelse**
	for-stop-el-ser
a cough	**hoste**
	hoosster
diarrhea	**diarre**
	dee-array
earache	**øreverk**
	er-rer-vark
flu	**influensa**
	influenssa
sore gums	**sårt tannkjøtt**
	sort tahn-shirt
*sunburn	**solbrenthet**
	sool-brent-hait
*toothache	**tannverk**
	tahn-vark
travel sickness	**reisesyke**
	racer-seeker

The following articles can normally only be bought at a *parfymeri*. Articles marked * can also be bought at supermarkets and groceries.

I need . . .	Jeg trenger . . .
	yay treng-er . . .
*some baby food	**noe bebymat**
	noo-er baby-maht
*some deodorant	**en deodorant**
	en day-odorant
*some disposable diapers	**papirbleier**
	papeer-blayer
*some hand cream	**noe håndkrem**
	noo-er hawn-kraim
*some lipstick	**leppestift**
	lepper-stift
some lip salve/chapstick	**leppomade**
	leppom-ahder

some make-up remover	**sminkefjerner**
	sm*i*nkerf-*ya*irner
*some paper tissues	**noen papirlommetørkler**
	n*oo*-en pap*ee*r-lommer-t*e*rk-ler
*some razor blades	**noen barberblader**
	n*oo*-en barb*air*-bl*ah*der
*some safety pins	**noen sikkerhetsnåler**
	n*oo*-en s*i*cker-haits-n*aw*ler
*some sanitary napkins	**sanitetsbind**
	sahnit*ai*ts-binn
*some shaving cream	**barberkrem**
	barb*air*-kraim
*some suntan lotion/oil	**solkrem/olje**
	s*oo*l-kraim/*o*l-yer
some talcum powder	**talkumpulver**
	t*ah*lkoom-p*oo*lver
*some Tampax	**tampax**
	t*ah*mpax
*some toilet paper	**noe toalettpapir**
	n*oo*-er twa-lett-pap*ee*r
*some toothpaste	**noe tannkrem**
	n*oo*-er t*ah*nn-kraim
*some Vaseline	**noe Vaseline**
	n*oo*-er vasser-l*ee*n

Holiday items

ESSENTIAL INFORMATION

- Normal opening hours: 9–5 Monday–Friday and 9–1 Saturdays.
- Places to shop and signs to look for:
  BOKHANDEL (stationery-bookshop) sell stamps and postcards, not toys, records etc.
  KODAK (films)
  KOLONIAL (general store, grocery)
  KIOSK sells postcards, stamps, newspapers, often films.
  STORMARKED (department store)

Norwegian

WHAT TO SAY

I'd like . . .	**Jeg vil ha . . .** yay vil ha . . .
a bag	**en bag** en b*a*g
a beach ball	**en badeball** en b*ah*der-b*ah*ll
a bucket	**en bøtte** en b*i*rtter
an English newspaper	**en engelsk avis** en *eng*-elsk ahv*ee*ss
some envelopes	**noen konvolutter** n*oo*-en kon-vo-l*u*tter
a guide book	**en reisehåndbok** en racer-h*aw*n-book
a map (of the area)	**et (lokal) kart** et (lok*ah*l)-kart
some postcards	**noen prospektkort** n*oo*-en prospekt-kort
a spade	**en spade** en spa-der
a straw hat	**en stråhatt** en str*aw*-hahtt
some sunglasses	**et par solbriller** et par s*oo*l-briller
an umbrella	**en paraply** en para-pl*ee*
some writing paper	**skrivepapir** skr*ee*ver-pap*ee*r
I'd like . . . [*show the camera*]	**Jeg vil ha . . .** yay vil ha . . .
a roll of color film	**en fargefilm** en f*a*r-gher-film
a roll of black and white film	**en svart/hvitt film** en svart/vitt film
for prints	**for fotografier** for footo-graf*ee*-er
for slides	**for lysbilder** for l*ee*ss-bilder
Please can you . . .	**Kan De . . .** kan dee . . .

develop/print this?	**fremkalle/kopiere denne?**
	fr*ai*m-kaller/kopee-*ay*rer d*e*nner
load the camera?	**sette inn filmen?**
	setter inn film-en

[*For other essential expressions, see 'Shop talk', p. 158*]

The tobacco shop

ESSENTIAL INFORMATION

- Tobacco, cigarettes etc. are sold in kiosks, candy shops, snack bars, groceries and supermarkets.
- Most international brands are available.
- All tobacco products are exceedingly expensive in Norway.
- Rolling and pipe tobacco, cigarette paper and other rolling equipment is readily available.

WHAT TO SAY

A pack of cigarettes . . .	**En pakke sigaretter . . .**
	en p*a*kker sigar*e*tt-er . . .
with filters	**med filter**
	may f*i*lter
without filters	**uten filter**
	*oo*ten f*i*lter
king size	**king size**
	k*i*ng size
menthol	**med mentol**
	may men-t*oo*l
Those up there . . .	**De der oppe . . .**
	dee dar *o*pper . . .
on the right	**til høyre**
	til h*ay*-rer
on the left	**til venstre**
	til v*e*nstrer
These [*point*]	**Disse**
	d*i*sser

Norwegian

Do you have . . .	**Har dere . . .** har dayrer . . .
English cigarettes?	**engelske sigaretter?** eng-elsker sigarett-er
rolling tobacco?	**rulletobakk?** rooler-tobakk
A packet of pipe tobacco	**En pakke pipetobakk** en pakker peeper-tobakk
That one [point]	**Den der** den dar
A cigar, please	**En sigar, takk** en sigar takk
This one [point]	**Denne** denner
Some cigars, please	**Noen sigarer, takk** noo-en sigar-er takk
Those [point]	**De der** dee dar
A box of matches	**En eske fyrstikker** en esker feer-stikker
A packet of flints [show lighter]	**En pakke flintesteiner** en pakker flinter-stainer
Lighter fluid	**Lighter bensin** lighter ben-seen
Lighter gas	**Lighter gass** lighter gahss

[*For other essential expressions, see 'Shop talk' p. 158*]

Buying clothes

ESSENTIAL INFORMATION

- Clothes are expensive but tend to be of high quality. Sales in January and August have genuine reductions and are good value for money.
- For clothes and shoes check shop windows or ask for:

DAMEKLÆR (women's clothes)
HERREKLÆR (men's clothes)
BARNEKLÆR (children's clothes)
SKOBUTIKK (shoe shop)
STORMARKED (department store)
- Most shops leave you to look around on your own and try things on.

WHAT TO SAY

I'd like . . .	**Jeg vil ha . . .**
	yay vil ha . . .
an anorak/parka	**en anorakk**
	en ahn-oor*ah*kk
a belt	**et belte**
	et b*e*lter
a bikini	**en bikini**
	en bik*i*ni
a bra	**en B.H.**
	en b*ay* h*aw*
a cap (swimming)	**en badehette**
	en b*ah*der-h*e*tter
a cap (skiing)	**en skilue**
	en sh*ee*-loo-er
a cardigan	**en ulljakke**
	en *oo*ll-yakker
a coat	⌈**en kåpe** (ladies)
	⎪en k*aw*-per
	⎪**en frakk** (men)
	⌊en fr*ah*kk
a dress	**en kjole**
	en sh*oo*ler
a jacket	**en jakke**
	en y*a*kker
a jumper/pullover	**en genser**
	en gh*e*n-ser
a nightgown	**en nattkjole**
	en n*a*tt-shooler
a raincoat	**en regnfrakk**
	en r*ai*n-frahkk
a shirt	**en skjorte**
	en sh*oo*rter

WHAT TO SAY

I'd like . . .	**Jeg vil ha . . .**
	yay vil ha . . .
a skirt	**et skjørt**
	et sh*i*rt
a suit	**en dress**
	en dr*e*ss
a swimsuit	**en badedrakt**
	en b*ah*der-drahkt
a T-shirt	**en T-skjorte**
	en t*ay*-shoorter
I'd like a pair of . . .	**Jeg vil ha et par . . .**
	yay vil ha et par . . .
shorts	**shorts**
	shorts
stockings	**strømper**
	str*i*rm-per
tights	**strømpebukser**
	str*i*rm-per-b*oo*kser
pajamas	**pyjamas**
	pee-sh*a*-mass
briefs	**truser** (women)
	tr*oo*sser
	korte underbukser (men)
	korter *oo*nder-b*oo*kser
gloves	**hansker**
	han-sker
jeans	**ola-bukser**
	*oo*la-b*oo*kser
socks	**sokker**
	s*o*cker
trousers	**bukser**
	b*oo*kser
shoes	**sko**
	skoo
sandals	**sandaler**
	san-d*ah*ler
skiing boots	**skistøvler**
	shee-st*i*rfler
smart shoes	**pen sko**
	p*ai*n skoo
warm boots	**varme støvler**
	v*a*rmer st*i*rfler

My size is . . . [*For numbers, see p. 205*]	**Jeg er størrelse . . .** yay ar stir-rel-ser
Can you measure me, please?	**Kan De måle meg?** kan dee m*a*w-ler may
Can I try it on?	**Kan jeg prøve den?** kan yay pr*i*rfer den
It's for a present	**Det er en gave** day ar en g*a*-ver
These are the measurements [*show written*]	**Dette er målene** detter ar m*a*w-len-er
bust	**byste** b*ee*ster
chest	**bryst** br*ee*st
hips	**hofter** h*o*fter
waist	**livvidde** l*ee*-vidder

Have you something . . .	**Har dere noe . . .** har d*a*yrer n*oo*-er . . .
in black?	**i svart?** ee svart
in white?	**i hvitt?** ee v*i*tt
in gray?	**i grått?** ee gr*a*wt
in brown?	**i brunt?** ee br*oo*nt
in pink?	**i rosa?** ee r*oo*-sa
in green?	**i grønt?** ee gr*er*nt
in red?	**i rødt?** ee r*er*t
in yellow?	**i gult?** ee g*oo*lt
in this color? [*point*]	**i denne fargen?** ee denner f*a*r-ghen
in cotton?	**i bomull?** ee b*o*m-ooll
in denim?	**i dongeri?** ee .d*u*ng-ree

Norwegian

Have you something . . .	**Har dere noe . . .**
	har dayrer noo-er . . .
in leather?	**i skinn?**
	ee shinn
in nylon?	**i nylon?**
	ee neelon
in suede?	**i semsket skinn?**
	ee sem-sket shinn
in wool?	**i ull?**
	ee ooll
in this material? [point]	**i dette stoffet?**
	ee detter stuffer

[For other essential expressions, see 'Shop talk', p. 158]

Replacing equipment

ESSENTIAL INFORMATION

- Look for the signs or ask for:
  JERNVAREFORRETNING (hardware)
  GLASSMAGASIN (crockery, cutlery, ornaments etc)
  ELEKTRISKE VARER (electrical goods)
- Many groceries and general stores sell basic household equipment.
  Also ask for **kjøkken** (kitchen department) or **jernvarer** (hardware) in a department store or supermarket.
- To ask the way to the shop, see p. 127.
- At a campsite try their shop first.

WHAT TO SAY

Have you got . . .	**Har dere . . .**
	har dayrer . . .
an adaptor?	**en overgangskontakt?**
[show appliance]	en awver-gang-skontahkt
a bottle of propane gas?	**en flaske propangass?**
	en flasker proopahn-gahss

a bottle opener?	**en flaskeåpner?**
	en fl*a*sker *a*wpner
a corkscrew?	**en korketrekker?**
	en k*o*rker-tr*e*kker
any disinfectant?	**et desinfeksjonsmiddel?**
	et d*e*ss-infeksh*oo*nss-m*i*ddel
any disposable cups?	**papirkopper?**
	pap*ee*r-kopper
any disposable plates?	**papirtallerkner?**
	pap*ee*r-tal-l*ai*rk-ner
a drying-up cloth?	**et oppvasdhåndkle?**
	et *o*p-vask-h*a*wn-kler
any forks?	**gafler?**
	g*a*f-ler
a fuse? [*show old one*]	**en sikring?**
	en s*i*ck-ring
insecticide spray?	**et insektmiddel?**
	et *i*nsekt-m*i*ddel
paper kitchen towels?	**en rull papirhandklær?**
	en rooll pap*ee*r-hawn-klair
any knives?	**kniver?**
	k-n*ee*ver
a light bulb? [*show old one*]	**en lyspære?**
	en l*ee*ss-parer
a plastic bucket?	**en plastikk-bøtte?**
	en pl*a*stikk-b*i*rt-ter
a plastic can?	**en plastik-kanne?**
	en pl*a*stikk-k*ah*nner
a scouring pad?	**en gryteskrubb?**
	en gr*ee*ter-skroob
a wrench?	**en skrunøkkel?**
	en skr*oo*-nirk-el
a sponge?	**en svamp?**
	en sv*ah*mp
any string?	**hyssing?**
	h*i*ssing
any tent pegs?	**teltplugger?**
	t*e*lt-pl*oo*gger
a can opener?	**en bokseåpner?**
	en b*o*kser-awpner
a flashlight?	**en lommelykt?**
	en l*o*mmer-leekt

Norwegian

Have you got . . .	**Har dere . . .**
	har d*a*yrer . . .
any flashlight batteries?	**lommelykt-batterier?**
	lommer-leekt-b*a*hteree-er
a universal plug (for the sink)?	**en universalplugg (til oppvaskkum)?**
	en ooniversh*a*hl-ploogg (til *o*p-vask-kum)
a washing line?	**en klesnor?**
	en kl*a*y-snoor
any laundry powder?	**vaskepulver?**
	v*a*sker-p*u*ll-ver
any liquid detergent?	**oppvaskmiddel?**
	*o*pvask-m*i*ddel
a scrub brush?	**en oppvaskbørste?**
	en *o*pvask-b*u*rster

[*For other essential information, see 'Shop talk' below*]

Shop talk

ESSENTIAL INFORMATION

- The illustrated coins are in wide circulation.
  Notes 10, 50, 100, 500, 1000 kroner (kr).
- Know how to say the important weights and measures.

50 grams	**en halv hekto**
	en hahl h*e*ktoo
100 grams	**en hekto**
	en h*e*ktoo
250 grams	**en kvart kilo**
	en kvart sh*ee*lo
500 grams	**en halv kilo**
	en hahl sh*ee*lo
1000 grams	**en kilo**
	en sh*ee*lo
2000 grams	**to kilo**
	too sh*ee*lo

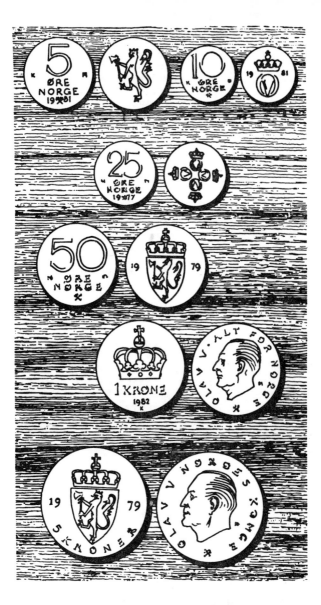

¼ litre	**en kvart liter**
	en kvart leeter
½ litre	**en halv liter**
	en hahl leeter
1 litre	**en liter**
	en leeter
2 litres	**to liter**
[*For numbers see p. 205*]	too leeter

CUSTOMER

I'm just looking	**Jeg bare ser**
	yay bar-er sair
Excuse me	**Unnskyld**
	oonshil
How much is this/that?	**Hvor mye koster denne/den?**
	vor mee-er koster denner/den
What is that? ⎤	**Hva er det?**
What are those? ⎦	va ar day
Is there a discount?	**Er det noen rabatt?**
	ar day noo-en rabaht
I'd like that, please	**Takk, jeg tar den**
	takk yay tar den
Not that	**Ikke den**
	ikker den
Like that	**Sånn**
	sonn
That's enough, thank you	**Takk, det er nok**
	takk day ar nok
More, please	**Litt mer takk**
	litt mair takk
Less	**Litt mindre**
	litt meendrer
That's fine	**Det er fint**
	day ar feent
O.K.	**O.K.**
	O.K.
I won't take it, thank you	**Nei takk, jeg tar den ikke**
	nay takk yay tar den ikker
It's not right	**Den passer ikke**
	den pahsser ikker
Have you got something . . .	**Har De noe . . .**
	har dee noo-er . . .
better?	**bedre?**
	bedrer

cheaper?	**billigere?**
	b*i*lli-rer
different?	**annet?**
	*ah*net
larger?	**større?**
	st*i*r-rer
smaller?	**mindre?**
	m*ee*ndrer
At what time do you . . .	**Når . . . dere?**
	nor . . . d*ay*rer
open?	**åpner**
	*aw*pner
close?	**stenger**
	st*e*ng-er
Can I have a bag, please?	**Kan jeg få en pose?**
	kan yay faw en p*oo*sser
Can I have a receipt?	**Kan jeg få en kvittering?**
	kan yay faw en kvitt*ai*ring
Do you take . . .	**Tar dere . . .**
	tar d*ay*rer . . .
English/American money?	**engelske/amerikanske penger?**
	*e*ng-elsker/ahmerik*ah*nsker p*e*ng-er
travelers' checks?	**reisesjekker?**
	racer-sh*e*cker?
credit cards?	**kreditt kort?**
	kred*i*tt kort
I'd like . . .	**Jeg vil ha . . .**
	yay vil ha . . .
one like that	**en sånn en**
	en s*o*nn en

SHOP ASSISTANT

Can I help you?	**Vær så god?**
	var saw goo
What would you like?	**Hva skal det være?**
	va skahl day v*a*rer
Will that be all?	**Er det det hele?**
	ar day day h*ai*ler
Is that all?	**Er det alt?**
	ar day *ah*lt
Anything else?	**Var det noe annet?**
	var day n*oo*-er *ah*net
Would you like it wrapped?	**Skal jeg pakke den inn?**
	skahl yay p*ah*kker den inn

Norwegian

Is it a present?	**Skal det værer en gave?**
	skal day varer en gahver
Sorry, none left	**Vi er dessverre utsolgt?**
	vee ar dess-varrer oot-salt
I haven't got any	**Jeg har ikke noen**
	yay har ikker noo-en
I haven't got any left	**Jeg har ikke flere igjen**
	yay har ikker flayrer ee-yen
How many do you want?	**Hvor mange vil De ha?**
	vor mahng-er vil dee ha
How much do you want?	**Hvor mye vil De ha?**
	vor mee-er vil dee ha
Is that enough?	**Er det nok?**
	ar day nok

Shopping for food

Bread

ESSENTIAL INFORMATION
- Finding a bakery, see p. 127.
- Key words to look for:
  BAKERI (bakery)
  BRØD (bread)
  CONDITORI (bakery with cake shop attached)
- Supermarkets, groceries and general stores always sell ready packed, unsliced bread.
- Opening hours as for other shops.
- Most characteristic are the following loaves of bread: **kneipbrød and vitabrød**, a whitish wheatgerm bread; **vanlig brød**, a large, greyish plain bread and **loff**, a finer white bread.
- You can also simply say **et brød** and point.

WHAT TO SAY

| A loaf (like that) | **Et (sånt) brød** |
| | et (sont) brer |

A homemade loaf	**Et hjemmebakt brød**
	et *y*emmer-ba*h*kt brer
A French loaf	**Et franskbrød**
	et fr*a*nsk-brer
A large one	**Et stort et**
	et st*oo*rt et
A small one	**Et lite et**
	et l*ee*ter et
A bread roll	**Et rundstykke**
	et r*oo*n-sticker
A crescent roll	**Et horn**
	et h*oo*rn
Two loaves	**To brød**
	too brer
Two homemade loaves	**To hjemmebakte brød**
	too *y*emmer-ba*h*kter brer
Four bread rolls	**Fire rundstykker**
	f*ee*rer r*oo*n-sticker
A sliced loaf	**Et oppskåret brød**
	et op-sk*aw*-ret brer
A wholemeal loaf	**Et helkornbrød**
	et h*ai*l-koorn-brer

[*For other essential expressions, see 'Shop talk' p. 158*]

Cakes

ESSENTIAL INFORMATION

- Key words to look for:
  BAKERI (bakery) sells cakes and bread
  KONDITORI (cake shop) sells cakes to take away or to be eaten on the premises. Coffee, tea and various soft drinks are also served.
  KAFÉ, KAFETERIA both sell a limited selection of cakes.
- Supermarkets, groceries and some kiosks sell prepacked cakes.
- To find a cake shop see p. 127.

Norwegian

WHAT TO SAY

The types of cakes you find in shops vary from region to region but the following are the most common.

berlinerbolle berleener-boller	doughnut
bolle boller	bun
bløtkake blert-kahker	cream gateau
honningkake honning-kahker	a heavy, brown spicy honey cake sold in thick slices
lefse lef-ser	a large, round, flat, soft and sweet bread. Served, folded up like a sandwich with butter, sugar and cinnamon
Napoleonskake napooleonss-kahker	custard slice
skolebrød skooler-brer	large, flattish wheat bun with coconut icing and egg custard on top
vafler vahf-ler	waffles
vannbakkels vahn-bakkelss	cream éclairs
wienerbrød veener-brer	Danish pastry
smultring smoolt-ring	doughnut ring

[*For other essential expressions, see 'Shop talk' p. 158*]

Ice cream and sweets

ESSENTIAL INFORMATION

- Prepacked ice cream is sold in kiosks, groceries, candy shops, snack bars and some gas stations. Look for **IS** (ice cream).
- There is always a poster with pictures of the various kinds of ice cream for sale.

- Many varieties come on sticks like ice cream bars. There are also prepacked cones, sandwiches, etc.
- Point to what you would like.
- Soft ice cream and scoop ice cream are available from machines – usually in snack bars and cafeterias.
- Prepacked sweets are available in groceries, supermarkets, kiosks and sweet shops.

WHAT TO SAY

A . . . ice, please	**En . . . is** en . . . eess
chocolate	**sjokolade** shooko-la*h*der
roasted nuts	**krokan** kruck-*ah*n
strawberry	**jordbær** yoor-bar
vanilla	**vanilje** va-neel-yer
An ice cream cone, please	**En kuleis** en kooler-eess
An ice cream bar, please	**En pinneis** en pinner-eess
A soft ice, please	**En soft is** en soft-eess
An ice cream like that	**En sånn is** en sonn eess
A lollipop, please	**En kjærlighet på pinne** en sharlee-hait paw pinner
A packet of . . .	**En pakke . . .** en pakker . . .
chewing gum	**tyggegummi** tigger-goommi
mints	**peppermynte** pepper-minter
Five/ten/twenty . . .	**Fem/ti/tjue . . .** fem/tee/shoo-er . . .
toffees	**karameller** kara-meller
chocolates	**små-sjokolader** smaw-shooko-la*h*der
A box of chocolates [*For other essential expressions,* *see 'Shop talk', p. 158*]	**En eske konfekt** en esker kon-fekt

Norwegian

Picnic food

ESSENTIAL INFORMATION

- Look for **DELIKATESSEN** or the cold meat counter in supermarkets.
- Supermarkets and groceries always sell a wide range of prepacked foods.

WHAT TO SAY

Two slices of . . .	To skiver . . .
	too sh*ee*ver . . .
ham	**kokt skinke**
	cookt sh*i*nker
roast pork	**stekt skinke**
	staykt sh*i*nker
spam	**skinkerull**
	sh*i*nker-r*oo*l
salami	**salami**
	salam*ee*
(parma) ham	**kokt svinekam**
	cookt sv*ee*ner-kahm
tongue	**tunge**
	t*oo*ng-er

You might also like to try some of these:

roastbiff	finely sliced, rare roast beef
r*oa*st-biff	
reker	fresh cooked shrimps/prawns, often
r*a*yker	bought and eaten at the harbour
rekesalat	salad with shrimps, sliced cabbage
r*a*yker-sal*ah*t	and mayonnaise
italiensk salat	salad with sliced ham, cabbage,
eetalee-*ai*nsk sal*ah*t	onion and mayonnaise
kalverull	boiled, finely sliced veal
k*ah*lver-r*oo*ll	
okserull	salty, boiled, finely sliced beef
*o*kser-r*oo*ll	

sursild s*oo*r-sill	pieces of salted herring, pepper and onions in water
krydddersild kr*i*dder-sill	pieces of salted herring, pepper and bayleaves in tomato sauce
røkt makrell rerkt ma-kr*e*ll	smoked mackerel
røkelaks r*e*rker-lahks	smoked salmon
gravlaks gr*ah*v-lahks	cured salmon with dill
røkt ørret rerkt *e*r-ret	smoked trout
leverpostei l*a*yver-pust*ay*	paté
flatbrød fl*a*tt-brer	crispy, unleavened paper-thin bread
multesyltetøy m*oo*lter-silter-t*ay*	cloudberry jam, yellow, sweet and tasty
brunost br*oo*n-ost	brown sweet cheese, of which there are numerous varieties some with goat's milk
nøkkelost n*e*rk-kel-ost	hard cheese with cloves and caraway seeds

Try some of these cured foods – salty, dry meat, eaten uncooked and finely sliced:

spekeskinke sp*a*yker-sh*i*nker	cured ham
spekepølse sp*a*yker-p*e*rl-ser	cured sausage, eaten in sandwiches
fenalår f*a*yna-l*o*r	cured leg of lamb
fårepølse forer-p*e*rl-ser	cured mutton sausage
spekesild sp*a*yker-sill	cured herring

Norwegian

Fruit and vegetables

ESSENTIAL INFORMATION

- Fruit (**FRUKT**) is bought in candy shops, some kiosks, groceries and supermarkets, and at the market place (**TORG**).
- Vegetables (**GRØNNSAKER**) are bought at supermarkets and groceries, some butchers and at the market place (**TORG**).
- Fruit and vegetables tend to be expensive in Norway and the selection is often limited.

WHAT TO SAY

1 kilo (2 lbs) of . . .	**En kilo . . .**
	ain sh*ee*lo . . .
apples	**epler**
	*e*pler
apricots	**aprikoser**
	ahpree-k*oo*-ser
bananas	**bananer**
	ba-n*a*-ner
cherries (sweet)	**moreller**
	mor*e*ller
cherries (slightly bitter)	**kirsebær**
	k*i*sher-b*a*r
grapes	**druer**
	dr*oo*-er
oranges	**appelsiner**
	appel-s*ee*ner
peaches	**ferskner**
	f*a*shk-ner
pears	**pærer**
	p*a*rer
plums	**plommer**
	pl*o*mmer
strawberries	**jordbær**
	y*oo*r-bar
A pineapple, please	**En ananas**
	en *a*nna-nass
A grapefruit	**En grapefrukt**
	en gr*a*pe-fr*oo*kt

A melon	**En melon**
	en meloon
A watermelon	**En vannmelon**
	en vahn-meloon
½ kilo of . . .	**En halv kilo . . .**
	en hahl sheelo . . .
carrots	**gulrøtter**
	gool-rert-ter
green beans	**franske bønner (haricots verts)**
	fransker burner (arrikaw var)
leeks	**purre**
	poor-rer
mushrooms	**sjampinjonger**
	shamping-yong-er
onions	**løk**
	lerk
potatoes	**poteter**
	pot-ayter
spinach	**spinat**
	spin-aht
tomatoes	**tomater**
	tom-ahter
A bunch of . . .	**En bunt . . .**
	en boont
parsley	**persille**
	pashiller
radishes	**redikker**
	red-ikker
garlic	**En hvitløk**
	en veet-lerk
A head of lettuce	**Et salathode**
	et salaht-hooder
cauliflower	**Et blomkålhode**
	et blom-kawl-hooder
A cucumber	**En slangeagurk**
	en shlang-er-agoork
Like that, please	**En sånn en**
	en sonn en

[*For other essential expressions, see 'Shop talk' p. 158*]

Norwegian

Meat

ESSENTIAL INFORMATION

- Key word to look for:
  KJØTTVARER (butcher's)
- Norwegian butchers never exhibit fresh meat in the window, only salami, cured sausages, cured hams etc. As meat is very expensive, the selection inside may be limited.
- Most supermarkets sell ready cut, prepacked meat. A shop with a wide selection of unpacked, uncut meat is hard to find. Few supermarkets and groceries and even fewer butchers sell chicken and other poultry.
- Kidneys are seldom eaten, hearts and brains never.
- The diagrams on p. 171 will help you to get the cuts you want. Point to the appropriate word on the diagram and the butcher will understand.

WHAT TO SAY

For a joint, choose the type of meat and then say how many people it is for:

Some beef, please	**Jeg skal ha litt oksekjøtt**
	yay skahl ha litt *okser*-sh*ir*tt
Some lamb	**Litt lammekjøtt**
	litt *lah*mmer-sh*ir*tt
Some mutton	**Litt fårekjøtt**
	litt *fo*rer-sh*ir*tt
Some pork	**Litt svinekjøtt**
	litt *svee*ner-sh*ir*tt
Some veal	**Litt kalvekjøtt**
	litt *kal*ver-sh*ir*tt
A joint of lamb/mutton	**En lamme/fårestek**
	en *lam*mer/*fo*rer-stayk
for two people	**til to personer**
	til *too* pesh*oo*ner
for four people	**til fire personer**
	til *fee*rer pesh*oo*ner
for six people	**til seks personer**
	til *seks* pesh*oo*ner

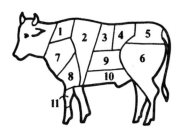

Beef Okse
1. Høyrygg
2. Entrekotkam
3. Oksekam (kotelett)
4. T. Benkam
5. Mørbrand
6. Lår
7. Bryst
8. Bog
9. Bibringe
10. Buklist (rulleskinn)
11. Skank

Veal Kalv
1. Høyrygg
2. Kotelettkam
3. T. Benkam
4. Lår
5. Bog
6. Rulleskinn
7. Kalveknoke

Pork Svin
1. Skinke
2. Kotelettkam
3. Nakkekotelett
4. Ribbe (buklist)
5. Bog
6. Labber

Lamb/Mutton Fam/Får
1. Lår (stek)
2. Rygg (sadel)
3. Nakke
4. Rulleskinn (ribbe)
5. Bog

Norwegian

For steak and liver do as above:

Some steak, please	**Jeg skal ha litt biff** y*ay* skahl ha litt b*i*ff
Some liver	**Litt lever** litt l*ay*ver
Some sausages	**Noen pølser** n*oo*-en p*er*l-ser
for three people	**til tre personer** til tr*ay* peshoon*er*
Two veal scallops, please	**To skiver kalvekjøtt** too sh*ee*ver k*a*hlver-sh*i*rtt
Three pork chops	**Tre svinekoteletter** tray sv*ee*ner-kotter-l*e*tter
Four mutton chops	**Fire fårekoteletter** f*ee*rer f*o*rer-kotter-l*e*tter
Five lamb chops	**Fem lammekoteletter** fem l*a*hmmer-kotter-l*e*tter
A small chicken	**En kylling** en sh*i*lling
A large chicken	**En broyler** en br*oi*ler
Please can you . . .	**Kan De . . .** kan dee . . .
mince it?	**male det?** m*a*hler day
dice it?	**skjære det i småbiter?** sh*a*rer day ee sm*aw*-beeter
trim the fat?	**skjære bort flesket?** sh*a*rer bort fl*e*sker

Fish

ESSENTIAL INFORMATION

- Sign to look for: **FISK** (fish).
- Fresh fish can be bought at fishmongers all over the country, and

in some open air markets particularly in Bergen where the fish is kept live.

- Supermarkets and groceries sell frozen fish much the same as at home. **Findus** and **Frionor** are well-known marks.
- Shrimps and prawns (**reker**) can often be purchased freshly caught and cooked at the harbour.

WHAT TO SAY

Purchase large fish and small shellfish by weight:

½ kilo of . . .	**En halv kilo . . .**
	en hahl sheelo . . .
cod	**torsk**
	toshk
whiting	**hvitting**
	vitting
dover sole	**sjøtunge**
	sher-tung-er
shrimps	**små reker**
	smaw rayker
prawns	**store reker**
	stoorer rayker
mussels	**blåskjell**
	blaw-shell
sardines	**sardiner**
	sardeener
haddock	**kolje**
	kol-yer
salmon	**laks**
	lahks
halibut	**hellefisk**
	heller-fisk

For some shellfish and pan fish, specify the numbers:

A crab, please	**En krabbe**
	en krahbber
A lobster	**En hummer**
	en hummer
A female crab	**En hunkrabbe**
	en hoon-krahbber
A big lobster	**En stor hummer**
	en stoor hummer

Norwegian

A trout	**En ørret**
	en *er*-ret
A sole	**En flyndre**
	en fl*i*ndrer
A mackerel	**En makrell**
	en ma-kr*e*ll
A hake	**En lysing**
	en l*ee*-sing

Other essential expressions [*see also p. 159*]

Please can you . . .	**Kan De . . .**
	kan dee . . .
take the heads off?	**skjære av hodene?**
	sh*a*rer ahv h*oo*dener
clean them?	**rense dem?**
	r*a*ynsser dem
fillet them?	**skjære bort bena?**
	sh*a*rer bort b*a*yna

Eating and drinking out

Ordering a drink

ESSENTIAL INFORMATION

- Places to ask for: **HOTELL, RESTAURANT, BAR**
  and **VERTSHUS**.
- Alcoholic beverages are expensive, so make full use of your duty
  free quota.
- Some Norwegian towns and counties, particularly in the West and
  South are 'dry'. However, big hotels in these counties often sell
  alcohol by special license.
- Beer and wine can be enjoyed all day. Liquor is only available
  between 3 and 11 p.m. and never on Sundays or public holidays. At
  11 p.m. an establishment may therefore stop selling liquor but
  continue to sell beer and wine, unless of course they hold a special
  license.

- Many establishments enforce a **spiseplikt** (duty to eat) – that is to say you cannot buy an alcoholic beverage without ordering food.
- Beer **øl** can be bought in most supermarkets unless you are in a 'dry' town; wine and spirits only in the state wine monopoly shops **Vinmonopolet**. These are found in towns with more than 4000 inhabitants. However there is only one shop to each minor town and no **Vinmonopol** in dry counties.
- Coffee is the most popular hot drink. Served black, accompanied by sugar and cream.
- Tea is less popular, served on demand with sugar and a slice of lemon. White tea is unknown, you will have to ask for milk and no lemon.
- In winter, try hot beefstock, hot blackcurrant juice or hot chocolate with whipped cream.
- BE WARNED! Driving and drinking is a serious offense. Random checks are frequent. More than a very small amount could mean the loss of your license and prison for 21 days.

WHAT TO SAY

I'll have . . . please	**Kan jeg få . . .**
	kan yay f*aw* . . .
a tea	**en te**
	en t*ay*
with milk	**med melk**
	may m*e*lk
with lemon	**med sitron**
	may sitr*oo*n
a glass of milk	**et glass melk**
	et glahss melk
a hot chocolate	**en kopp sjokolade**
	en kopp shooko-l*ah*der
with/without cream	**med/uten krem**
	may/*oo*ten kraim
a glass of water	**et glass vann**
	et glahss vahnn
a lemonade (fizzy)	**en sitronbrus**
	en sitr*oo*n-brooss
a Coca-Cola	**en coca cola**
	en coca-c*oo*la
an orangeade (fizzy)	**en appelsinbrus**
	en appel-s*ee*n-brooss

Norwegian

an orange juice	**et glass appelsinsaft**
	et glahss appel-*see*n-saft
an apple juice	**et glass eplesaft**
	et glahss *epp*ler-saft
a blackcurrant juice	**et glass solbærsaft**
	et glahss s*oo*l-bar-saft
a milkshake	**en milk shake**
	en milk shake
Do you serve beer or wine?	**Serverer dere øl eller vin?**
	serv*ay*-rer d*ay*rer erl *ell*er veen
A lager	**En pils**
	en pilss
A glass of draught lager	**Et glass fatøl**
	et glahss f*a*-terl
A pint of draught lager	**Et stort glass fatøl**
	et st*oo*rt glahss f*a*-terl
A brown ale	**En bukkøl**
	en b*oo*kk-erl
A glass of . . .	**Et glass . . .**
	et glahss . . .
red wine	**rødvin**
	r*er*-veen
white wine	**hvitvin**
	v*ee*t-veen
rosé wine	**rosévin**
	ross*ay*-veen
dry/sweet wine	**tørr/søt vin**
	terr/s*i*rt veen
A bottle of . . .	**En flaske . . .**
	en fl*a*sker . . .
sparkling wine	**sprudlende vin**
	spr*oo*dlen-er veen
champagne	**champagne**
	shamp*ah*g-ner
A whisky	**En whisky**
	en wh*i*sky
with water	**med vann**
	may v*ah*nn
with ice	**med isbiter**
	may *ee*ss-beeter
with soda	**med soda**
	may s*oo*da

A gin | **En gin**
| en gin
and tonic | **og tonic**
| aw tonic
with lemon | **med sitron**
| may sitroon
A brandy/cognac | **En brandy/cognac**
| en brandy/conyac

These are drinks you may like to try:

Lagerøl/Brigg | nonalcoholic lager
lager-erl/brigg |
Vørterøl | a sweet, heavy, nonalcoholic ale –
virter-erl | good for the stomach
Pils | Norwegian lager
pilss |
Export | a stronger kind of lager
export |
Bayer | strong dark ale
ba-yer |
Bokkøl | a stronger, darker version of Bayer
bokk-erl |
Akevitt | Norwegian firewater (40%
ahk-ker-vitt | alcohol), served chilled with
| heavy dishes and often chased
| down with beer
Solo | a fizzy, not too sweet orangeade
soolo |
Selters | a kind of soda water
seltesh. |
Buljong | hot beefstock
bull-yong |

Other essential expressions:

The bill, please | **Kan jeg få regningen**
| kan yay faw raining-en
How much does that come to? | **Hvor mye kommer det på?**
| vor mee-er kommer day paw
Is the service included? | **Er service inkludert?**
| ar service inkloo-dairt
Where is the toilet, please? | **Hvor er toalettet?**
| vor ar twa-letter

Norwegian

Ordering a snack

ESSENTIAL INFORMATION

- Look for **KIOSK, SNACKBAR, KONDITORI, KAFÉ, KAFETERIA, KRO** and **VEIKRO**
  (the last four sell complete meals as well).
- Kiosks and snack bars throughout Norway are good places for inexpensive snacks. They all sell tasty hot dogs and potato chips, and many sell chicken, cakes and pizza.
- For cakes see p. 163.
- For ice cream see p. 164.
- For picnic-type snacks see p. 166.

WHAT TO SAY

I'll have . . . please	**Jeg vil ha . . .**
	yay vil ha . . .
a cheese sandwich	**et ostesmørbrød**
	et *oo*ster-sm*i*r-brer
a ham sandwich	**et skinkesmørbrød**
	et sh*i*nker-sm*i*r-brer
an egg and tomato sandwich	**et egg og tomat smørbrød**
	et *e*gg aw tom*ah*t sm*i*r-brer

These are some other snacks you may like to try

en pølse med lompe/brød	a steamed frankfurter sausage with potato cake/soft roll
en p*e*rl-ser may l*u*mper/brer	
en grillpølse med sennep og ketchup	a thick, grilled frankfurter with mustard and ketchup
en gr*i*ll-perl-ser may s*e*nnep aw ketchup	
en pose potetgull	a bag of potato chips
en p*oo*sser pot*ai*t-gooll	
en pizza	a pizza
en pizza	
et rekesmørbrød	an open prawn sandwich
et r*ay*ker-sm*i*r-brer	
et roastbiffsmørbrød	an open sandwich with slightly underdone roast beef
et r*oa*st-biff-sm*i*r-brer	

et rundstykke med gaudaost/ brunost	half a largish roll with gouda or brown cheese on top
et *roon*-sticker may *gou*da-ost/ br*oo*n-ost	
et smørbrød med eggerøre	open sandwich with scrambled egg
et sm*ir*-brer may *egg*er-r*ir*-er	
pommes frites	french fries
pom frit	

In a restaurant

ESSENTIAL INFORMATION

- The place to ask for:
  EN RESTAURANT [see p. 128]
- You can eat in these places or where you see this sign
  RESTAURANT
  CAFÉ
  KAFETERIA
  SNACK BAR
  KRO (reasonable self-service establishments)
  VEIKRO (reasonable self-service establishments)
  GRILLRESTAURANT (various grilled foods)
- The menus are not always displayed in the window. The look of a restaurant is therefore the best indication you'll have of whether it will suit you. Norwegian restaurants tend to be expensive.
- Service charges are often included. Tipping is at your discretion: small change after a snack and maybe 5% after a good meal.
- You can choose between large and small portions, a large portion often being very large.
- In self-service establishments, snacks can be purchased all day and hot dinner type meals from midday onwards.
- Expensive restaurants often serve buffets and open sandwiches for lunch and dinner from 7 p.m.
- A starter is by no means universal. Norwegians tend to be satisfied

by a main course and a dessert followed by coffee. Soup is the most frequent form of starter.
• And remember no alcohol with your meal if you are driving!

WHAT TO SAY

May I book a table?	**Kan jeg bestille et bord?** kan yay bestiller et boor
I've booked a table	**Jeg har bestilt et bord** yay har bestilt et boor
A table . . .	**Et bord . . .** et boor . . .
for one	**for en person** for ain peshoon
for three	**for tre personer** for tray peshooner
The à la carte menu, please	**Kan jeg få à la carte menyen** kan yay faw ah la cart men-ee-en
Today's special menu	**Dagens meny** dahg-enss menee
What is this, please? [point to the menu]	**Hva er det?** va ar day
Do you serve beer and wine?	**Serverer dere øl og vin?** servay-rer dayrer erl aw veen
The wine list, please	**Kan jeg få vinkartet** kan yay faw vin-karter
A carafe of wine, please	**En karaffel vin** en karaffel veen
A half carafe	**En halv karaffel** en hahl karaffel
A bottle	**En flaske** en flasker
A half bottle	**En halv flaske** en hahl flasker
A litre	**En liter** en leeter
Red/white/rosé/house wine	**Rød/hvit/rosé/husets vin** rer/veet/rossay/hooss-ess veen
Some more bread, please	**Kan jeg få litt mer brød** kan yay faw litt mair brer
Some more wine	**Litt mer vin** litt mair veen

Some oil	**Litt olje**
	litt *o*l-yer
Some vinegar	**Litt eddik**
	litt *e*ddik
Some salt	**Litt salt**
	litt s*ah*lt
Some pepper	**Litt pepper**
	litt p*e*pper
Some water	**Litt vann**
	litt v*ah*nn
How much does that come to?	**Hvor mye kommer det på?**
	vor m*ee*-er kommer day paw
Is service included?	**Er service inkludert?**
	ar s*e*rvice inkloo-d*ai*rt
The bill, please	**Regningen takk**
	r*ai*ning-en takk
Can you give me a receipt?	**Kan jeg få en kvittering?**
	kan yay f*aw* en kvitt*ai*ring

Key words for courses as seen on some menus: [*Only ask the
question if you want the waiter to remind you of the choice*]

What have you got in the way of . . .	**Hva slags . . . har dere?**
	va shl*ah*gss . . . har d*ay*rer
STARTERS?	**FORRETTER?**
	f*o*r-retter
SOUP?	**SUPPE?**
	s*oo*pper
EGG DISHES?	**EGGRETTER?**
	*e*gg-retter
MEAT?	**KJØTTRETTER?**
	sh*i*rtt-retter
GAME?	**VILTRETTER?**
	v*i*lt-retter
FOWL?	**FUGLERETTER?**
	f*oo*gler-retter
VEGETABLES?	**GRØNNSAKER?**
	gr*er*n-sahker
CHEESE?	**OST?**
	ost
FRUIT?	**FRUKT?**
	fr*oo*kt

Norwegian

ICE CREAM?	**ISKREM?**
	*ee*ss-kra*im*
DESSERT?	**DESSERT?**
	dess*ar*

UNDERSTANDING THE MENU

- You will find the names of the principal ingredients of most dishes
  on these pages:

Starters p. 167	Fruit p. 168
Meat p. 170	Dessert p. 163–164
Fish p. 172	Cheese p. 167
Vegetables p. 169	Ice cream p. 164

- Used together with the following lists of cooking and menu terms,
  they should help you to decode the menu.
- The following cooking and menu terms are for understanding only
  – not for speaking aloud.

Cooking and menu terms

blandet	mixed
blodig	rare
brunet i smør	sautéed
dampet	steamed
fløte	unwhipped cream
forlorent	poached
frityrstekt	deep fried in breadcrumbs
fyllt	stuffed
godt stekt	well done
griljert/grillet	grilled
grytestekt	braised
hermetisk	canned
kokt	boiled
krem	whipped cream
marinert	marinated
medium	medium
med/uten løk	with/without fried onion
ovnstekt	baked/roasted
revet	grated
ristet	toasted
røkt	smoked
rå	raw/rare

saft	juice
salted/speket	cured
saus	sauce/gravy
hvit saus	white, creamy sauce
remulade saus	mayonnaise sauce with diced pickled gherkins
rød/bringebær saus	red/raspberry sauce
vaniljesaus	custard (cold)
sur	bitter
søt	sweet

Further words to help you understand the menu

asparges	asparagus
bayonskinke	cooked ham (for dinner)
betasuppe	soup consisting of chunks of meat, marrow bones and vegetables
blandet kjøttgryte	different meats roasted together
blomkålsuppe	cream of cauliflower soup
dyrestek/reinsdyrstek	roast reindeer
eggerøre	scrambled egg
elgstek	roast moose
erter	peas
ertesuppe	thick yellow pea soup with ham
fenalår	cured leg of mutton
fersk suppe	hearty meat and vegetable soup
fiskegrateng	fish in thick, creamy, white sauce
fiskesuppe	fish soup
fjellørret	mountain trout
franske poteter/pommes frites	french fries
gravlaks	cured salmon with dill
gås	goose
gåselever	goose liver
hønsefrikassé	chicken stew
kalvefrikassé	veal stew
karamellpudding	cream caramel
karbonade	beefburger
kjøttkaker (med surkål)	meat balls (with sweet and sour cabbage)
klippfisk	boiled, dried, salty fish
klubb	potato dumpling with bacon
kålrabi	swede

Norwegian

kålruletter	stuffed cabbage leaves
kålstuing	creamed cabbage
lapskaus	beef stew
lever	liver
lutefisk	cod soaked in lye, then boiled; jelly like when served
mandelpudding	vanilla blancmange with almonds
medisterkaker	pork meatballs
medisterpølser	thick pork sausages
middagspølser	thick, smoked sausages
multer	arctic cloudberries
oksehalesuppe	oxtail soup
potetstappe	mashed potato
rakørret	semi fermented salmon/trout (mostly for daring nationals)
ribbe	roast pork rib
risgrøt	hot rice pudding, served with butter, sugar and cinnamon
riskrem	cold rice pudding, made with whipped cream
rosenkål	brussels sprouts
ryper	roast grouse/ptarmigan
rødbeter	beetroot
rødkål	red cabbage
røkelaks	smoked salmon
rømmegrøt	porridge made with sour cream, semolina or wheat flour
seifillet	fried fillet of coalfish, often served with fried onions
semulepudding	semolina pudding
sjokoladepudding	chocolate blancmange
smørgrøt	cream porridge made with wheat flour
spinatsuppe	cream of spinach soup
surkål	sweet and sour cabbage
syltelabber	pigs trotters
tomatsuppe	tomato soup
torskerogn	cod roe
tyttebær	cranberry
wienerschnitzel	fillet of pork, fried in breadcrumbs with anchovy and capers

Health

ESSENTIAL INFORMATION

- Be sure to have medical insurance.
- Norwegians stay free of charge in hospitals. But doctors do charge a consultation fee, be it in a doctor's office, your own abode or the emergency ward at a hospital. You will need to produce your passport.
- In remote areas doctors may be few and far between.
- In towns doctors are on duty day and night Ask for **LEGEVAKT**.
- There is no one common telephone number for medical emergencies throughout Norway. Look under **LEGER** (doctors) in the classified directory or ask a Norwegian.
- Also look for **SYKEBIL/AMBULANSE** (ambulance) on the inside of the front cover of the telephone directory.
- Take your own first aid kit with you.
- A pharmacist, **apotek**, will suggest treatment for minor disorders.
- For asking your way to a doctor, dentist or drugstore, see p. 127.

What's the matter?

I have a pain . . .	**Jeg har vondt . . .**
	yay har voont . . .
in my abdomen	**i underlivet**
	ee *oo*nner-l*ee*ver
in my ankle	**i ankelen**
	ee *a*nkel-en
in my arm	**i armen**
	ee *a*rm-en
in my back	**i ryggen**
	ee r*i*ggen
in my bladder	**i urinblæren**
	ee oor*ee*n-blaren
in my bowels	**i tarmene**
	ee t*a*rmen-er

I have a pain . . .	**Jeg har vondt . . .**
	yay har voont . . .
in my breast	**i et bryst**
	ee et br*i*st
in my chest	**i brystet**
	ee br*i*ster
in my ear	**i øret**
	ee *e*r-rer
in my eye	**i øyet**
	ee *e*rer
in my foot	**i foten**
	ee f*oo*ten
in my head	**i hodet**
	ee h*oo*der
in my heel	**i hælen**
	ee h*ai*len
in my kidney	**i nyret**
	ee n*ee*rer
in my leg	**i benet**
	ee b*ai*ner
in my lung	**i en lunge**
	ee en l*u*ng-er
in my neck	**i nakken**
	ee n*ah*kken
in my penis	**i penis**
	ee p*ai*niss
in my shoulder	**i skulderen**
	ee sk*oo*lderen
in my stomach	**i maven**
	ee m*ah*ven
in my testicle	**i testikelen**
	ee test*i*ck-el-en
in my throat	**i halsen**
	ee h*ah*l-sen
in my vagina	**i skjeden**
	ee sh*ay*-den
in my wrist	**i håndleddet**
	ee h*aw*n-ledder
I have a pain here [*point*]	**Jeg har vondt her**
	yay har voont har
I have a toothache	**Jeg har tannverk**
	yay har t*ah*nn-vark
I have broken . . .	**Jeg har ødelagt . . .**
	yay har *e*r-derl*a*gt

my dentures	**gebisset mitt**
	ghe*bi*sser mitt
my glasses	**brillene mine**
	br*i*ll-en-er m*ee*ner
I have lost . . .	**Jeg har mistet . . .**
	yay har m*i*ss-tet . . .
my contact lenses	**kontaktlinsene mine**
	kont*a*hkt-lin-sen-er m*ee*ner
a filling	**en plumbe**
	en pl*oo*m-ber
My child is ill	**Barnet mitt er sykt**
	b*a*rn-er mitt ar s*ee*kt
He/she has a pain in his/her ...	**Han/hun har vondt i . . .**
	han/hun har v*oo*nt ee . . .
ankle [*see list above*]	**ankelen**
	*a*nkel-en

How bad is it?

I'm ill	**Jeg er syk**
	yay ar s*ee*k
It's serious	**Det er alvorlig**
	day ar ahl-v*o*rlee
It's not serious	**Det er ikke alvorlig**
	day ar *i*kker ahl-v*o*rlee
It hurts (a lot)	**Det gjør (veldig) vondt**
	day yer (v*e*ldee) v*oo*nt
I've had it for . . .	**Jeg har hatt det i . . .**
	yay har h*a*tt day ee . . .
one hour/one day	**en time/en dag**
	en t*ee*mer/en d*a*hg
It's a . . .	**Det er en . . .**
	day ar ain . . .
sharp pain	**skarp smerte**
	skarp sm*a*rter
dull ache	**dump smerte**
	domp sm*a*rter
nagging pain	**nagende smerte**
	n*a*hg-en-er sm*a*rter
I feel . . .	**Jeg føler meg . . .**
	yay f*e*rler may . . .
dizzy	**svimmel**
	sv*i*mmel
sick/weak	**kvalm/svak**
	kvalm/svahk

Norwegian

I think I have a fever	**Jeg tror jeg har feber** yay troor yay har fayber

Already under treatment for something else?

I take . . . regularly [show]	**Jeg tar . . . regelmessig** yay tar . . . ray-ghel-messy
this medicine	**denne medisinen** denner mediceenen
these pills	**disse pillene** disser pill-en-er
I have . . .	**Jeg har . . .** yay har . . .
a heart condition	**hjertefeil** yarter-fail
hemorrhoids	**hemorroider** hem-orreeder
rheumatism	**gikt** yeekt
I am . . .	**Jeg er . . .** yay ar . . .
diabetic	**diabetiker** dee-ah-bayticker
asthmatic	**astmahtiker** ahst-ma-ticker
allergic to penicillin	**allergisk mot penicillin** allarghisk moot penicileen
pregnant	**gravid** gra-veed

Other essential expressions

Please can you help?	**Kan De hjelpe meg?** kan dee yelper may
A doctor, please	**Jeg trenger en lege** yay treng-er en laygher
I need a dentist	**Jeg trenger en tannlege** yay treng-er en tahnn-laygher
I don't speak Norwegian	**Jeg snakker ikke norsk** yay snakker ikker noshk

From the doctor: key sentences to understand

Take this . . .	**Ta dette . . .**
	ta detter . . .
every day/hour	**hver dag/time**
	var dahg/teemer
twice/three times a day	**to/tre ganger om dagen**
	too/tray gang-er um dahg-en
Stay in bed	**Hold sengen**
	hawl seng-en
Don't travel , , ,	**Ikke reis . . .**
	ikker race . . .
for . . . days/weeks	**før om . . . dager/uker**
	fir om . . . dahg-er/ooker
You must go to the hospital	**De må legges inn på sykehus**
	dee maw legg-ess in paw seeker-hooss

Problems: complaints, loss, theft

ESSENTIAL INFORMATION

- Problems with:
  camping facilities, see p. 140
  household appliances, see p. 156
  health, see p. 185
  the car, see p. 156
- If the worst comes to the worst, find the police station. To ask the way, see p. 126
- Look for **POLITI**
- If you lose your passport, report the loss to the police and contact your country's embassy.
- There is no one common telephone number for fire and police covering all Norway. Therefore, look for **BRANN** (fire) and **POLITI** (police) inside the front cover of telephone directory.
- If you have lost something on the bus or train, go to the station of the appropriate service and ask for **HITTEGODS** (lost property) or go to the police.

Norwegian

COMPLAINTS

I bought this . . .	**Jeg kjøpte denne . . .**
	yay shirp-ter denner . . .
today	**i dag**
	ee dahg
yesterday	**i går**
	ee gor
on Monday [see p. 208]	**på mandag**
	paw mahn-dahg
It's no good	**Den er ikke riktig**
	den ar ikker riktee
Look	**Se**
	say
Here [point]	**Her**
	har
Can you . . .	**Kan De . . .**
	kan dee . . .
change it?	**bytte den?**
	bitter den
mend it?	**reparere den?**
	repar-rairer den
give me a refund?	**gi meg pengene tilbake?**
	yee may peng-en-er til-bahker
Here is the receipt	**Her er kvitteringen**
	har ar kvittairing-en

LOSS
[See also 'Theft' below: the lists are interchangeable]

I have lost . . .	**Jeg har mistet . . .**
	yay har miss-tet . . .
my bag	**vesken min**
	vess-ken meen
my bracelet	**armbåndtet mitt**
	arm-bonner mitt
my car keys	**bilnøklene mine**
	beel-nerk-len-er meener
my car logbook	**vognkortet mitt**
	vogn-korter mitt
my driver's license	**sertifikatet mitt**
	sartifik-ahter mitt
my insurance certificate	**forsikringsattesten min**
	for-sick-ringss-attest-en meen

THEFT
[*See 'Loss' above: the lists are interchangeable*]

Someone has stolen . . .	Noen har stjålet . . .
	noo-en har st-yaw-let . . .
my car	**bilen min**
	beelen meen
my luggage	**bagasjen min**
	ba-gashen meen
my money	**pengene mine**
	peng-en-er meener
my purse	**pungen min**
	poong-en meen
my tickets	**billettene mine**
	bill-aitten-er meener
my travelers' checks	**reisesjekkene mine**
	racer-shecken-er meener
my wallet	**lommeboken min**
	lommer-booken meen
my watch	**klokken min**
	klokken meen

LIKELY REACTIONS: key words to understand

Wait	**Vent**
	vent
When?	**Når**
	nor
Name?	**Navn?**
	nahvn
Address?	**Adresse?**
	ah-dresser
I can't help you	**Jeg kan ikke hjelpe Dem**
	yay kan ikker yelper dem
Nothing to do with me	**Jeg har ikke noe med det**
	yay har ikker noo-er may day

Norwegian

The post office

ESSENTIAL INFORMATION

- Look for the word **POST** and this sign
- Stamps can also be purchased in kiosks, bookshops and stationers.
  Ask for **FRIMERKER** (stamps).
- Telegrams can be sent from the post office or by dialling 013 on the telephone.
- Telexes can be sent from major post offices only.
- Letterboxes are red.

WHAT TO SAY

To England, please
Til England
til *e*ng-lahn
[*Hand letters, cards or parcels over the counter*]

To Australia
Til Australia
til owstr*a*-lee-ah

To the United States
Til De Forente Stater/USA
til dee for*ay*nter st*ah*ter/oo-ess-ah

[*For other countries, see p. 211*]

Airmail
Luftpost
l*oo*ft-posst

Surface mail
Ikke luftpost
*i*kker l*oo*ft-posst

Telephoning

ESSENTIAL INFORMATION

- Unless you read or speak Norwegian well, it's best not to make the call yourself. Go to a post office or snack bar, write the town and number you want on a piece of paper and add **PERSONLIG SAMTALE** if you want a person to person call or **NOTERINGS-OVERFØRING** if you want to reverse the charges.
- Telephone boxes are grey or red. Put the appropriate coins in the slot on top of the telephone, they will fall in automatically when the call is answered. Put more coins in the slot, and they will fall through automatically when needed.
- For dialling direct to the U.K. dial 095 then 44 then the code of your town etc. For the U.S.A. dial 095 and then check the rest of the codes in the telephone directory under *De Forente Stater*.
- Alternatively look in the telephone directory for the heading 'How to telephone in Norway' or dial 093 for an English speaking operator.
- To ask the way to public telephone or post office, see p. 126.

WHAT TO SAY

I'd like this number . . .	**Jeg trenger dette nummeret . . .**
[*show number*]	yay treng-er detter noommerer . . .
in England	**i England**
	ee eng-lahn
in Canada	**i Kanada**
	ee ka-na-da
Can you dial it for me, please?	**Kan De slå det for meg?**
	kan dee slaw day for may
May I speak to . . .?	**Kan jeg få snakke med . . .?**
	kan yay faw snakker may . . .
Extension . . .	**Linje . . .**
	lin-yer
Do you speak English?	**Snakker De engelsk?**
	snakker dee eng-elsk
Thank you, I'll phone back	**Takk, jeg ringer igjen siden**
	takk yay ring-er ee-yen seeden

LIKELY REACTIONS

That's . . .	**Det er . . .** day ar . . .
Cabin number (3) [For numbers, see p. 205]	**Avlukke nummer (tre)** *ahv*-lookker n*oo*mmer (tray)
Don't hang up	**Ikke legg på** *i*kkgr legg paw
I'm trying to connect you	**Jeg skal sette Dem over** yay skahl setter dem *aw*ver
You're through	**Vær så god** var saw goo
There's a delay	**Han er opptatt** han ar *o*pp-tahtt
I'll try again	**Jeg kan forsøke igjen** yay kan for-s*ir*ker ee-y*e*n

Cashing checks and changing money

ESSENTIAL INFORMATION

- Finding your way to a bank or currency exchange, see p. 127.
- Look for these words on buildings: **BANK, VEKSLEKONTOR, EXCHANGE.**
- International credit cards are not as widely used as in other countries. Only major department stores, shops and restaurants are likely to be familiar with them. Traveler's checks are easier to cash. In towns most shops will accept them. In the countryside and off the beaten track, use cash.
- Banks are open from Monday to Friday. Opening hours vary from town to country and from one city to another. The safest is to seek a bank between 8.30 a.m. and 3 p.m.
- Always have your passport handy for identification.

WHAT TO SAY

I'd like to cash . . .	**Jeg vil løse inn . . .** yay vil l*ir*-ser inn . . .

this travelers' check	**denne reisesjekken**
	denner racer-shecken
this check	**denne sjekken**
	denner shecken
I'd like to change this into Norwegian crowns	**Jeg vil veksle disse i norske kroner**
	yay vil veksler disser ee noshker krooner

For excursions into neighbouring countries

I'd like to change this . . .	**Jeg vil veksle disse . . .**
[*show bank notes*]	yay vil veksler disser . . .
into Swedish/Danish crowns	**i svenske/danske kroner**
	ee svensker/dahn-sker krooner
into Finnish marks/Russian rubles	**i finske mark/russiske rubler**
	ee finsker mark/rooss-isker roobler

LIKELY REACTIONS

Your passport, please	**Kan jeg få se passet Deres**
	kan yay faw say passer dayress
Sign here	**Vil De skrive under her**
	vil dee skreever oonner har
Your banker's card, please	**Kan jeg få se bankkortet Deres**
	kan yay faw say bank-korter dayress
Go to the cash desk	**Gå til kassen**
	gaw til kahssen

Car travel

ESSENTIAL INFORMATION

- Finding a filling station or garage, see p. 128.
- Grades of gasoline:
  SUPER (98 octane) **NORMAL** (96 octane) **REGULÆR** (93 octane)
- 1 gallon is about 4½ litres (accurate enough up to 6 gallons).

Norwegian

- Types of garages: for filling station
  BENSINSTASJON look for the
  names of oil companies like, **BP**,
  MOBIL, **SHELL**, **TEXACO** etc.
  Filling stations are
  helpful with minor problems but do
  not handle major repairs, for that
  you need a garage **VERKSTED**,
  look for this sign

- Filling stations are open from
  7 a.m. to 8 p.m. on weekdays and
  from 8 a.m. to 8 p.m. on Sundays
  and most holidays. Most filling stations have self-service, look for
  SELVBETJENING, **SELVTANK**.
- When driving through the vast, thinly populated areas, be sure to
  start out with a full tank.

WHAT TO SAY
[*for numbers, see p. 205*]

(9) litres of . . .	(Ni) liter . . .
	(nee) leeter . . .
(100) crowns of . . .	. . . for (hundre) kroner
	. . . for (hoondrer) krooner
four star/premium	**super/98 octan**
	sooper/nitti awtter octahn
two star/regular	**regulær/93 octan**
	regular/nitti tray octahn
diesel	**diesel**
	deessel
Fill it up, please	**Fyll opp tanken**
	fill opp tahnken
Will you check . . .	**Kan De sjekke . . .**
	kan dee shecker . . .
the oil?	**oljen?**
	ol-yen?
the battery?	**batteriet?**
	bahtteree-er
the radiator?	**radiatoren?**
	rahdee-ahtooren
the tires?	**dekkene?**
	dekken-er

I've run out of gasoline	**Jeg har kjørt tom for bensin**
	yay har shirt tom for ben-*seen*
Can I borrow a can, please?	**Kan jeg få låne en kanne?**
	kan yay faw *law*ner en *kan*ner
My car has broken down	**Bilen min har fått motorstopp**
	*bee*len meen har fott *moo*tor-stop
Can you help me, please?	**Kan De hjelpe meg?**
	kan dee *yel*per may
Do you do repairs?	**Foretar dere reparasjoner?**
	*for*er-tar *day*rer rep-ahra-sh*oo*ner
I have a puncture	**Jeg har punktert**
	yay har poong-*tairt*
I have a broken windshield	**Jeg har knust frontruten**
	yay har k-*noosst* front-*roo*ten
I think the problem is here . . . [*point*]	**Jeg tror feilen er her . . .**
	yay troor *fai*len ar har . . .
Can you . . .	**Kan De . . .**
	kan dee . . .
repair the fault?	**reparere feilen?**
	rep-ahr*ay*-rer *fai*len
come and look?	**komme og se?**
	*kom*mer aw say
estimate the cost?	**gi et overslag over kostnadene?**
	yee et *aw*ver-shlahg *aw*ver kost-*nah*den-er
write it down?	**skrive det ned?**
	*skree*ver day naid
How long will the repair take?	**Hvor lang tid tar reparasjonen?**
	vor lang *tee* tar rep-ahra-sh*oo*nen
This is my insurance document	**Dette er forikringspapirene mine**
	*det*ter ar for-*sick*-ringss-pap*ee*rener *mee*ner

RENTING A CAR

Can I rent a car?	**Kan jeg leie en bil?**
	kan yay *lay*er en beel
I need a car . . .	**Jeg trenger en bil . . .**
	yay *treng*-er en beel . . .
for five people	**for fem personer**
	for fem pesh*oo*ner
for a week	**for en uke**
	for en *oo*ker

Can you write down . . .	**Kan De skrive ned . . .**
	kan dee skr*ee*ver na*i*d . . .
the deposit to pay?	**depositum?**
	dep*o*ssit-um
the charge per kilometre?	**prisen per kilometer?**
	pr*ee*-sen pair sh*ee*lo-maiter
the daily charge?	**prisen per dag?**
	pr*ee*-sen pair d*ah*g
the cost of insurance?	**prisen på forsikringen?**
	pr*ee*-sen paw for-s*i*ck-ring-en
Can I leave it in (Oslo)?	**Kan jeg levere den i (Oslo)?**
	kan yay lev*a*yrer den ee (*o*shlo)
What documents do I need?	**Hva slags papierer trenger jeg?**
	va shl*ah*gss pap*ee*erer treng-er yay

LIKELY REACTIONS

We don't do repairs	**Vi foretar ikke reparasjoner**
	vee forer-tar *i*kker rep-ahra-sh*oo*ner
Where is your car?	**Hvor er bilen Deres?**
	vor ar b*ee*len d*a*yress
What make is it?	**Hva slags merke er den?**
	va shl*ah*gss m*a*rker ar den
Come back tomorrow/on Monday	**Kom igjen i morgen/på mandag**
	kom ee-yen ee m*o*ren/paw m*ah*ndahg

[*For days of the week see p. 208*]

We don't rent cars	**Vi leier ikke ut biler**
	vee l*a*yer *i*kker oot b*ee*ler
Your driver's license, please	**Kan jeg få se sertifikatet Deres**
	kan yay faw say sertifi-k*ah*ter d*a*yress
The mileage is unlimited	**De kan kjøre så mye De vil**
	dee kan sh*i*r-er saw m*ee*-er dee v*i*l

Public transport

ESSENTIAL INFORMATION

- Finding the way to a bus station, a bus stop, a tram stop, a railway station and a taxi stand, see p. 129.
- People usually line up for buses, particularly in towns.
- Most towns and cities have taxi stands. Taxis rarely cruise for passengers. Find a taxi stand or look under **DROSJER** (taxis) in the telephone directory. You can hail a taxi with the 'taxi free' sign up. All taxis are metered and expensive.
- There is a national train network called **NSB** (Norwegian State Railways). From Oslo trains run to all parts of Norway with connections to local lines. There are also trains going to Sweden with connections to the Continent.
- Buses and coach services between neighboring towns and tourist centers in populated parts of the country are good and frequent. In sparsely populated parts, less frequent.
- Oslo is serviced by trolleys, buses and two small subway networks. In Oslo's trolleys and buses there is a single fare system. A ticket allows you to interchange once within the hour. Trolley, bus and subway tickets are bought as you enter, or from a roving conductor. Train tickets are bought at the railway station.
- In Oslo there is a '**universalkort**' (special ticket) which gives un-limited travel within city limits for either two weeks or a month. In Bergen there is a 48 hour tourist ticket for buses and trolley buses available from the Tourist Information Office and most hotels.
- Many smaller towns have their own airport, and local flights are becoming increasingly popular.
- Key words and signs to look for:
  BILLETTER (tickets)   **TOGTABELL** (train timetable)
  INNGANG (entrance)   **RUTETABELL** (bus timetable)
  UTGANG (exit)
  ADGANG FORBUDT (no entry)
  PLATTFORM/SPOR (platform)
  TURISTINFORMASJON (tourist information)
  VEKSLEKONTOR (exchange)
  OPPBEVARING (left luggage)
  BUSSHOLDEPLASS (regular bus stop)
  STOPPER PÅ SIGNAL (stops on request)

Norwegian

WHAT TO SAY

Where does the train for (Oslo) leave from?	**Hvor går toget til (Oslo) fra?** vor gor tawg-er til (oshlo) fra
At what time does the train leave for (Oslo)?	**Når går toget til (Oslo)?** nor gor tawg-er til (oshlo)
At what time does the train arrive in (Oslo)?	**Når kommer toget til (Oslo)?** nor kommer tawg-er til (oshlo)
Is this the train for (Oslo)?	**Er dette toget til (Oslo)?** ar detter tawg-er til (oshlo)
Where does the bus for (Hønefoss) leave from?	**Hvor går (Hønefoss) bussen fra?** vor gor (hern-erfoss) boossen fra
Is this the bus for (Hønefoss)?	**Er dette (Hønefoss) bussen?** ar detter (hern-erfoss) boossen
Do I have to change?	**Må jeg bytte?** maw yay bit-ter
Where can I get a taxi?	**Hvor kan jeg finne en drosje?** vor kan yay finner en drosher
Can you put me off at the right stop, please?	**Kan De si fra når jeg må gå av?** kan dee see fra nor yay maw gaw ahv
Can I book a seat?	**Kan jeg bestille en plass?** kan yay best-iller en plahss
A single	**Én vei** ain vay
A return	**Tur-retur** toor-ret-toor
First class	**Første klasse** firster klahsser
Second class	**Annen klasse** annen klahsser
One adult	**En voksen** ain vaksen
Two adults	**To voksne** too vaksner
and one child	**og et barn** aw et barn
and two children	**og to barn** aw too barn
How much is it?	**Hvor mye koster det?** vor mee-er koster day

LIKELY REACTIONS

Over there	**Der borte** dar borter
Here	**Her** har
Platform (1) [*For times, see p. 207*]	**Plattform/spor (en)** platform/spoor (ain)
Change at (Dombås)	**Bytt på (Dombås)** bitt paw (dombawss)
Change at (the town hall)	**Bytt ved (rådhuset)** bitt vaid (rawd-hoosser)
There is only tourist class	**Det er bare turistklasse** day ar bahrer toorist-klahsser
There is a supplement	**Det er et tillegg** day ar et till-egg

Leisure

ESSENTIAL INFORMATION

- Finding your way to a place of entertainment, see p. 127, 129.
- For times of day, see p. 207.
- Smoking is not permitted in cinemas, theatres, etc. during performances. You may, however, smoke during intervals, away from the seating area.
- Foreign films have subtitles and are not dubbed.
- No usherettes in cinemas as lights are on when you enter.
- In theatres it is customary to leave one's coat in the cloakroom.

WHAT TO SAY

At what time does . . . open?	**Når åpner . . .?** nor *aw*pner . . .
the museum	**museet** moos*say*-er

Norwegian

At what time does . . . close?	**Når stenger . . .?**
	nor st*e*ng-er . . .
the art gallery	**kunstmuseet/galleriet**
	k*oo*nst-mooss*ay*-er/galler*ee*-er
At what time does . . . start?	**Når begynner . . .?**
	nor be-y*i*nr . . .
the concert	**konserten**
	kons*e*rt-en
the film	**filmen**
	f*i*lmen
the match	**kampen**
	k*ah*mpen
the performance/play	**forestillingen**
	forer-st*i*lling-en
How much is it . . .	**Hvor mye koster det . . .**
	vor m*ee*-er k*o*ster day . . .
for an adult?	**for en voksen?**
	for en v*o*ksen
for a child?	**for et barn?**
[*state the price, if there's a choice*]	for et barn
Stalls/circle/upper circle/sun/shade	**Parkett/losje/balkong/sol/skygge**
	par-k*e*t/l*oo*sher/balk*o*ng/sool/sh*i*hgg-er
Do you have . . .	**Har De . . .**
	har dee . . .
a program /guidebook?	**et program?**
	et pru-gr*ah*m
I would like lessons in . . .	**Jeg vil ha . . . timer**
	yay vil ha . . . t*ee*mer
skiing	**ski**
	shee
sailing	**seile**
	s*ai*ler
waterskiing	**vannski**
	v*ah*nn-shee
Can I rent . . .	**Kan jeg leie . . .**
	kan yay l*ay*-er . . .
some skis?	**ski?**
	shee
some ski boots?	**skistøvler?**
	sh*ee*-stirfler

a boat?	**en båt?**
	en b*a*wt
a fishing rod?	**en fiskestang?**
	en f*i*sker-stahng
a sun lounger?	**en solseng?**
	en s*oo*l-seng
a beach chair?	**en fluktstol?**
	en fl*oo*kt-stool
a sun umbrella?	**en solparasoll?**
	en s*oo*l-para-soll
the necessary equipment?	**nødvendig utstyr?**
	n*i*rd-vendee *oo*t-steer
How much is it . . .	**Hvor mye koster det . . .**
	vor m*ee*-er k*o*st-er day . . .
per day/per hour?	**per dag/per time?**
	pair d*a*hg/pair t*ee*mer
Do I need a license?	**Trenger jeg tillatelse?**
	tr*e*ng-er yay till-*ah*tel-ser

Asking if things are allowed

ESSENTIAL INFORMATION

- May one smoke here?
  May we smoke here?   **Kan man røke her?**
  May I smoke here?   kan man r*i*rk-er har
  Can one smoke here?
  Can I smoke here?
- All these English variations can be expressed in one way in Norwegian. To save space, only the first English version (May one . . .?) is shown below.

WHAT TO SAY

Excuse me, please	**Unnskyld meg**
	*oo*nshil may

May one . . .	Kan man . . .
	kan man . . .
camp here?	**sette opp telt her?**
	setter opp telt har
come in?	**gå inn?**
	gaw inn
dance here?	**danse her?**
	dancer har
fish here?	**fiske her?**
	fisker har
get a drink here?	**få en drink her?**
	faw en drink har
get out this way?	**gå ut denne veien?**
	gaw oot denner vay-en
get something to eat here?	**få noe å spise her?**
	faw noo-er aw speesser har
eat something here?	**spise her?**
	speesser har
leave one's things here?	**legge igjen sakene sine her?**
	legger ee-yen sahkener seener har
look around?	**se seg om?**
	say say um
park here?	**parkere her?**
	park-airer har
picnic here?	**sette seg og spise her?**
	setter say aw speesser har
sit here?	**sitte her?**
	sitter har
smoke here?	**røke her?**
	rirker har
swim here?	**bade her?**
	bahder har
telephone here?	**låne telefonen?**
	lawner telefoonen
take photos here?	**ta bilder her?**
	ta bilder har
wait here?	**vente her?**
	venter har

LIKELY REACTIONS

Yes, certainly	**Ja, selvfølgelig**
	ya sell-firl-gaylee

Help yourself	**Ja, vær så god**	ya va*r* saw goo
I think so	**Ja, jeg tror det**	ya yay tro*or* day
Of course	**Selvfølgelig**	sell-f*ir*l-gaylee
Yes, but be careful	**Ja, men vær forsiktig**	ya men var for-s*i*ktee
No, certainly not	**Nei, det er ikke tillatt**	nay day ar *i*kker till-att
I don't think so	**Nei, jeg tror ikke det**	nay yay tro*or i*kker day
Not normally	**Nei, ikke vanligvis**	nay, *i*kker va*h*nlee-veess
Sorry	**Beklager**	bay-kla*h*g-er

Reference

NUMBERS
Cardinal numbers

0	**null**	nooll
1	**en**	ain
2	**to**	too
3	**tre**	tray
4	**fire**	feerer
5	**fem**	fem
6	**seks**	seks
7	**sju**	shoo
8	**åtte**	*aw*tter
9	**ni**	nee
10	**ti**	tee
11	**elleve**	*e*lver
12	**tolv**	tawl
13	**tretten**	tretten
14	**fjorten**	f-yorten

15	**femten**	f*e*mten
16	**seksten**	s*ay*sten
17	**søtten**	s*i*rtten
18	**atten**	*ah*tten
19	**nitten**	n*i*tten
20	**tjue**	sh*oo*-er
21	**tjueen**	sh*oo*-er-a*i*n
22	**tjueto**	sh*oo*-er-t*oo*
23	**tjuetre**	sh*oo*-er-tray
24	**tjuefire**	sh*oo*-er-f*ee*rer
25	**tjuefem**	sh*oo*-er-fem
26	**tjueseks**	sh*oo*-er-seks
27	**tjuesju**	sh*oo*-er-shoo
28	**tjueåtte**	sh*oo*-er-*aw*tter
29	**tjueni**	sh*oo*-er-nee
30	**tretti**	tretti
31	**trettien**	tretti-a*i*n
32	**trettito**	tretti-t*oo*
33	**trettitre**	tretti-tray
34	**trettifire**	tretti-f*ee*rer
35	**trettifem**	tretti-fem
40	**førti**	f*i*rty
45	**førtifem**	f*i*rty-fem
50	**femti**	femti
55	**femtifem**	f*e*mti-fem
60	**seksti**	seksti
66	**sekstiseks**	seksti-seks
70	**søtti**	s*i*rtti
77	**søttisju**	s*i*rtti-shoo
80	**åtti**	*aw*tti
88	**åttiåtte**	*aw*tti-*aw*tter
90	**nitti**	n*i*tti
99	**nittini**	n*i*tti-nee
100	**hundre**	h*oo*ndrer
101	**hundreogen**	h*oo*ndrer-aw-*ai*n
102	**hundreogto**	h*oo*ndrer-aw-t*oo*
125	**hundreogtjuefem**	h*oo*ndrer-aw-sh*oo*-er-fem
150	**hundreogfemti**	h*oo*ndrer-aw-f*e*mti
175	**hundreogsøttifem**	h*oo*ndrer-aw-s*i*rtti-fem
200	**to hundre**	t*oo*-h*oo*ndrer
300	**tre hundre**	tray-h*oo*ndrer
400	**fire hundre**	f*ee*rer h*oo*ndrer
500	**fem hundre**	fem h*oo*ndrer

1000	**tusen**	*too*-sen
2000	**to tusen**	too *too*-sen
10,000	**ti tusen**	tee *too*-sen
100,000	**hundre tusen**	hoondrer *too*-sen
1,000,000	**en million**	ain milli-*oon*

Ordinal numbers

1st	**første (1.)**	*fir*ster
2nd	**andre (2.)**	*ahn*drer
3rd	**tredje (3.)**	tr*ai*d-yer
4th	**fjerde (4.)**	f-*ya*rder
5th	**femte (5.)**	*fem*ter
6th	**sjette (6.)**	*shet*ter
7th	**sjuende (7.)**	sh*oo*-en-er
8th	**åttende (8.)**	*aw*ttener
9th	**niende (9.)**	n*ee*-en-er
10th	**tiende (10.)**	t*ee*-en-er
11th	**ellevte (11.)**	*el*lefter
12th	**tolvte (12.)**	t*aw*lf-ter

TIME

What time is it?	**Hvor mange er klokken?**
	vor m*ah*ng-er ar kl*o*kken
It's . . .	**Klokken er . . .**
	kl*o*kken ar . . .
one o'clock	**ett**
	*ai*tt
two o'clock	**to**
	t*oo*
three o'clock	**tre**
	tr*ay*
It's noon	**Den er tolv**
	den ar t*aw*l
It's midnight	**Det er midnatt**
	day ar m*i*d-natt
It's . . .	**Den er . . .**
	den ar . . .
five past five	**fem over fem**
	fem *aw*ver fem
twenty to six	**tjue på seks**
	sh*oo*-er paw s*e*ks
ten to six	**ti på seks**
	t*ee* paw s*e*ks

Norwegian

At what time . . . (does the train leave)?	**Når . . . (går toget)?**
	nor . . . (gor tawg-er)
At . . .	**Klokken . . .**
	klokken . . .
13.00	**tretten**
	tretten
22.45	**tjueto førtifem**
	shoo-er-too firty-fem
0.55	**null femtifem**
	nooll femti-fem

DAYS

Sunday	**søndag**
	sirn-dahg
Monday	**mandag**
	mahn-dahg
Tuesday	**tirsdag**
	teesh-dahg
Wednesday	**onsdag**
	onss-dahg
Thursday	**torsdag**
	toosh-dahg
Friday	**fredag**
	fray-dahg
Saturday	**lørdag**
	ler-dahg
last Monday	**forrige mandag**
	forree-er mahn-dahg
next Tuesday	**neste tirsdag**
	nester teesh-dahg
on Wednesday	**på onsdag**
	paw onss-dahg
on Thursdays	**på torsdagene**
	paw toosh-dahg-en-er
until Friday	**til fredag**
	til fray-dahg
before Saturday	**før lørdag**
	fir ler-dahg
after Sunday	**etter søndag**
	etter sirn-dahg
the day before yesterday	**i forgårs**
	ee for-gorss
two days ago	**for to dager siden**
	for too dahg-er seeden

yesterday	**i går** ee gor
yesterday morning	**i går morges** ee gor mor-res
yesterday afternoon	**i går ettermiddag** ee gor ettermiddag
last night	**i natt** ee natt
today	**i dag** ee dahg
this morning	**i dag morges** ee dahg mor-res
this afternoon	**i ettermiddag** ee ettermiddag
tonight	**i natt** ee natt
tomorrow	**i morgen** ee moren
tomorrow morning	**i morgen tidlig** ee moren teelee
tomorrow afternoon	**i morgen ettermiddag** ee moren ettermiddag
tomorrow evening	**i morgen kveld** ee moren kvel
tomorrow night	**i morgen natt** ee moren natt
the day after tomorrow	**overimorgen** *aw*ver-ee-moren

MONTHS AND DATES

January	**januar** yan-oo-ar
February	**februar** febroo-ar
March	**mars** marsh
April	**april** ahpreel
May	**mai** my
June	**juni** yoonee

Norwegian

July	**juli**	y*oo*lee
August	**august**	owg*oo*st
September	**september**	september
October	**oktober**	okt*oo*ber
November	**november**	november
December	**desember**	december
last month	**forrige måned**	f*o*rree-er m*aw*ner
in spring	**om våren**	om v*o*ren
in summer	**om sommeren**	om s*o*mmer-en
in autumn	**om høsten**	om h*e*rssten
in winter	**om vinteren**	om v*i*nter-en
this year	**i år**	ee or
last year	**i fjor**	ee f-y*oo*r
next year	**neste år**	n*e*ster or
in 1985	**i nitten åttifem**	ee n*i*tten *aw*tti-f*e*m
What's the date today?	**Hvilken dato er det i dag?**	v*i*lken d*a*htoo ar day ee dahg
It's the 6th of March	**Det er den sjette mars**	day ar den sh*e*tter m*a*rsh

Public holidays

● Offices, shops and schools are all closed on the following days

(NB Christmas eve and the day before Easter have half day closing.)

January 1	**Nyttårsdag**	New Year's Day
. . .	**Skjærtorsdag**	Maundy Thursday
. . .	**Langfredag**	Good Friday
. . .	**Annen påskedag**	Easter Monday

May 1	**Arbeidets dag**	Labour Day
May 17	**Nasjonaldagen**	Constitution Day
. . .	**Kristi Himmelfartsdag**	Ascension Day
. . .	**Annen pinsedag**	Whit Monday
December 25	**Første Juledag**	Christmas Day
December 26	**Annen Juledag**	Boxing Day

COUNTRIES AND NATIONALITIES
Countries

Australia	**Australia** owstra-lee-ah
Austria	**Østerrike** erster-reeker
Belgium	**Belgia** bel-ghee-ah
Britain	**Storbritannia** stoor-britannia
Canada	**Kanada** ka-na-da
East Africa	**Øst-Afrika** erst ahfreeka
Eire/Ireland	**Eire** eye-ray
England	**England** eng-lahn
France	**Frankrike** frahnk-reeker
Greece	**Hellas** hell-ahss
India	**India** india
Italy	**Italia** eeta-lee-ah
Luxembourg	**Luksemburg** looks-emburg
Netherlands	**Nederland/Holland** naider-lahn/holl-ahn
New Zealand	**New Zealand** new sealahn
Northern Ireland	**Nord-Irland** noor-eer-lahn
Pakistan	**Pakistan** pakee-stahn

Portugal	**Portugal**
	portoo-gahl
Scotland	**Skotland**
	skot-lahn
South Africa	**Sør-Afrika**
	sir-ahfreeka
Spain	**Spania**
	spahn-ee-ah
Switzerland	**Sveits**
	svaits
United States	**De Forente Stater/USA**
	dee forainter stahter/oo-ess-ah
Wales	**Wales**
	wales
West Germany	**Vest-Tyskland**
	vest-tisk-lahn

Nationalities

American	**amerikansk**
	ahmeri-kahnsk
Australian	**australiensk**
	owstra-lee-ainsk
British	**britisk**
	brittisk
Canadian	**kanadisk**
	ka-na-disk
East African	**øst-afrikansk**
	erst-ahfree-kahnsk
English	**engelsk**
	eng-elsk
Indian	**indisk**
	in-disk
Irish	**irsk**
	eeshk
New Zealander	**new zealandsk**
	new sea-lahnsk
Pakistani	**pakistansk**
	pa-kistahnsk
Scottish	**skotsk**
	skotsk
South African	**sør-afrikansk**
	sir-ahfree-kahnsk
Welsh	**walesisk**
	va-lay-sisk

Do it yourself

Some notes on the language

This section does not deal with 'grammar' as such. The purpose here is to explain some of the most obvious and elementary nuts and bolts of the language, based on the principal phrases included in the book. This information should enable you to produce numerous sentences of your own making.

There is no pronunciation guide in the first part of this section partly because it would get in the way of the explanations and partly because you have to do it yourself at this stage, if you are serious: work out the pronunciation from all the earlier examples in the book.

THE

All nouns in Norwegian belong to one of three genders: masculine, feminine or neuter, irrespective of whether they refer to living beings or inanimate objects. Most feminine words can also be used as masculine words, but never the other way round.

The in Norwegian is tagged on to the end of the word, so that instead of *the boy* they say *boy the*. That is *boy* – **gutt**, *the boy* – **gutten**. *The* is **-en** after a masculine noun, **-a** after a feminine noun and **-et** after a neuter noun.

The	masculine	feminine	neuter
the address	**adressen**		
the apple			**eplet**
the bill	**regningen**		
the cup of tea	**tekoppen**		
the glass of beer			**ølglasset**
the key	**nøkkelen**		
the luggage	**bagasjen**		
the menu	**menyen**		
the newspaper		**avisa**	
the receipt	**kvitteringen**		
the ham sandwich			**skinke-smørbrødet**
the suitcase	**kofferten**		
the telephone directory	**telefon-katalogen**		
the train timetable	**togtabellen**		

Norwegian

Important things to remember

- There is no easy way of predicting if a noun is masculine, feminine or neuter. You just have to learn and remember its gender. But it may help you to know that most words are masculine, and that you can, if you like, eliminate the feminine gender altogether.
- Does it matter? Not unless you want to make a serious attempt to speak correctly and scratch beneath the surface of the language. You would be understood if you said **eplen** or **nøkkelet** provided your pronunciation was good.

Plural

the addresses	**adressene**
the apples	**eplene**
the bills	**regningene**
the bus timetables	**rutetabellene**
the cups of tea	**tekoppene**
the glasses of beer	**ølglassene**
the keys	**nøklene**
the menus	**menyene**
the newspapers	**avisene**
the receipts	**kvitteringene**
the ham sandwiches	**skinkesmørbrødene**
the suitcases	**koffertene**
the telephone directories	**telefonkatalogene**

Important things to remember

- In plural most words end in **-ene** irrespective of gender.
- However, some Norwegian nouns do not follow the above rule. Their endings may be slightly different and their vowels may change in the singular and plural like 'ox' and 'goose' in English. In Norwegian we have *the daughter – the daughters* = **datteren – døtrene**. The rules for these exceptions are too many and too complicated to be explained here. Besides, there is no great harm done if you should happen to say **datterene** instead of **døtrene**. You will be understood provided your pronunciation is good.

Practice saying and writing these sentences in Norwegian. Notice that the verb remains unchanged from singular to plural.

Where is the key?	**Hvor er nøkkelen?**
Where is the receipt?	**Hvor er . . .?**

Where is the address?
Where is the luggage?
Where are the keys?   **Hvor er nøklene?**
Where are the ham sandwiches?   **Hvor er . . .?**
Where are the newspapers?
Where are the apples?

Now make up more sentences along these lines.

Practice saying and writing these sentences in Norwegian:

Have you got the key?   **Har De nøkkelen?**
Have you got the suitcase?   **Har De . . .?**
Have you got the luggage?
Have you got the telephone directory?
Have you got the menu?
I'd like the key   **Kan jeg få nøkkelen?**
I'd like the train timetable
I'd like the receipt
I'd like the keys
Where can I get the key?   **Hvor kan man få nøkkelen?**
Where can I get the address?
Where can I get the bus timetables?

Now make up more sentences along these lines.

A/an	masculine	feminine	neuter
an address	**en adresse**		
an apple			**et eple**
a bill	**en regning**		
a cup of tea	**en kopp te**		
a glass of beer			**et glass øl**
a key	**en nøkkel**		
a menu	**en meny**		
a newspaper		**ei avis**	
a receipt	**en kvittering**		
a ham sandwich			**et skinke-smørbrød**
a suitcase	**en koffert**		
a telephone directory	**en telefon-katalog**		
a train timetable	**en togtabbell**		

Norwegian

Important things to remember

- *A* or *an* is **en** before masculine nouns, **ei** before feminine nouns and **et** before neuter nouns.
- The plural for *some* or *any* is **noen** irrespective of gender when referring to an indefinite number of a certain thing, and **noe** irrespective of gender, when referring to an unknown quantity.
- The plural ending is **-er**, irrespective of gender, except for one syllable neuter words (**et brød – noen brød**) which don't get any ending at all.
- You may have noticed that in the restaurant and shopping sections, **noen** and **noe** have on occasions been omitted, sometimes substituted with **en** or **et** and sometimes with **litt** (a little). The rules that dictate these irregularities are many and complicated and to give a full description of them here would only lead to confusion. When looking up a given phrase in this book, use the given phrase. When making your own phrase, use **noen** and **noe** according to the above rules. Your phrase will then be basically if not absolutely correct, and you will be understood.

some/any (plural) indefinite number

some addresses	**noen adresser**
some apples	**noen epler**
some bills	**noen regninger**
some bus timetables	**noen rutetabeller**
some cups of tea	**noen kopper te**
some glasses of wine	**noen glass vin**
some keys	**noen nøkler**
some menus	**noen menyer**
some receipts	**noen kvitteringer**
some sandwiches	**noen smørbrød**
some suitcases	**noen kofferter**
some telephone directories	**noen telefonkataloger**

some/any part of a larger quantity

some butter	**noe smør**
some meat	**noe kjøtt**
some paper	**noe papir**
some toothpaste	**noe tannkrem**

Practise writing and saying these sentences in Norwegian:

Have you got a receipt?	**Har De en kvittering?**
Have you got a menu?	
I'd like a telephone directory	**Kan jeg få en telefonkatalog?**
I'd like some sandwiches	**Kan jeg få noen smørbrød?**
Where can I get some newspapers?	**Hvor kan jeg få noen aviser?**
Where can I get a cup of tea?	
Is there a key?	**Er det en nøkkel?**
Is there a train timetable?	
Are there any keys?	**Er det noen nøkler?**
Are there any newspapers?	

Now make up more sentences along these lines.

THIS AND THAT

There are two different sets of words for *this* and *that* in Norwegian according to the gender of the word they are referring to.

Masculine/feminine	*Neuter*
denne this	**dette** this
den that	**det** that

- If you don't know the gender of the object that you are referring to or even its name, it does not really matter. You will be understood even if you use the wrong gender. Just point and say:

Jeg vil ha denne/dette	I'd like this
Jeg vil ha den/det	I'd like that
Jeg trenger denne/dette	I need this

HELPING OTHERS

There is really no adequate and easy way in which to say *I'd like* in Norwegian. There is a rather long phrase which is somewhat daunting for the inexperienced speaker of the language and the phrase **jeg vil ha . . .** (I'll have) which in some cases may seem a little abrupt. What Norwegians often do is to say **kan jeg få . . .?** (may I have?) when what they really mean is *I'd like*. This is why *I'd like* in this book is sometimes translated by **jeg vil ha . . .** and sometimes by **kan jeg få . . .?**

You can help yourself with phrases such as:

I'd like . . . a sandwich	**Jeg vil ha . . . et smørbrød**
Where can I get . . . a cup of tea?	**Hvor kan jeg få . . . en kopp te?**
I'll have . . . a glass of wine	**Jeg vil ha et glass vin**
I need . . . a receipt	**Jeg trenger . . . en kvittering**

If you come across a compatriot having trouble making himself or herself understood, you should be able to speak to the Norwegian on their behalf.

He'd like . . .	**Han vil ha et skinkesmørbrød**
	han vil ha et sh*i*nker-smir-brer
She'd like . . .	**Hun vil ha et skinkesmørbrød**
	hun vil ha et sh*i*nker-smir-brer

Strictly speaking, **kan man . . .?** means *can one . . .?* and normally serves instead of *can I . . .?* (**kan jeg . . .?**), *can he . . .?*, *can she . . .?*, *can they . . .?* and *can we . . .?* However, all the above-mentioned variations in Norwegian are included in the remainder of this section because of their potential usefulness.

Where can he get . . .?	**Hvor kan han få en kopp te?**
	vor kan han f*a*w en kopp t*a*y
Where can she get . . .?	**Hvor kan hun få en kopp te?**
	vor kan hun faw en kopp t*a*y
He'll have . . .	**Han vil ha et glass øl**
	han vil ha et glahss *e*rl
She'll have . . .	**Hun vil ha et glass øl**
	hun vil ha et glahss *e*rl
He needs . . .	**Han trenger en kvittering**
	han treng-er en kvitt*ai*ring
She needs . . .	**Hun trenger en kvittering**
	hun treng-er en kvitt*ai*ring

You can also help a couple or a group if *they* are having difficulties. The Norwegian word for *they* is **de**. Note that **De** written with a capital is also the polite form of *you*.

They'd like . . .	**De vil ha ost**
	dee vil ha *o*st
Where can they get . . .?	**Hvor kan de få noe smør?**
	vor kan dee faw n*oo*-er sm*i*r

They'll have . . .	**De vil ha vin**
	d*ee* vil ha v*ee*n
They need . . .	**De trenger vann**
	d*ee* treng-er v*a*hnn

What about the two of you? No problem the word for *we* is **vi**.

We'd like . . .	**Vi vil ha vin**
	v*ee* vil ha v*ee*n
Where can we get . . .?	**Hvor kan vi få vann?**
	vor kan vee faw v*a*hnn
We'll have . . .	**Vi vil ha noe smør**
	v*ee* vil ha n*oo*-er sm*i*r
We need . . .	**Vi trenger sukker**
	v*ee* treng-er s*oo*kker

Try writing out your own checklist for these four useful phrase-starters, like this:

Jeg vil ha . . .	**Vi vil ha . . .**
Han vil ha . . .	**De vil ha . . .**
Hun vil ha . . .	
Hvor kan jeg . . . få?	**Hvor . . . vi . . .?**
Hvor kan han . . . få?	**Hvor . . . hun . . .?**
Hvor . . . hun . . . få?	

You may have noticed that the verb never changes from one person to another: **jeg vil, han vil, hun vil, vi vil** etc.

MORE PRACTICE

Here are some Norwegian names of things. See how many different sentences you can make up, using the various points of information given earlier in this section.

		singular	plural
1	ashtray	**askebeger** (*m*)	**askebegrene**
2	ballpoint pen	**kulepenn** (*m*)	**kulepennene**
3	bag	**veske** (*f*)	**veskene**
4	bottle	**flaske** (*f*)	**flaskene**
5	car	**bil** (*m*)	**bilene**
6	cigarette	**sigarett** (*m*)	**sigarettene**
7	corkscrew	**korketrekker** (*m*)	**korketrekkerne**
8	egg	**egg** (*n*)	**eggene**
9	house	**hus** (*n*)	**husene**

Norwegian

		singular	plural
10	knife	**kniv** (*m*)	**knivene**
11	mountain	**fjell** (*n*)	**fjellene**
12	plate	**tallerken** (*m*)	**tallerknene**
13	postcard	**prospektkort** (*n*)	**prospektkortene**
14	room	**rom** (*n*)	**rommene**
15	shoe	**sko** (*m*)	**skoene**
16	stamp	**frimerke** (*n*)	**frimerkene**
17	street	**gate** (*f*)	**gatene**
18	ticket	**billett** (*m*)	**billettene**
19	train	**tog** (*n*)	**togene**
20	wallet	**lommebok** (*f*)	**lommebøkene**

Norwegian Index

Swedish

Swedish

D. L. Ellis,

Pronunciation **Dr J. Baldwin**

Useful address

Swedish/Norwegian National Tourist Office
75 Rockefeller Plaza
New York, NY 10019
(212) 582-2802

Contents

Swedish

Everyday expressions

[See also 'Shop talk', p. 266]
● There is no word that corresponds exactly with 'please' in Swedish. **Tack** (thank you) is used instead. When handing over something, the phrase 'please' is **var så god**.

Hello (informal)	**Hej** hay
Goodbye (informal)	**Hej då** hay daw
Goodbye (formal)	**Adjö** ah-yer
Good morning	**God morgon** goo morron
Good afternoon	**God middag** goo mid-da
Good day (formal)	**God dag** goo da
Good evening	**God afton** goo af-ton
Good night	**God natt** goo naht
Yes	**Ja** ya
Please [see above]	**Var så god/tack** var saw goo/tak
Thank you	**Tack** tak
Thank you very much	**Tack så mycket** tak saw mee-ket
That's right	**Det är riktigt** det air rik-tit
No	**Nej** nay
No, thank you	**Nej tack** nay tak
I disagree	**Jag håller inte med** ya holler inter med
Excuse me	**Ursäkta mig** yoo-shek-ta may

That's good	**Det är bra**
	det air bra
That's no good	**Det är inte bra**
	det air *i*nter bra
I know	**Jag vet**
	ya vet
It doesn't matter	**Det gör ingenting**
	det yer *i*ng-en-ting
Where's the toilet, please?	**Var är toaletten?**
	var air toh-ah-*let*-ten
Do you speak English?	**Talar ni engelska?**
	ta-lar nee *e*ng-el-ska
I'm sorry ...	**Tyvärr ...**
	tee-*va*ir ...
I don't speak Swedish	**jag talar inte svenska**
	ya *ta*-lar *i*nter sven-ska
I don't understand	**jag förstår inte**
	ya fer-*sto*r *i*nter
Please can you ...	**Kan ni ... tack**
	kan nee ... tak
repeat that?	**säga om det?**
	say-ah om det
speak more slowly?	**tala långsammare?**
	ta-la *lo*ng-sam-ah-rer
write it down?	**skriva ner det?**
	skr*ee*va nair det?
What is this called in Swedish?	**Vad heter det här på svenska?**
[*point*]	vad h*ai*ter det hair paw sven-ska

Crossing the border

ESSENTIAL INFORMATION

- Don't waste time just before you leave rehearsing what you are going to say to the border officials – the chances are that you won't have to say anything at all, especially if you travel by air.
- It's more useful to check that you have your documents handy for

Swedish

the journey: passports, tickets, money, travelers' checks, insurance
documents, driver's license and car registration documents.
● Look out for these signs:
TULL (customs)
GRÄNS (border)
GRÄNSPOLIS (frontier police)
● You may be asked routine questions by the customs officials [*see
below*]. If you have to give personal details, see 'Meeting people'
p. 233. The other important answer to know is 'Nothing':
Ingenting (ing-en-ting).

ROUTINE QUESTIONS

Passport?	**Pass?**
	pass
Insurance?	**Försäkring?**
	fer-*saik*-ring
Registration document? (logbook)	**Registreringsbevis?**
	reg-ee-str*ai*r-ings-bay-vees
Ticket, please	**Biljetten, tack**
	bil-*yet*-ten tak
Have you anything to declare?	**Har ni något att deklarera?**
	har nee *naw*-got aht deklah-r*ai*ra
Where are you going?	**Vart är ni på väg?**
	vart air nee paw v*ai*g
How long are you staying?	**Hur länge stannar ni?**
	hoor l*ai*ng-er st*a*n-nar nee
Where have you come from?	**Var kommer ni ifrån?**
	var k*o*m-mer nee *ee*-frawn

Meeting people

[See also 'Everyday expressions', p. 230]
Breaking the ice

How are you?	**Hur mår ni?**
	hoor mor nee
I am here . . .	**Jag är här . . .**
	ya air hair . . .
on vacation	**på semester**
	paw se-mes-ter
on business	**i affärer**
	ee af-fairer
Can I offer you . . .	**Kan jag få bjuda . . .**
	kan ya faw b-yoo-da . . .
a drink?	**på en drink?**
	paw en drink
a cigarette?	**på en cigarrett?**
	paw en cigarett
a cigar?	**på en cigarr?**
	paw en cigar
Are you staying long?	**Stannar ni länge?**
	stan-nar nee laing-er

Name

What's your name?	**Vad heter ni?**
	vad haiter nee
My name is . . .	**Mitt namn är . . .**
	mitt namn air . . .

Family

Are you married?	**Är ni gift?**
	air nee yeeft
I am . . .	**Jag är . . .**
	ya air . . .
married	**gift**
	yeeft
single	**ogift**
	o-yeeft

Swedish

This is . . .	**Det här är . . .**
	det hair air . . .
my wife	**min fru**
	min froo
my husband	**min man**
	min man
my son	**min son**
	min sawn
my daughter	**min dotter**
	min dot-ter
my boyfriend	**min pojkvän**
	min poyk-ven
my girlfriend	**min flickvän**
	min flick-ven
my colleague (male or female)	**min kollega**
	min kol-lai-ga
Do you have any children?	**Har ni några barn?**
	har nee nora barn
I have . . .	**Jag har . . .**
	ya har . . .
one daughter	**en dotter**
	en dot-ter
one son	**en son**
	en sawn
two daughters	**två döttrar**
	tvaw dert-rar
three sons	**tre söner**
	tray sern-er
No, I haven't any children	**Nej, jag har inga barn**
	nay ya har inga barn

Where you live

Are you . . .	**Är ni . . .**
	air nee . . .
Swedish?	**svensk/svenska?***
	svensk/sven-ska
Norwegian?	**norsk/norska?***
	norsk/nor-ska
Danish?	**dansk/danska?***
	dansk/dan-ska

*Use the first alternative for men, the second for women

I am . . .   **Jag är . . .**
ya air . . .

   American   **amerikan/amerikanska***
am-ree-kahn/am-ree-kahn-ska

   English   **engelsman/engelska***
eng-els-man/eng-el-ska

[*For other nationalities, see p. 320*]

I live . . .   **Jag bor . . .**
ya boor . . .

   in America   **i Amerika**
ee amair-reeka

   in Canada   **i Kanada**
ee kan-ah-da

   in the north (of Sweden)   **i norra (Sverige)**
ee nor-ra (svair-yer)

   in the south   **i södra**
ee serd-ra

   in the west   **i västra**
ee vaist-ra

   in the east   **i östra**
ee erst-ra

   in the center (of Stockholm)   **i centrum (av Stockholm)**
ee centrum (ahv stock-holm)

For the businessman and woman

I'm from . . . (firm's name)   **Jag kommer från . . .**
ya kom-mer frawn . . .

I have an appointment with   **Jag har ett möte med . . .**
. . .   ya har ett merter med . . .

May I speak to . . .?   **Kan jag få tala med . . .?**
kan ya faw ta-la med . . .

This is my card   **Här är mitt kort**
hair air mitt kort

I'm sorry, I'm late   **Jag är ledsen, att jag är sen**
ya air led-sen aht ya air sain

Can I make another   **Kan jag bestämma ett nytt möte**
  appointment?   kan ya be-stem-ma ett neet merter

I am staying at the hotel . . .   **Jag bor på hotell . . .**
ya boor paw hotell . . .

*First alternative for men, second for women

Swedish

Asking the way

ESSENTIAL INFORMATION

● Keep a lookout for all these place names as you will find them on
shops, maps and signs.

WHAT TO SAY

Excuse me, please	**Ursäkta mig** yoo-shek-ta may
How do I get . . .	**Hur kommer jag . . .** hoor kom-mer ya . . .
to the airport?	**till flygplatsen?** till fleeg-platsen
to the beach?	**till stranden?** till stran-den
to the bus station?	**till busshållplatsen?** till booss-holl-platsen
to Gothenburg?	**till Göteborg?** till yerter-bory
to the market?	**till torget?** till tor-yet
to the police station?	**till polisstationen?** till police-sta-shonen
to the post office?	**till posten?** till pos-ten
to the railway station?	**till tågstationen?** til tawg-sta-shonen
to the sports stadium?	**till sportstadion?** till sport-stad-ee-on
to the Stora Hotel?	**till Stora hotellet?** till stoora hotellet
to the tourist information office?	**till turist informationen?** till toorist-informa-shonen
to the town center?	**till centrum?** till centrum
to the town hall?	**till rådhuset?** till rawd-hoos-et
Excuse me, please	**Ursäkta mig** yoo-shek-ta may

Is there . . . near by?	**Finns det . . . i närheten?**
	finss det . . . ee nair-haiten
an art gallery	**ett konstgalleri**
	ett konst-galleree
a bakery	**ett bageri**
	ett bahg-er-ree
a bank	**en bank**
	en bank
a bar	**en bar**
	en bar
a botanical garden	**en botanisk trädgård**
	et bot-ahn-eesk traid-gord
a bus stop	**en busshållplats**
	en booss-holl-platss
a butcher's	**en slaktare**
	en slakta-rer
a café	**ett kafé**
	ett café
a cake shop	**ett konditori**
	ett kondit-oree
a campsite	**en campingplats**
	en kamping-plats
a car park	**en parkeringsplats**
	en park-airings-plats
a currency exchange	**ett växelkontor**
	ett vaik-sel-kontor
a chemist's/drugstore	**ett apotek**
	ett ap-o-taik
a church	**en kyrka**
	en sheer-ka
a cinema/movie theater	**en biograf**
	en bee-oo-graf
a delicatessen	**en delikatessaffär**
	en delee-ka-tess-af-fair
a dentist's	**en tandläkare**
	en tand-laik-arer
a department store	**ett varuhus**
	ett va-roo-hoos
a disco	**ett diskotek**
	ett disko-tek
a doctor's office	**en läkarmottagning**
	en laik-ar-mot-tag-ning

Swedish

Is there . . . near by?	Finns det . . . i närheten?
	finss det . . . ee nair-haiten
a dry cleaner's	**en kemtvätt**
	en shaim-tvet
a fishmonger's	**en fiskaffär**
	en fisk-af-fair
a garage	**en bilverkstad**
	en beel-vairk-stad
a greengrocer's	**en grönsaksaffär**
	en grern-saks-af-fair
a hairdresser	**en hårfrisör**
	en hor-free-ser
a hardware shop	**en järnaffär**
	en yairn-af-fair
a Health and Social Security office	**en försäkringskassa**
	en fer-saik-rings-kas-sa
a hospital	**ett sjukhus**
	ett shook-hoos
a hotel	**ett hotell**
	ett hotell
an ice-cream parlour	**en glassbar**
	en glass-bar
a laundry	**en tvätt**
	en tvet
a museum	**ett museum**
	ett moo-say-um
a night club	**en nattklubb**
	en naht-klubb
a park	**en park**
	en park
a petrol/gasoline station	**en bensinstation**
	en ben-seen-sta-shon
a post box/mailbox	**en brevlåda**
	en braiv-law-da
a restaurant	**en restaurang**
	en resto-rang
a (snack) bar	**en (grill)-bar**
	en (grill)-bar
a sports ground	**en idrottsplats**
	en eedrots-plats
a supermarket	**ett snabbköp**
	ett snahb-kerp

a sweet/candy shop	**en godisaffär**
	en go-dees-af-fair
a swimming pool	**en swimming pool**
	en swimming pool
a telephone (booth)	**en telefon (kiosk)**
	en telefon (shee-osk)
a theater	**en teater**
	en tay-ah-ter
a tobacco shop	**en tobaksaffär**
	en toh-baks-af-fair
a toilet	**en toalett**
	en toh-ah-let
a travel agent's	**en resebyrå**
	en raiser-bee-raw
a youth hostel	**ett vandrarhem**
	ett vand-rar-hem
a zoo	**en djurpark**
	en yoor-park

DIRECTIONS

- Asking where a place is, or if a place is near by, is one thing; making sense of the answer is another.
- Here are some of the most important key directions and replies.

Left	**Vänster**
	venster
Right	**Höger**
	herg-er
Straight on	**Rakt fram**
	rakt fram
There	**Där**
	dair
First left/right	**Första vänster/höger**
	fer-sta ven-ster/herg-er
Second left/right	**Andra vänster/höger**
	andra venster/herg-er
At the crossroads	**I korsningen**
	ee korsning-en
At the traffic lights	**Vid trafikljusen**
	veed tra-feek-yoos-en
At the traffic rotary	**Vid rondellen**
	veed rond-ellen

Swedish

At the level crossing	**Vid järnvägsövergången**
	veed yairn-vaigs-erver-gawng-en
It's near/far	**Det är nära/långt**
	det air naira/lawngt
One kilometre	**En kilometer**
	en kilo-maiter
Two kilometres	**Två kilometer**
	tvaw kilo-maiter
Five minutes . . .	**Fem minuter . . .**
	fem min-ooter . . .
on foot/by car	**till fots/med bil**
	till foots/med beel
Take . . .	**Ta . . .**
	ta . . .
the bus	**bussen**
	boossen
the train	**tåget**
	taw-get
the underground/subway	**tunnelbanan**
	toon-nel-ba-nan
the tram/trolley	**spårvagnen**
	spor-vang-nen

[*For public transport, see p. 306*]

The tourist information office

ESSENTIAL INFORMATION

- There are tourist information offices in over 200 locations throughout Sweden.
- Look out for this sign or the following words:
  TURISTBYRÅ
  TURIST INFORMATION
- Tourist offices offer you free information in the form of maps and brochures.

- You may have to pay for some types of documents, but this is not usual.
- There is usually a hotel booking service, **RUMSFÖRMEDLING** or **HOTELLCENTRAL** attached to the tourist office where you can get help finding overnight accommodation in a hotel, in a private home, or where you can rent a chalet **STUGA**.
- For finding a tourist office, see p. 236.

WHAT TO SAY

Please, have you got . . .	**Har ni . . .**
	har nee . . .
a plan of the town?	**en karta över staden?**
	en k*a*rta *e*rver st*a*-den
a list of hotels?	**en lista på hotell?**
	en l*ee*sta paw hotell
a list of campsites?	**en lista på campingplatser?**
	en l*ee*sta paw k*a*mping-plats-er
a list of restaurants?	**en lista på restauranger?**
	en l*ee*sta paw resto-r*a*ng-er
a list of events?	**en lista på evenemang?**
	en l*ee*sta paw *ev*-en-emang
a leaflet of the town?	**en broschyr om staden?**
	en bro-sh*eer* om st*a*-den
a leaflet on the region?	**en broschyr om regionen?**
	en bro-sh*eer* om reg-ee-*o*nen
a railway/bus timetable?	**en tåg/busstidtabell?**
	en t*a*wg/b*oo*ss-teed-tah-bell
In English, please	**På engelska, tack**
	paw *e*ng-el-ska tak
How much do I owe you?	**Hur mycket är jag skyldig?**
	hoor m*ee*-ket air ya sh*ee*l-dig

LIKELY ANSWERS

You need to understand when the answer is 'No'. You should be able to tell by the assistant's facial expression, tone of voice and gesture; but there are some language clues, such as:

No	**Nej**
	nay
I'm sorry	**Tyvärr**
	tee-v*air*

I don't have a list of hotels	**Jag har ingen lista på hotell** ya har *ing*-en *lee*sta paw ho*tell*
I haven't got any left	**Jag har inga kvar** ya har *ing*a kvar
It's free	**Det är gratis** det air *gra*tis

Accommodation

Hotel

ESSENTIAL INFORMATION

- If you want hotel-type
  accommodation, all the following
  words in capital letters are worth
  looking for on name boards:
  HOTELL
  MOTELL
  PENSIONAT (boarding house)
  VÄRDSHUS (type of inn with a
  limited number of rooms)
  RUM (room to let in a private house,
  bed and breakfast) or look for this sign
- A list including all types of accommodation except **RUM** in the
  town or district can be obtained at the local tourist information
  office [see p. 236].
- Not all hotels and boarding houses provide meals apart from
  breakfast; inquire about this on arrival.
- The cost of the room is per night and not per person. It includes
  service charges, VAT and usually breakfast.
- Almost all hotels provide a substantial Swedish breakfast where
  you help yourself to a wide choice of cereals, yoghurts, eggs,
  cheese and cold meats, bread, jam and fruit juices.
- On arrival you will be asked to complete a registration document
  and the receptionist will want to see your passport.
- It is customary to tip the porter.
- Finding a hotel, [see p. 238].

WHAT TO SAY

I have a reservation	**Jag har beställt**
	ya har be-ste*ll*t
Have you any vacancies, please?	**Har ni några lediga rum?**
	har nee n*o*ra la*i*d-eega room
Can I book a room?	**Kan jag beställa ett rum?**
	kan ya beste*l*-la ett room
It's for . . .	**Det är för . . .**
	det air fer . . .
one person	**en person**
	en per-s*oo*n
two people	**två personer**
[*For numbers, see p. 313*]	tvaw per-s*oo*n-er
It's for . . .	**Det är för . . .**
	det air fer . . .
two nights	**två nätter**
	tvaw n*ai*t-ter
one week	**en vecka**
	en v*ai*ka
two weeks	**två veckor**
	tvaw v*ai*k-or
I would like . . .	**Jag ska be att få . . .**
	ya ska bay aht faw . . .
a room	**ett rum**
	ett room
two rooms	**två rum**
	tvaw room
a room with a single bed	**ett enkelrum**
	ett *e*n-kel-room
a room with two single beds	**ett dubbelrum**
	ett d*oo*b-bel-room
with toilet	**med toalett**
	med toh-ah-l*e*t
with bathroom	**med badrum**
	med b*a*d-room
with shower	**med dusch**
	med doosh
with cot	**med barnsäng**
	med b*a*rn-seng
with balcony	**med balkong**
	med b*a*l-kong

Swedish

I would like . . .
Jag ska be att få . . .
ya ska bay aht faw . . .

full board
helpension
h*ail*-pan-shoon

half board
halvpension
h*a*lv-pan-shoon

bed and breakfast
övernattning med frukost
*e*rver-nattning med fr*oo*-kost

Do you serve meals?
Serverar ni mat?
serv*air*-ar nee mat

At what time is . . .
När serveras . . .
nair serv*air*-as . . .

breakfast?
frukost?
fr*oo*-kost

lunch?
lunch?
lunch

dinner?
middag?
m*i*d-da

How much is it?
Hur mycket kostar det?
hoor m*ee*-ket kostar det

Can I look at the room?
Kan jag få titta på rummet?
kan ya faw t*i*t-ta paw r*oo*m-et

I'd prefer a room . . .
Jag föredrar ett rum . . .
ya f*e*rer-drar ett room . . .

at the front/the back
på framsidan/baksidan
paw fr*a*m-seed-an/b*a*k-seed-an

OK, I'll take it
Tack, jag tar det
tak ya tar det

No thanks, I won't take it
Nej tack, jag tar det inte
nay tak ya tar det *i*nter

The key to number (10), please
Nyckeln till nummer (10), tack
n*ee*k-eln till n*oo*m-mer (t*ee*-oo) tak

Please, may I have . . .
Kan jag få . . .? Tack
kan ya faw . . . tak

a coat hanger?
en klädhängare?
en kl*ai*d-heng-arer

a towel?
en handduk?
en h*a*nd-dook

a glass?
ett glas?
ett glass

some soap?
lite tvål?
l*ee*ter tvawl

an ashtray?	**ett askfat?**
	ett *a*sk-fat
another pillow?	**en kudde till?**
	en k*oo*d-der till
another blanket?	**en filt till?**
	en filt till
Come in!	**Kom in!**
	kom in
One moment, please!	**Ett ögonblick!**
	ett *e*rgon-blick
Please can you . . .	**Kan ni . . .**
	kan nee . . .
do this laundry/dry-cleaning?	**ta hand om min tvätt/kemtvätt?**
	ta hand om min tvet/sh*ai*m-tvet
call me at . . .?	**väcka mig klockan . . .?**
	v*ai*ka may klock-an . . .
help me with my luggage?	**hjälpa mig med bagaget?**
	y*e*lpa may med ba-g*a*-shet
call me a taxi for . . .?	**ringa efter en taxi till . . .?**
	r*i*nga *e*fter en t*a*xi till . . .
The bill, please	**Notan, tack**
	n*o*-tan tak
Is service included?	**Ingår dricks?**
	in-gor dricks
I think it is wrong	**Jag tror att den är fel**
	ya troor aht den air fel
May I have a receipt?	**Kan jag få ett kvitto?**
	kan ya faw ett kv*i*t-to
At breakfast	
Some more . . . please	**Lite till . . . tack**
	l*ee*ter till . . . tak
coffee	**kaffe**
	k*a*f-fer
tea	**te**
	tay
bread/butter	**bröd/smör**
	brerd/smer
jam	**marmelad**
	mar-mer-l*a*d
May I have a boiled egg?	**Kan jag få ett kokt ägg?**
	kan ya faw ett kookt egg

LIKELY REACTIONS

Have you an identity document, please?
Har ni ett pass eller någon annan identitetshandling?
har nee ett pass el-ler naw-gon an-an eedent-eetaits-handling

What's your name? [*see p. 233*]
Vad heter ni?
vad haiter nee

Sorry, we're full
Tyvärr, vi har fullt
tee-vair vee har fullt

I haven't any rooms left
Jag har inga rum kvar
ya har inga room kvar

Do you want to have a look?
Vill ni titta på det?
vill nee tit-ta paw det

How many people is it for?
För hur många personer är det?
fer hoor monga per-sooner air det

From (7 o'clock) onwards
Från och med (klockan sju)
frawn ock med (klock-an shoo)

From (midday) onwards
[*For times, see p. 314*]
Från och med (klockan tolv)
frawn ock med (klock-an tolv)

It's (350) crowns
Det blir (350) kronor
det bleer (tray-hoondra-fem-tee-oo) kroon-or

Camping and youth hostelling

ESSENTIAL INFORMATION
Camping

- There are some 600 campsites in Sweden, all approved and classified by the Swedish Tourist Board.
- Look out for this sign
  or the word:
  CAMPINGPLATS
- Be prepared to have to pay:
  per person
  for electricity

for the car (if applicable)
for the tent or camper plot
At some places there are small charges for showers, laundry etc.

- You must provide proof of identity, such as your passport.
- A camping carnet is required at most camping sites. It is issued at the first camping site you visit and is then valid throughout the whole season. Holders of the 'Camping International' card do not need the Swedish camping carnet.
- Sites are classified from one to three stars; a third of Sweden's campsites are three star establishments.
- LPG (liquid petroleum gas) is called **GASOL** in Sweden. Butane gas is not available, only propane gas. When refilling your **LPG** bottle in Sweden, please make sure that propane gas is not filled into a butane gas bottle as this is dangerous. Try to bring enough gas with you or buy an expendable **LPG** bottle for attachment to your camping equipment.
- A number of campsites also have camping cabins for hire. These usually have 2–6 beds, a cooking range and kitchen utensils. You must, however, provide your own bedclothes. It is advisable to book these cabins in advance.

Youth hostels

- Look for the word **VANDRARHEM** or the sign on pages 31 and 138.
- There are some 200 youth hostels run by the Swedish Touring Club in Sweden.
- Membership cards of youth hostel organizations affiliated to the **IYHF** (International Youth Hostel Federation) are valid in all the Swedish youth hostels. Otherwise you have to buy an international guest card (season ticket) or a 'one night' guest card.
- The youth hostels are open to anyone irrespective of age. Rates vary according to standards.
- Bring your own linen (or it can be rented). Sleeping bags are not allowed.
- All youth hostels have facilities for cooking your own meals, a few offer full meal service.
- Cleaning up is compulsory in the bedrooms, washrooms and kitchen.
- Most youth hostels are open only during the summer season (mid June – mid August). You are advised to book in advance.
- The maximum length of stay is 5 nights in each location but this can be extended according to availability.
- For buying or replacing equipment, see p. 264.

Swedish

WHAT TO SAY

Have you any vacancies?	**Har ni något ledigt?**
	har nee naw-got laid-it
It's for . . .	**Det är för . . .**
	det air fer . . .
one adult/person	**en vuxen/person**
	en vooksen/per-soon
two adults/people	**två vuxna/personer**
	tvaw vooks-na/per-sooner
and one child	**och ett barn**
	ock ett barn
and two children	**och två barn**
	ock tvaw barn
It's for . . .	**Det är för . . .**
	det air fer . . .
one night	**en natt**
	en naht
one week	**en vecka**
	en vaika
How much is it . . .	**Hur mycket kostar det . . .**
	hoor mee-ket kostar det . . .
for the tent?	**för tältet?**
	fer telt-et
for the camper?	**för husvagnen?**
	fer hoos-vang-nen
for the car?	**för bilen?**
	fer beelen
for the electricity?	**för elektriciteten?**
	fer elek-tree-see-taiten
per person?	**per person?**
	per per-soon
per day/night?	**per dag/natt?**
	per da/naht
May I look around?	**Kan jag se mig omkring?**
	kan ya say may om-kring
Do you provide anything . . .	**Serverar ni något . . .**
	servair-ar nee naw-got . . .
to eat?	**att äta?**
	aht aita
to drink?	**att dricka?**
	aht dricka

Do you have . . .   **Har ni . . .**
har nee . . .

  a bar?   **en bar?**
en bar

  hot showers?   **dusch med varmt vatten?**
doosh med varmt vat-ten

  a kitchen?   **ett kök?**
ett sherk

  a laundry?   **en tvättinrättning**
en tvet-in-ret-tning

  a restaurant?   **en restaurang?**
en resto-rang

  a shop?   **en butik?**
en boot-eek

  a swimming pool?   **en swimming pool?**
en swimming pool

[*For food shopping, see p. 270,
and for eating and drinking out,
see p. 283*]

Where are . . .   **Var är . . .**
var air . . .

  the wastebaskets?   **soptunnorna?**
soop-toon-or-na

  the showers?   **duscharna?**
doosh-ar-na

  the toilets?   **toaletterna?**
toh-ah-let-ter-na

At what time must one . . .   **När måste man . . .**
nair mos-ter man . . .

  go to bed?   **gå och lägga sig?**
gaw ock leg-ga sig

  get up?   **gå upp?**
gaw oop

Please, have you got . . .   **Har ni . . .**
har nee . . .

  a broom?   **en sopborste?**
en soop-borster

  a corkscrew?   **en korkskruv?**
en kork-skroov

  a drying-up cloth?   **en trasa?**
en tra-sa

  a fork?   **en gaffel?**
en gaffel

Swedish

Please, have you got . . .	**Har ni . . .**
	har nee . . .
a fridge?	**en kyl?**
	en sheel
a frying pan?	**en stekpanna?**
	en staik-pan-na
an iron?	**ett strykjärn?**
	ett streek-yairn
a knife?	**en kniv?**
	en k-neev
a plate?	**en tallrik?**
	en tal-rick
a saucepan?	**en kastrull?**
	en ka-strool
a teaspoon?	**en tesked?**
	en tay-shaid
a can opener?	**en konservöppnare?**
	en kon-sairv-erpna-rer
any liquid detergent?	**något tvättmedel?**
	naw-got tvet-maid-el

Problems

The toilet	**Toaletten**
	toh-ah-let-ten
The shower	**Duschen**
	doosh-en
The razor outlet	**Uttaget för rakapparaten**
	oot-ta-get fèr rak-ap-parah-ten
The light	**Ljuset**
	yoos-et
. . . is not working	**. . . fungerar inte**
	foong-airar inter
My camping gas has run out	**Min gas har tagit slut**
	min gas har ta-geet sloot

LIKELY REACTIONS

Have you an identity document?	**Har ni någon identitets-handling?**
	har nee naw-gon eedent-eetaits-handling
Your membership card, please	**Ert medlemskort, tack**
	airt maid-lems-kort tak

What's your name? [see p. 233]	**Vad heter ni?**
	vad haiter nee
How many people is it for?	**För hur många personer är det?**
	fer hoor monga per-soon-er air det
How many nights is it for?	**För hur många nätter är det?**
	fer hoor monga naiter air det
It's (80) crowns . . .	**Det blir (åttio) kronor . . .**
	det bleer (ot-tee-oo) kroon-or . . .
per day/night	**per dag/natt**
[For numbers, see p. 313]	per da/naht

Rented accommodation: problem solving

ESSENTIAL INFORMATION

- If you are looking for accommodation to rent, look out for:
  STUGA (cottage)
  STUGBY (cottage village)
  VÅNING (flat)
  ATT HYRA (to let)
  RUM (rooms)
- For arranging details of your let, see 'Hotel' p. 242.
- Key words you will need if renting on the spot:
  deposition (deposit)
  deposee-shoon
  nyckel (key)
  nee-kel
- Having arranged your own accommodation and arrived with the key, check the obvious basics that you take for granted at home.
  Electricity: Voltage? Razors and small appliances brought from home may need adjusting. You may need an adaptor.
  Cooker: Don't be surprised to find the grill inside the oven, or no grill at all.
  Toilet: Mains drainage or septic tank? Don't flush disposable diapers or anything else down the toilet if you are on a septic tank.

Swedish

Water: Find the stopcock. Check taps and plugs – they may not operate in the way you are used to. Check how to turn on the hot water.

Windows: Check the method of opening and closing windows and shutters.

Insects: Is an insecticide spray provided? If not, get one locally.

Equipment: See p. 264 for buying or replacing equipment.

- You will probably have an official agent, but be clear in your own mind who to contact in an emergency, even if it is only a neighbour in the first instance.

WHAT TO SAY

My name is . . .	**Mitt namn är . . .** mitt namn air . . .
I'm staying at . . .	**Jag bor på . . .** ya boor paw . . .
They've cut off . . .	**De har stängt av . . .** day har stengt ahv . . .
the electricity	**elektriciteten** elek-tree-see-taiten
the gas	**gasen** gas-en
the water	**vattnet** vat-net
Is there . . . in the area?	**Finns det . . . i närheten?** finss det . . . ee nair-haiten
an electrician	**en elektriker** en elek-tree-ker
a plumber	**en rörmokare** en rer-mok-arer
Where is . . .	**Var är . . .** var air . . .
the fuse box?	**proppskåpet?** prop-skawpet
the tap?	**huvudkranen?** hoov-od-kra-nen
the boiler?	**oljepannan?** ol-yer-pan-nan
Is there . . .	**Finns det . . .** finss det . . .

a septic tank?	**en septisk tank?** en septisk tank
central heating?	**centralvärme?** central-vairmer
The cooker	**Spisen** speesen
The hairdryer	**Hårtorken** hor-tor-ken
The heating	**Värmen** vairmen
The iron	**Strykjärnet** streek-yairnet
The pilot light	**Kontroll-lampan** kon-trol-lampa
The refrigerator	**Kylskåpet** sheel-skawpet
The telephone	**Telefonen** tele-fonen
The toilet	**Toaletten** toh-ah-let-ten
The washing machine	**Tvättmaskinen** tvet-masheenen
. . . is not working	**. . . fungerar inte** . . . fong-airar inter
Where can I get . . .	**Var kan jag få tag på . . .** var kan ya faw tag paw . . .
an adaptor for this?	**en adaptor till den här?** en ah-dap-tor till den hair
a fuse?	**en propp?** en prop
insecticide spray?	**en insektsspray?** en insekts-spray
a light bulb?	**en glödlampa?** en glerd-lampa
The drains	**Rören** rer-ren
The sink	**Diskhon** disk-hoon
The toilet	**Toaletten** toh-ah-let-ten
. . . is blocked	**Det är stopp i . . .** det air stop ee . . .

Swedish

The gas is leaking	**Gasen läcker**
	gas-en laiker
Can you mend it right away?	**Kan ni laga det meddetsamma?**
	kan nee la-ga det med-det-samma
When can you mend it?	**När kan ni laga det?**
	nair kan nee la-ga det
How much do I owe you?	**Hur mycket blir jag skyldig?**
	hoor mee-ket bleer ya sheel-dig
When is the rubbish collected?	**När hämtas soporna?**
	nair hem-tas soop-orna

LIKELY REACTIONS

What's your name?	**Vad heter ni?**
	vad haiter nee
What's your address?	**Vad har ni för adress?**
	vad har nee fer ah-dress
There's a shop . . .	**Det finns en affär . . .**
	det fins en af-fair . . .
in town	**i staden**
	ee sta-den
in the village	**i byn**
	ee been
I can't come . . .	**Jag kan inte komma . . .**
	ya kan inter kom-ma . . .
today	**idag**
	ee-da
this week	**den här veckan**
	den hair vaikan
until Monday	**förrän på måndag**
	fer-ren paw mon-da
I can come . . .	**Jag kan komma . . .**
	ya kan kom-ma . . .
on Tuesday	**på tisdag**
	paw tees-da
when you want	**när ni vill**
	nair nee vill
Every day	**Varje dag**
	var-yer da
Every other day	**Varannan dag**
	var-an-an da
On Wednesdays	**På onsdagar**
	paw oons-dahg-ar

[*For days of the week, see p. 315*]

General shopping

The drugstore/The chemist's

ESSENTIAL INFORMATION

- Look out for the word **APOTEK** or this sign
- Medicines are available only at the *apotek*.
- Toiletries can also be bought at department stores, supermarkets and perfumeries.
- **Apotek** are open weekdays 9.00 a.m. to 6.00 p.m. and Saturdays 9.00 a.m. to 1.00 p.m.

- Try the pharmacist before going to the doctor's as they are usually qualified to treat minor ailments.
- Finding a drugstore, see p. 237.

WHAT TO SAY

I'd like . . .	**Jag ska be att få . . .**
	ya ska bay aht faw . . .
some Alka Seltzer	**lite Alka Seltzer**
	leeter alka seltzer
some antiseptic	**lite antiseptiskt**
	leeter anti-*sep*-tiskt
some aspirin	**lite aspirin**
	leeter aspi-*reen*
some bandage	**lite bandage**
	leeter band-*ash*
some cotton wool	**lite bomull**
	leeter bom-ool
some eye drops	**lite ögondroppar**
	leeter *er*gon-droppar
some inhalant	**lite näsdroppar**
	leeter *nais*-droppar
some insect repellent	**lite myggspray**
	leeter *meeg*-spray
some lip salve/chapstick	**lite läppsalva**
	leeter *lep*-sal-va
some sticking plaster	**lite plåster**
	leeter pl*aws*-ter
some throat lozenges	**lite halstabletter**
	leeter h*a*ls-tab-let-ter
some Vaseline	**lite vaselin**
	leeter-va-ser-*leen*

Swedish

I'd like something for . . .	**Jag ska be att få något för . . .**
	ya ska bay aht faw naw-got fer . . .
bites/stings	**bett**
	bett
burns	**brännsår**
	bren-sor
a cold	**förkylning**
	fer-sheel-ning
constipation	**förstoppning**
	fer-stop-ning
a cough	**hosta**
	hos-ta
diarrhea	**diarré**
	dee-ah-rer
earache	**örsprång**
	er-sprong
flu	**influensa**
	in-floo-en-sa
sore gums	**ömt tandkött**
	ermt tand-shert
sunburn	**solbränna**
	sool-bren-na
travel sickness	**ressjuka**
	rais-shooka
I need . . .	**Jag behöver . . .**
	ya bay-herver . . .
some baby food	**lite barnmat**
	leeter barn-mat
some contraceptives	**lite preventivmedel**
	leeter preven-teev-maidel
a deodorant	**en deoderant**
	en deo-der-rant
some disposable diapers	**lite engångsblöjor**
	leeter en-gongs-bler-yor
some hand cream	**lite handkräm**
	leeter hand-kraim
some lipstick	**lite läppstift**
	leeter lep-stift
some make-up remover	**lite rengöringskräm**
	leeter rain-yer-ings-kraim
some paper tissues	**lite ansiktsservietter**
	leeter an-sikts-servietter

some razor blades	**lite rakblad**
	leeter rak-blad
some safety pins	**lite säkerhetsnålar**
	leeter saiker-haits-naw-la
some sanitary napkins	**lite dambindor**
	leeter dahm-beend-or
some shaving cream	**lite rakkräm**
	leeter rak-kraim
some soap	**lite tvål**
	leeter tvawl
some suntan oil/lotion	**lite sololja/solkräm**
	leeter sool-ol-ya/sool-kraim
some talcum powder	**lite talk**
	leeter talk
some Tampax	**lite Tampax**
	leeter tam-pax
some (soft) toilet paper	**lite (mjukt) toalettpapper**
	leeter (m-yookt) toh-ah-let-pap-per
some toothpaste	**lite tandkräm**
	leeter tand-kraim

[*For other essential expressions, see 'Shop talk', p. 266*]

Holiday items

ESSENTIAL INFORMATION

- Places to shop at and signs to look for:
  BOKHANDEL (bookshop, stationery)
  PAPPERSHANDEL (stationery)
  FOTOHANDEL (films)
  and of course department stores such as:
  DOMUS
  NK
  TEMPO
  ÅHLENS
- In the countryside look out for **HEMSLÖJD**, handicraft centres which sell local crafts.

Swedish

WHAT TO SAY

I'd like . . .	**Jag ska be att få . . .**
	ya ska bay aht faw . . .
a bag	**en väska**
	en *va*iska
a beach ball	**en strandboll**
	en strand-bol
a bucket	**en hink**
	en hink
an English newspaper	**en engelsk tidning**
	en *e*ng-elsk *tee*-ning
some envelopes	**några kuvert**
	n*o*ra koo-v*ai*r
a guide book	**en guidebok**
	en g*ui*de-book
a map (of the area)	**en karta (över området)**
	en k*ar*-ta (*e*rver om-raw-det)
some postcards	**några vykort**
	n*o*ra v*ee*-kort
a spade	**en spade**
	en sp*a*-der
a straw hat	**en stråhatt**
	en str*a*w-hat
some sunglasses	**ett par solglasögon**
	ett par s*oo*l-glas-ergon
an umbrella	**ett paraply**
	ett para-pl*ee*
some writing paper	**lite skrivpapper**
	l*ee*ter skr*ee*v-pap-per
I'd like . . . [*show camera*]	**Jag ska be att få . . .**
	ya ska bay aht faw . . .
a roll of color film	**en färgfilm**
	en f*ai*ry-film
a roll of black and white film	**en svart/vit film**
	en svart/v*ee*t film
for prints	**för papperskopior**
	fer p*a*p-pers-kopee-or
for slides	**för dia**
	fer d*ee*-ah
Please can you . . .	**Kan ni . . .**
	kan nee . . .

develop/print this? **framkalla/kopiera?**
fram-kal-la/kopee-*a*ira

load the camera for me? **sätta in filmen åt mig, tack?**
set-ta in film-en awt may tak

[*For other essential expressions, see 'Shop talk' p. 266*]

The tobacco shop

ESSENTIAL INFORMATION

- Tobacco is sold where you see these signs:
  TOBAK   TOBAKSHANDEL
- To ask if there is one near by, see p. 239.
- Most usual brands of tobacco, cigars and cigarettes may be bought at supermarkets and at **PRESSBYRÅN**, a chain of kiosks which also sell newspapers, magazines, sweets and fruit.

WHAT TO SAY

A pack of cigarettes . . .	**Ett paket cigarretter . . .** ett pa-*kait* cigar*et*-ter . . .
with filters	**med filter** med filter
without filters	**utan filter** *oo*tahn filter
king size	**king size** king size
menthol	**mentol** ment-*ol*
Those up there . . .	**De där uppe . . .** day dair *oo*per . . .
on the right	**till höger** till herg-er
on the left	**till vänster** till venster
These [*point*]	**De här** day hair

Swedish

Have you got . . .	**Har ni . . .** har nee . . .
English cigarettes?	**engelska cigarretter** eng-elska cigaret-ter
rolling tobacco?	**rulltobak?** rool-toh-bak
A packet of pipe tobacco	**Ett paket piptobak** ett pa-kait peep-toh-bak
This one [*point*]	**Den här** den hair
A cigar, please	**En cigarr, tack** en cigar tak
Some cigars, please	**Några cigarrer, tack** nora cigar-rer tak
A box of matches	**En ask tändstickor** en ask tend-stick-or
A packet of pipe cleaners	**Ett paket piprensare** ett pa-kait peep-rensa-rer
A packet of flints [*show lighter*]	**Ett paket stift till tändare** ett pa-kait stift till tenda-rer
Lighter fluid	**Bensin till tändare** ben-seen til tenda-rer
Lighter gas, please	**Gas till tändare, tack** gas till tenda-rer tak

[*For essential expressions, see 'Shop talk', p. 266*]

Buying clothes

ESSENTIAL INFORMATION

- Look for:
  DAMKLÄDER (women's clothes)
  HERRKLÄDER (men's clothes)
  BARNKLÄDER (children's clothes)
  SKOAFFÄR (shoe shop)
- Don't buy without being measured first or without trying things on.
- If you are buying for someone else, take their measurements with you.

WHAT TO SAY

I'd like . . .	**Jag ska be att få . . .**
	ya ska bay aht faw . . .
an anorak/parka	**en anorak**
	en *a*n-no-rak
a belt	**ett bälte**
	ett b*e*ll-ter
a bikini	**en bikini**
	en bik*i*ni
a bra	**en behå**
	en bay-haw
a cap (swimming)	**en badmössa**
	en b*a*d-mers-sa
a cap (skiing)	**en skidmössa**
	en sh*ee*d-mers-sa
a cardigan	**en kofta**
	en k*o*fta
a coat	**en kappa**
	en k*a*p-pa
a dress	**en klänning**
	en kl*e*n-ning
a hat	**en hatt**
	en hat
a jacket	**en jacka**
	en y*a*cka
a jumper	**en jumper**
	en y*oo*mper
a nightgown	**ett nattlinne**
	ett n*a*ht-linner
a pullover	**en tröja**
	en tr*er*-ya
a pair of pajamas	**en pyjamas**
	en pee-y*a*-mas
a raincoat	**en regnrock**
	en r*ai*ng-n-rock
a shirt	**en skjorta**
	en sh*oo*rta
a suit	**en kostym**
	en kos-t*ee*m
a swimsuit	**en baddräkt**
	en b*ah*d-drekt
a T-shirt	**en T-shirt**
	en t*ee*-shirt

Swedish

I'd like a pair of . . .	**Jag ska be att få ett par . . .**
	ya ska bay aht faw ett par . . .
gloves	**handskar**
	hand-skar
socks (short/long)	**sockor (korta/långa)**
	sock-or (korta/longa)
stockings	**strumpor**
	stroom-por
tights	**trikåbyxor**
	trickaw-beek-sor
trousers	**långbyxor**
	long-beek-sor
underpants	**kalsonger**
	kal-song-er
shoes	**skor**
	skoor
canvas shoes	**tygskor**
	teeg-skoor
sandals	**sandaler**
	san-da-ler
beach shoes	**strandskor**
	strand-skoor
smart shoes	**finskor**
	feen-skoor
boots	**stövlar**
	sterv-lar
moccasins	**moccasiner**
	mocca-seener
My size is . . .	**Min storlek är . . .**
[*For numbers see p. 313*]	min stoor-laik air . . .
Can you measure me, please?	**Kan ni se vad jag har för storlek?**
	kan nee say vad ya har fer
	stoorlaik
Can I try it on?	**Kan jag få prova?**
	kan ya faw proova
It's for a present	**Det är en present**
	det air en pres-ent
These are the measurements	**Det här är måtten . . .**
. . . [*show written*]	det hair air mawt-ten . . .
bust/chest	**byst/bröst**
	beest/brerst
collar	**krage**
	krahg-er

hip	**höft**
	herft
leg	**ben**
	bain
waist	**midja**
	meed-ya
Have you something . . .	**Har ni något . . .**
	har nee naw-got . . .
in black?	**i svart?**
	ee svart
in white?	**i vitt?**
	ee veett
in gray?	**i grått?**
	ee grawtt
in blue?	**i blått?**
	ee blawtt
in brown?	**i brunt?**
	ee broont
in pink?	**i rosa?**
	ee rawsa
in green?	**i grönt?**
	ee grernt
in red?	**i rött?**
	ee rert
in yellow?	**i gult?**
	ee goolt
in this color? [*point*]	**i den här färgen?**
	ee den hair fair-yen
in cotton?	**i bomull?**
	ee bom-ool
in denim?	**i denim?**
	ee denim
in leather?	**i läder?**
	ee laider
in nylon	**i nylon?**
	ee neel-awn
in suede?	**i mocka?**
	ee mokka
in wool?	**i ull?**
	ee ool
in this material?	**i det här materialet?**
	ee det hair mat-ree-ah-let

[*For other essential expressions, see 'Shop Talk', p. 266*]

Swedish

Replacing equipment

ESSENTIAL INFORMATION

- Look out for these shops and signs:
  JÄRNHANDEL/JÄRNAFFÄR (hardware)
  ELAFFÄR (electrical shop)
  ELARTIKLAR (electrical goods)
  HUSHÅLLSARTIKLAR (household articles)
  KEMISKA ARTIKLAR (household cleaning materials)
- To ask the way to the shop, see p. 236.
- At a campsite try their shop first.

WHAT TO SAY

Have you got . . . **Har ni . . .**
har nee . . .

an adaptor? **en adaptor?**
[show appliance] en adap-tor
a bottle of propane gas? **en flaska propangas?**
en flaska prop-ahn-gahs
a bottle opener? **en flasköppnare?**
en flask-erpna-rer
a corkscrew? **en korkskruv?**
en kork-skroov
any disinfectant? **något desinficeringsmedel?**
naw-got des-infee-sairings-maidel
any disposable cups? **några engångskoppar?**
nora en-gongs-kop-par
a drying-up cloth? **en trasa?**
en tra-sa
any forks? **några gafflar?**
nora gafflar
a fuse? [show old one] **en propp?**
en prop
insecticide spray? **en insektsspray?**
en insekts-spray
paper kitchen towels? **en hushållspappersrulle?**
en hoos-hols-pap-pers-rooler
any knives? **några knivar?**
nora k-nee-var

a light bulb? [*show old one*]	**en glödlampa?**
	en glerd-*lampa*
a plastic bucket?	**en plasthink?**
	en pl*ast*-hink
a plastic can?	**en plastburk?**
	en pl*ast*-boork
a scouring pad?	**en skurtrasa?**
	en sk*oo*r-tra-sa
a wrench?	**en skruvnyckel?**
	en skr*oo*v-neekel
a sponge?	**en tvättsvamp?**
	en tv*et*-svamp
any string?	**något snöre?**
	n*aw*-got sn*er*-rer
any tent pegs?	**några tältpinnar?**
	n*o*ra t*e*lt-pin-nar
a can opener?	**en konservöppnare?**
	en kon-s*airv*-erpna-rer
a flashlight?	**en ficklampa?**
	en f*ic*k-lampa
any flashlight batteries?	**några ficklampsbatterier?**
	n*o*ra fick-lamps-bat-ter-r*ee*-er
a washing line?	**en tvättlina?**
	en tv*et*-leena
any laundry powder?	**något tvättmedel?**
	n*aw*-got tv*et*-maidel
a scrub brush?	**en diskborste?**
	en d*i*sk-borster
any liquid detergent?	**något diskmedel?**
	n*aw*-got d*i*sk-maidel

[*For other essential expressions, see 'Shop talk', p. 266*]

Shop talk

ESSENTIAL INFORMATION

- Coins: see illustration. The crown is divided into 100 ören.
  Notes: 10, 50, 100, 1000, 10 000 kronor (crowns).
- Know how to say the important weights and measures. You will
  hear **grams**, **kilos** and **hektos** being used in shops and supermarkets. **Ett hekto (1 hg)** = 100 grams.

50 grams	**femtio gram/ett halvt hekto** fem-tee-oo gram/ett halvt hek-to
100 grams	**hundra gram/ett hekto** hoon-dra gram/ett hek-to
200 grams	**tvåhundra gram** tvaw-hoon-dra gram
250 grams	**tvåhundrafemtio gram** tvaw-hoon-dra-fem-tee-oo gram
½ kilo	**ett halvt kilo** ett halvt kilo
1 kilo	**ett kilo** ett kilo
2 kilos	**två kilo** tvaw kilo
½ litre	**en halv liter** en halv lee-tair
1 litre	**en liter** en lee-tair
2 litres [For numbers, see p. 313]	**två liter** tvaw lee-tair

CUSTOMER

I'm just looking	**Jag tittar bara** ya tit-tar ba-ra
Excuse me	**Ursäkta mig** yoo-shek-ta may
How much is that/this?	**Hur mycket kostar den där/den här** hoor mee-ket kostar den dair/den hair
What's that?	**Vad är det?** vad air det

What are those?	**Vad är de här?**
	vad air day hair
Is there a discount?	**Har ni någon rabatt?**
	har nee naw-gon ra-bat
I'd like that, please	**Jag ska be att få det, tack**
	ya ska bay aht faw det tak
Not that	**Inte det**
	inter det
Like that	**Som det**
	som det
That's enough, thank you	**Det räcker, tack**
	det raiker tak
More, please	**Mer, tack**
	mair tak
Less, please	**Mindre, tack**
	min-drer tak
That's fine	**Det är bra**
	det air bra
OK	**OK**
	okay
I won't take it, thank you	**Jag tar det inte, tack**
	ya tar det inter tak
It's not right	**Det är inte rätt**
	det air inter raitt
Have you something . . .	**Har ni något . . .**
	har nee naw-got . . .
better?	**bättre?**
	bet-rer
cheaper?	**billigare?**
	bil-lee-ga-rer
different?	**annorlunda?**
	an-nor-loonda
larger?	**större?**
	ster-rer
smaller?	**mindre?**
	min-drer
At what time do you . . .	**När . . . ni?**
	nair . . . nee
open?	**öppnar**
	erp-nar
close?	**stänger**
	steng-er

Can I have a bag, please	**Kan jag få en påse, tack**
	kan ya faw en pawser tak
Can I have a receipt?	**Kan jag få ett kvitto**
	kan ya faw ett kvit-to
Do you take . . .	**Tar ni . . .**
	tar nee . . .
English/American money?	**engelska/amerikanska pengar**
	eng-el-ska/am-ree-kahn-ska pengar
travelers' checks?	**resecheckar?**
	raiser-checkar
credit cards?	**kreditkort?**
	kred-eet-koort
I'd like . . .	**Jag ska be att få . . .**
	ya ska bay aht faw . . .
one like that	**en sån där**
	en sawn dair

SHOP ASSISTANT

Can I help you?	**Kan jag hjälpa er?**
	kan ya yelpa ehr
What would you like?	**Vad önskar ni?**
	vad ern-skar nee
Will that be all?	**Är det allt?**
	air det allt
Anything else?	**Något annat?**
	naw-got an-nat
Would you like it wrapped?	**Vill ni ha det inslaget?**
	vill nee ha det in-sla-get
Sorry, none left	**Tyvärr, inga kvar**
	tee-vair inga kvar
I haven't got any	**Jag har inga**
	ya har inga
I haven't got any more	**Jag har inga fler**
	ya har inga flair
How many do you want?	**Hur många vill ni ha?**
	hoor monga vill nee ha
How much do you want?	**Hur mycket vill ni ha?**
	hoor mee-ket vill nee ha
Is this enough?	**Räcker det här?**
	raiker det hair

Swedish

Shopping for food

Bread

ESSENTIAL INFORMATION

- Finding a bakery, see p. 237.
- Key words to look for:
  BAGERI (bakery)
  BAGARE (baker)
  BRÖD (bread)
- Supermarkets of any size and general stores nearly always sell bread.
- Opening times are usually 9.00 a.m. to 6.00 p.m. weekdays and 9.00 a.m. to 1.00 or 2.00 p.m. on Saturdays.
- The most characteristic loaves are **limpa**, a type of rye bread, and **hårt bröd**, hard bread.
- Most bread is sold unsliced in bakeries but can sometimes be sliced on request. Supermarkets normally sell both sliced and unsliced bread.

WHAT TO SAY

A loaf (like that)	**(Ett sådant) bröd** (ett sawnt) brerd
A French loaf	**En långfranska** en long-fran-ska
A tin loaf	**Ett formbröd** ett form-brerd
A rye bread loaf	**En limpa** en lim-pa
A wholemeal loaf	**Ett fullkornsbröd** ett full-korns-brerd
A packet of hard bread	**Ett paket hårt bröd** ett pa-kait hort brerd
A packet of pumpernickel	**Ett paket pumpernickel** ett pa-kait poomper-nickel
A bread roll	**En småfranska** en smaw-fran-ska
Two packets of rusks	**Två paket skorpor** tvaw pa-kait skor-por

A bun (plain)	**En vetebulle**
	en v*ai*ter-bool-ler
A bun (spiced with cinnamon)	**En kanelbulle**
	en kan-*ai*l-bool-ler
Wheat bread (spiced with saffron and raisins)	**Ett saffransbröd**
	ett s*a*f-rans-brerd
Wheat bread (spiced with cardamon)	**Ett kardemummabröd**
	ett karder-m*oo*ma-brerd

[*For other essential expressions, see 'Shop talk' p. 266*]

Cakes

ESSENTIAL INFORMATION

● Key words to look for:
  BAGERI (bread and cake shop)
  KONDITORI (cake shop, often with a tea room in the back)
  KAKOR (cakes)
  BAKELSER (pastries)
● To find a cake shop, see p. 237.

WHAT TO SAY

The following are the most common cakes and pastries. Cakes are sold per **hekto** (**1 hekto** = 100 grams, see also p. 266) and pastries are bought per slice or piece.

småkakor	small butter cakes, many different
sm*a*w-ka-kor	types available
pepparkakor	gingerbread
p*e*p-par-ka-kor	
mazarin	'mazarin', small tart with sweet
ma-za-r*ee*n	pastry base and hard sugar topping
chokladbiskvi	almond cake topped with chocolate
shok-l*a*-bee-skvee	cream
sockerkaka	sponge cake
soccer-k*a*-ka	

Swedish

jordgubbstårta
yoord-goobs-torta
prinsesstårta
princess-torta
toscatårta
tosca-torta
wienerbröd
veener-brerd
gräddtårta
graid-torta

strawberry cake

vanilla/cream/marzipan gateau

gateau with caramel glaze

'Danish' pastry

cream gateau

Ice cream and sweets

ESSENTIAL INFORMATION

- Key words to look for:
  GLASS (ice cream)
  GLASSKIOSK (ice cream stand)
  GLASSBAR (ice cream parlour)
  KONDITORI (cake/pastry shop)
  GODIS (sweets)
  GODISAFFÄR (sweet shop)
- Best known ice cream brand-name is: **GB**
- When buying ice cream, specify what price cone or tub you want.
- Prepacked sweets and ice cream are available in general stores, supermarkets and at **PRESSBYRÅN** (see p. 259).

WHAT TO SAY

A cone with . . . ice, please	**En strut med . . . glass, tack** en stroot med . . . glass tak
A waffle/tub with . . . ice, please	**En våffla/bägare med . . . glass, tack** en voff-la/baig-arer med . . . glass tak
banana	**banan** ba-nahn

chocolate	**choklad**
	shok-l*a*
mocha	**mokka**
	m*o*kka
pistachio	**pistasch**
	pist-*ah*sh
strawberry	**jordgubbs**
	yo*o*rd-goobs
vanilla	**vanilj**
	van-*i*l-ee
One (4 crown) cone	**En (fyra kronors) strut**
	en (f*ee*ra kr*oo*n-ors) stroot
Two (5 crown) waffles	**Två (fem kronors) våfflor**
	tvaw (fem kr*oo*n-ors) v*o*ff-lor
A lollipop	**En klubba**
	en kl*oo*b-ba
A packet of . . .	**Ett paket . . .**
	ett pa-k*ai*t . . .
100 grams of . . .	**Hundra gram . . .**
	h*oo*n-dra gram . . .

[*For further details of Swedish weights, see 'Shop talk' p. 266*]

chewing gum	**tuggummi**
	t*oo*g-goom-mee
chocolates	**chokladbitar**
	shok-l*a*-beetar
licorice (sweet/salt)	**lakrits (söt/salt)**
	l*a*k-rits (sert/salt)
mints	**mintkarameller**
	m*i*nt-ka-ra-m*e*l-ler
candies	**karameller**
	ka-ra-m*e*l-ler
toffees	**kola**
	k*aw*la

[*For other essential expressions, see 'Shop talk' p. 266*]

Swedish

Picnic food

ESSENTIAL INFORMATION

- Key words to look for:
  DELIKATESSER (delicatessen)
  MATAFFÄR (supermarket)
- Prepared picnic food can be found in every supermarket. Major supermarkets usually have a special delicatessen counter.

WHAT TO SAY

Two slices of . . .	**Två skivor . . .**
	tvaw sk*ee*vor . . .
roast beef	**rostbiff**
	r*o*st-biff
smoked ham	**rökt skinka**
	r*e*rkt shinka
boiled ham	**kokt skinka**
	k*oo*kt shinka
tongue	**tunga**
	t*oo*nga
salami	**salami**
	sal-l*a*-mee
liver paste	**leverpastej**
	l*ai*ver-pastay
150 grams of . . .	**Hundrafemtio gram . . .**
	h*oo*n-dra fem-tee-oo gram . . .

[*For further details of Swedish weights, see 'Shop talk', p. 266*]

potato salad	**potatissallad**
	po-ta-tis-sal-lad
herring salad	**sillsallad**
	s*i*ll-sal-lad
green salad	**grönsallad**
	gr*er*n-sal-lad
coleslaw	**kålsallad**
	k*aw*l-sal-lad
olives	**oliver**
	ool*ee*-ver

You might also like to try some of these:

lite kaviar	'Swedish caviar' smoked cod roe
leeter kav-yar	
lite löjrom	black roe
leeter ler-y-rom	
en strömming	a type of herring
en strerm-ming	
lite sill	some herring
leeter sill	
lite böckling	some smoked herring
leeter berk-ling	
lite rökt makrill	some smoked mackerel
leeter rerkt mak-rill	
lite sardiner	some sardines
leeter sar-deener	
lite rökt ål	some smoked eel
leeter rerkt awl	
lite rökt lax	some smoked salmon
leeter rerkt laks	
lite rökt renkött	some smoked venison
leeter rerkt rain-shert	
lite köttbullar	some meatballs
leeter shert-bool-lar	
lite västkustsallad	some shrimp/mussel/mushroom salad
leeter vest-koost-sal-lad	
lite kycklingsallad	some chicken salad
leeter sheek-ling-sal-lad	
lite ost-och skinksallad	some cheese and ham salad
leeter oost-ock shink-sal-lad	
Herrgårdsost	semi-hard cheese with a mild to medium strength flavour
herr-gords-oost	
Grevéost	Grevé cheese
graiver-oost	
Västerbottenost	pungent cheese from Northern Sweden
vester-bot-ten-oost	
Sveciaost	Svecia cheese – semi-hard with strong flavour
svay-see-ah-oost	
mjukost	soft white cheese
m-yeek-oost	

Fruit and vegetables

ESSENTIAL INFORMATION

- Key words to look for:
  FRUKT (fruit)
  FRUKTHANDEL (fruit store)
  GRÖNSAKER (vegetables)
  GRÖNSAKSHANDEL (greengrocer)
  [*For further details of Swedish weights, see 'Shop talk'. p. 266*]

WHAT TO SAY

1 kilo (2 lbs) of . . .	**Ett kilo . . .**
	ett kilo . . .
apples	**äpplen**
	*e*pp-len
apricots	**aprikoser**
	apree-*koo*ser
bananas	**bananer**
	ba-*nah*-ner
bilberries	**blåbär**
	bl*aw*-bair
cherries	**körsbär**
	sh*e*rs-bair
cloudberries	**hjortron**
	y*o*rt-ron
grapes (black/white)	**vindruvor (blå/gröna)**
	veen-dr*oo*vor (blaw/gr*e*rna)
oranges	**apelsiner**
	ap-pel-s*ee*ner
peaches	**persikor**
	p*e*r-see-kor
pears	**päron**
	p*ai*r-on
plums	**plommon**
	pl*o*m-mon
raspberries	**hallon**
	h*a*l-lon
strawberries	**jordgubbar**
	y*o*rd-goob-bar
wild strawberries	**smultron**
	sm*oo*lt-ron

A pineapple, please	**En ananas, tack**
	en *a*n-na-nas tak
A grapefruit	**En grapefrukt**
	en gr*a*pe-frookt
A melon	**En melon**
	en mer-l*oo*n
A watermelon	**En vattenmelon**
	en v*a*t-ten-mer-loon
½ kilo of . . .	**Ett halvt kilo . . .**
	ett halvt kilo . . .
artichokes	**kronärtskocka**
	kr*oo*n-airts-kocka
asparagus	**sparris**
	sp*a*r-ris
aubergines	**auberginer**
	*o*ber-shee-ner
beans	**bönor**
	b*e*r-nor
beetroot	**rödbetor**
	r*e*rd-bet-or
Brussels sprouts	**brysselkål**
	br*ee*ssel-kawl
carrots	**morötter**
	mo-r*e*rt-er
green beans	**haricots verts**
	haree-ko-vair
leeks	**purjolök**
	p*e*r-yo-lerk
mushrooms	**svamp**
	svamp
onions	**lök**
	lerk
peas	**ärtor**
	*ai*r-tor
potatoes	**potatis**
	po-t*a*-tis
red cabbage	**rödkål**
	r*e*rd-kawl
spinach	**spenat**
	spay-n*ah*t
tomatoes	**tomater**
	to-m*a*-ter

Swedish

A bunch of . . .	**En knippa . . .**
	en k-nip-pa . . .
parsley	**persilja**
	per-sil-ya
radishes	**rädisor**
	raidee-sor
A head of lettuce	**En vitlök**
	en veet-lerk
cauliflower	**Ett salladshuvud**
	ett sal-lads-hoov-od
cabbage	**Ett blomkålshuvud**
	ett blom-kawls-hoov-od
garlic	**Ett kålhuvud**
	ett kawl-hoov-od
A cucumber	**En gurka**
	en gurka
Like that, please	**Sån där, tack**
	sawn dair tak

Vegetables and fruit which may not be familiar:

kantareller	chanterelles (a type of mushroom –
kan-ta-rel-ler	yellow and funnel-shaped)
murklor	morels (type of mushroom)
murk-lor	

[*For other essential expressions, see 'Shop talk' p. 266*]

Meat

ESSENTIAL INFORMATION

- Key words to look for:
  KÖTT (meat)
  KÖTTAFFÄR (butcher's)
  SLAKTARE (butcher)
- Larger supermarkets usually have special meat departments.
- The diagrams opposite are to help you make sense of labels on counters, windows and supermarket displays, and decide which cut or joint to have.

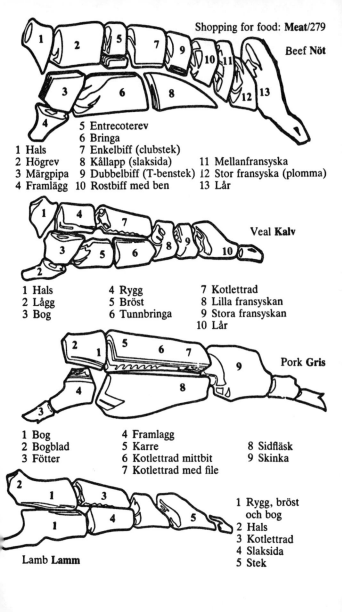

Beef Nöt

1 Hals
2 Högrev
3 Märgpipa
4 Framlägg
5 Entrecoterev
6 Bringa
7 Enkelbiff (clubstek)
8 Kållapp (slaksida)
9 Dubbelbiff (T-benstek)
10 Rostbiff med ben
11 Mellanfransyska
12 Stor fransyska (plomma)
13 Lår

Veal Kalv

1 Hals
2 Lågg
3 Bog
4 Rygg
5 Bröst
6 Tunnbringa
7 Kotlettrad
8 Lilla fransyskan
9 Stora fransyskan
10 Lår

Pork Gris

1 Bog
2 Bogblad
3 Fötter
4 Framlagg
5 Karre
6 Kotlettrad mittbit
7 Kotlettrad med file
8 Sidfläsk
9 Skinka

Lamb Lamm

1 Rygg, bröst och bog
2 Hals
3 Kotlettrad
4 Slaksida
5 Stek

WHAT TO SAY

For a joint, choose the type of meat and then say how many people
it is for:

Some beef, please	**Lite oxkött, tack**
	l*ee*ter *oo*ks-shert tak
Some lamb	**Lite lamm**
	l*ee*ter lam
Some mutton	**Lite fårkött**
	l*ee*ter for-shert
Some pork	**Lite griskött**
	l*ee*ter gr*ee*s-shert
Some veal	**Lite kalvkött**
	l*ee*ter k*a*lv-shert
A joint . . .	**En . . . -stek**
	en . . . staik
for two people	**för två personer**
	fer tvaw per-s*oo*ner
Some steak, please	**Lite biffstek, tack**
	l*ee*ter b*i*ff-staik tak
Some liver	**Lite lever**
	l*ee*ter l*a*iver
Some kidneys	**Lite njure**
	l*ee*ter n-y*oo*rer
Some sausages	**Lite korv**
	l*ee*ter korv
Two veal chops	**Två kalvkotletter**
	tvaw k*a*lv-kot-let-ter
Three pork chops	**Tre fläskkotletter**
	tray fl*a*isk-kot-let-ter
Four mutton chops	**Fyra fårkotletter**
	f*ee*ra for-kot-let-ter
Five lamb chops	**Fem lammkotletter**
	fem l*a*m-kot-let-ter

You may also want:

A chicken	**En kyckling**
	en sh*ee*kling
A hare	**En hare**
	en h*a*-rer
A pheasant	**En fasan**
	en f*a*-san

A tongue   **En tunga**
     en toonga

Other essential expressions [see also p. 266]:

Please can you . . .	**Kan ni . . .**
	kan nee . . .
mince it?	**mala det?**
	ma-la det
slice it?	**skiva det?**
	sheeva det
trim the fat?	**ta bort fettet?**
	ta bort fet-tet

Fish

ESSENTIAL INFORMATION

● The place to ask for: **EN FISKAFFÄR** (a fishmonger's).
● Markets and large supermarkets usually have fresh fish stalls.

WHAT TO SAY

Purchase large fish and small shellfish by weight:

½ kilo of . . .	**Ett halv kilo . . .**
	ett halvt kilo . . .
cod	**torsk**
	torsk
eel	**ål**
	awl
haddock	**kolja**
	kol-ya
herring	**sill**
	sill
pike	**gädda**
	yed-da

½ kilo of . . .	**Ett halv kilo . . .**
	ett halvt kilo . . .
plaice	**rödspätta**
	r*e*rd-spet-ta
turbot	**piggvar**
	p*i*g-var
mussels	**musslor**
	m*oo*s-lor
crayfish	**kräftor**
	kr*e*f-tor
shrimps	**räkor**
	r*ai*kor
One slice of . . .	**En skiva . . .**
	en sh*ee*va . . .
salmon	**lax**
	laks
tuna	**tonfisk**
	t*oo*n-fisk

For some shellfish and pan fish specify the number you want:

A crab, please	**En krabba, tack**
	en kr*a*-ba tak
A lobster	**En hummer**
	en h*oo*m-mer
A whitefish	**En sik**
	en seek
A trout	**En forell**
	en for-r*e*ll
A sole	**En sjötunga**
	en sh*e*r-toonga
A mackerel	**En makrill**
	en m*a*k-rill

Other essential expressions [*see also p. 266*]:

Please can you . . .	**Kan ni . . .**
	kan nee . . .
take the heads off?	**ta bort huvudena?**
	ta bort h*oo*v-od-en-ah
clean them?	**tvätta dem?**
	tv*e*t-ta dem
fillet them?	**filéa dem?**
	feel*ay*-ah dem

Eating and drinking out

Ordering a drink

ESSENTIAL INFORMATION

- The places to ask for:
  EN BAR
  EN RESTAURANG
  ETT KONDITORI
- You must be aged over 18 years to order alcoholic drinks and strong beers **starköl** (alcoholic content above 2.8%).
- Wine, liquor and strong beers are only sold through the state-owned monopoly, **systembolaget**, and the minimum age limit for buying alcoholic beverages is 20 years.
- The most popular drinks in Sweden are the lager and pilsner-type of beers. They come in two strengths – ordinary beer **folköl** (maximum alcohol content of 2.8%) and light beer **lättöl** (maximum alcohol content of 1.8%).
- **Aquavit** is the local liquor, usually drunk chilled.
- When the bill is presented the amount will be inclusive of service and VAT (**moms**). Tipping is therefore optional.
- Heavy fines are levied on motorists driving under the influence of alcohol and other stimulants. Even a very low level of alcohol in the blood (50 mg/100 ml) is sufficient to lead to prosecution. Two cans of beer may be enough to bring you up to this level. Be careful!
- **Konditori** do not serve alcoholic drinks.

WHAT TO SAY

I'll have . . . please	**Jag ska be att få . . . tack**
	ya ska bay aht faw . . . tak
a cup of coffee	**en kopp kaffe**
	en kop k*a*f-fer
a cup of tea	**en kopp te**
	en kop tay
with milk	**med mjölk**
	med m-yerlk
with lemon	**med citron**
	med see-tr*oo*n

Swedish

I'll have . . . please
Jag ska be att få . . . tack
ya ska bay aht faw . . . tak

a glass of milk
ett glas mjölk
ett glass m-yerlk

a cup of hot chocolate
en kopp varm choklad
en kop varm shok-la

a glass of chilled chocolate
ett glas kall choklad
ett glass kall shok-la

a glass of mineral water
ett glas mineralvatten
ett glass min-nair-ahl-vat-ten

a soft drink
en läsk
en lesk

a glass of fruit drink
ett glas saft
ett glass saft

a Coca-Cola
en Coca-Cola
en coca-cola

an orange juice
en apelsinjuice
en ap-pel-seen-yoos

an apple juice
en äppeljuice
en eppel-yoos

a beer
en öl
en erl

one light beer
en lättöl
en let-erl

one ordinary beer
en folköl
en folk-erl

one strong beer
en starköl
en stark-erl

A glass of . . .
Ett glas . . .
ett glass . . .

red wine
rödvin
rerd-veen

white wine
vitt vin
vitt-veen

rosé
rosé
rosé

dry/sweet
torrt/sött
torrt/sert

A bottle of . . .
En flaska . . .
en flas-ka . . .

sparkling wine
mousserande vin
moo-sair-ander veen

champagne	**champagne** cham-p*a*n-y
A whisky . . .	**En whisky . . .** en whisky . . .
with ice	**med is** med ees
with water	**med vatten** med v*a*t-ten
with soda	**med sodavatten** med s*oo*da-v*a*t-ten
A gin . . .	**En gin . . .** en yin . . .
and tonic	**och tonic** ock tonic
with lemon	**med citron** med see-tr*oo*n
A brandy/cognac	**En konjak** en kon-y*a*k

The following are local drinks you may like to try:

brännvin br*e*n-veen	aquavit
besk besk	bitter-tasting aquavit
glögg glerg	sweet, hot Christmas punch

Other essential expressions:

Cheers!	**Skål!** skawl
The bill, please	**Notan, tack** n*oo*-tan tak
How much does that come to?	**Hur mycket blir det?** hoor m*ee*-ket bleer det
Is service included?	**Är dricksen inräknad?** air dr*i*ck-sen *i*n-raik-nad
Where is the toilet, please?	**Var ligger toaletten?** var l*i*g-ger toh-ah-l*e*t-ten

Swedish

Ordering a snack

ESSENTIAL INFORMATION

- Look for any of these places:
  CAFETERIA (snack bar)
  GRILLBAR (grilled meat, fish and sausages)
  GRILLKIOSK (hamburger and sausage stall)
  KORVKIOSK (sausage stall)
  HAMBURGERBAR (hamburger bar)
- For cakes, see p. 270.
- For ice creams, see p. 272.
- For picnic-type snacks, see p. 274.

WHAT TO SAY

I'll have . . . please	**Jag ska be att få . . . tack** ya ska bay aht faw . . . tak
a cheese sandwich	**en ostsmörgås** en *oo*st-smer-gaws
a ham roll	**en småfranska med skinka** en sm*a*w-fran-ska med sh*i*nka
a hamburger	**en hamburgare** en h*a*m-boor-ya-rer
an omelet	**en omelett** en ommel-*et*
with mushrooms	**med svamp** med svamp
with ham	**med skinka** med sh*i*nka
with cheese	**med ost** med *oo*st

These are some other snacks you might like to try:

en räksmörgås en r*ai*k-smer-gaws	a shrimp sandwich
en grillkorv en gr*i*ll-korv	a hot dog
. . . med bröd . . . med brerd	. . . with bread
. . . med pommes frites . . . med pom frit	. . . with french fries

. . . **med potatismos**	. . . with mashed potatoes
. . . med po-*tat*is-moos	
. . . **med senap/ketchup**	. . . with mustard/ketchup
. . . med sain-*ap*/ketchup	
ett stekt ägg med skinka	a fried egg with ham
ett staikt egg med sh*i*nka	
en halstrad råbiff	a grilled beef steak tartare
en h*a*l-strad r*a*w-bif	
en smörgås med leverpastej	a sandwich with liver paste
en sm*e*r-gaws med l*ai*ver-pastay	
en grönsakssoppa	vegetable soup
en gr*e*rn-saks-sop-pa	
en tomatsoppa	tomato soup
en to-m*ah*t-sop-pa	
en ärtsoppa	pea soup
en *ai*rt-sop-pa	

[*For other essential expressions, see 'Ordering a drink', p. 283*]

In a restaurant

ESSENTIAL INFORMATION

- The place to ask for: **EN RESTAURANG** [*see p. 238*].
- You can eat at the following places:
  RESTAURANG
  VÄRDSHUS (an inn)
  HOTELL/MOTELL
  PUB (sometimes serves food)
- A service charge is always added to the bill. Tipping is therefore optional.
- Some 250 restaurants and inns around Sweden offer a 'Tourist Menu' at a fixed price during the period mid-June to mid-September.
- Swedes tend to eat earlier e.g. restaurants serve lunch from 11.30 a.m. and if you're touring and looking for a hotel or evening meal don't leave it much later than 6 p.m.

Swedish

- Alcohol is served from 12 p.m. onwards.
- **Smörgåsbord**, the famous Swedish cold table: offers a variety of dishes from appetizers to cold meats, smoked and pickled fish and usually a hot dish – meatballs or omelette. Followed by fruit salad, cheeses and of course crispbreads.

WHAT TO SAY

May I reserve a table?	**Kan jag få beställa ett bord?**
	kan ya faw bestel-la ett boord
I have reserved a table	**Jag har beställt ett bord**
	ya har bestellt ett boord
A table . . .	**Ett bord . . .**
	ett boord . . .
for one	**för en**
	fer en
for three	**för tre**
	fer tray
The menu, please	**Matsedeln, tack**
	mat-said-eln tak
What's today's set menu?	**Vad är dagens rätt?**
	var air dahg-ens ret
Do you have a menu in English?	**Har ni en matsedel på engelska?**
	har nee en mat-saidel paw eng-el-ska
What's this, please? [point to menu]	**Var är det här?**
	vad air det hair?
The wine list	**Vinlistan**
	veen-listan
A glass of wine	**Ett glas vin**
	ett glass veen
A half-bottle	**En halv flaska**
	en halv flaska
A bottle	**En flaska**
	en flaska
A litre	**En liter**
	en lee-tair
Red/white/rosé/house wine	**Rött/vitt/rosé/husets vin**
	rert/veet/rosé/hoos-ets veen
Some more bread, please	**Lite mera bröd, tack**
	leeter maira brerd tak
Some more wine	**Lite mera vin**
	leeter maira veen

Some salad dressing	**Lite salladsås**
	l*ee*ter s*a*l-lads-saws
With/without garlic	**Med/utan vitlök**
	med/*oo*t-an v*ee*t-lerk
Some water	**Lite vatten**
	l*ee*ter v*a*t-ten
How much does that come to?	**Hur mycket blir det?**
	hoor m*ee*-ker bleer det
Is service included?	**Ingår dricks?**
	*i*n-gor dricks
Waiter!	**Hovmästaren!**
	h*o*v-mais-taren
The bill, please	**Notan, tack**
	n*oo*-tan tak

Key words for courses, as seen on some menus [*Only ask this question, if you want the waiter to remind you of the choice*]

What have you got in the way of . . .	**Vad har ni för . . .**
	vad hahr nee fer . . .
STARTERS?	**FÖRRÄTTER?**
	fer-rait-ter
SOUP?	**SOPPA?**
	s*o*p-pa
EGG DISHES?	**ÄGGRÄTTER?**
	*e*gg-rait-ter
FISH?	**FISK?**
	fisk
MEAT?	**KÖTT?**
	shert
GAME?	**VILT?**
	veelt
FOWL?	**FÅGEL?**
	f*a*wg-el
VEGETABLES?	**GRÖNSAKER?**
	gr*e*rn-sa-ker
CHEESE?	**OST?**
	oost
FRUIT?	**FRUKT?**
	frookt
ICE-CREAM?	**GLASS?**
	glass
DESSERT?	**DESSERT?**
	des-s*ai*r

Swedish

UNDERSTANDING THE MENU

● You will find the names of the principal ingredients of most dishes
  on these pages:

Starters see p. 275

Fruit see p. 276

Meat see p. 278

Cheese see p. 275

Fish see p. 281

Ice-cream see p. 272

Vegetables see p. 277

Dessert see p. 271

● Used together with the following lists of cooking and menu
terms, they should help you decode the menu.

● These cooking and menu terms are for understanding – not
for speaking aloud.

Cooking and menu terms

aladåb	aspic
ångkokt	steamed
aptitlig	savoury
blandad	mixed
blodig	underdone
bräserad	braised
buljong	bouillon
filéad	filleted
förlorat ägg	poached
fylld	stuffed
garnerad	garnished
genomstekt	well-done
glacerad	glazed
gratinerad	au gratin
gravad	cured (salmon and herring)
grillad	grilled
halstrad	grilled
i gelé	jellied
kokad	boiled
kräm	cream
kryddad	spiced
lagom	medium
marinerad	marinated
mosad	mashed
osträtter	cheese dishes
panerad	dressed with eggs and breadcrumbs
rimmad	lightly salted (salmon)

riven	grated
rostad	toasted
rotmos	mashed
rå	raw
rökt	smoked
sallad	salad
saltad	salted
sås	gravy
smörfräst	sautéed
söt	sweet
stekt i gryta	braised
stekt	fried
stuvad	stewed
sufflé	soufflé
sur	sour
tillaga	dressed
ungsbakad	baked
ungstekt	roasted
välstekt	well-done

Further words to help you understand the menu

äggröra	scrambled eggs
älg	elk
and	duck
ansjovis	anchovies
avacado	avocado
bakad potatis	baked potatoes
bönor	beans
bröst	breast
bruna bönor med fläsk	sauce of brown beans served with thick bacon
färs	minced meat
färsk potatis	new potatoes
fasan	pheasant
fisksoppa	fish soup
fläskpannkaka	thick pancake with bacon
fruktsallad	fruit salad
gås	goose
gräddfil	sour cream
gröna ärter	peas
gryta	casserole

Swedish

hare	hare
haricots verts	string beans
kalla rätter	cold dishes
kalops	chunks of beef braised with bouillon, onions, allspice and bay leaves
kalvkött	veal
kokt potatis	boiled potatoes
kotlett	cutlet
kotletter	chops
kroppkakor	potato dumplings (stuffed with mince pork and onions)
köttbullar	meatballs
kroppkakor	potato dumplings (stuffed with mince pork and onions)
kyckling	chicken
pannbiff	mince beef cooked in a casserole or fried
paprika (fylld)	green/red paprika (stuffed)
persilja	parsley
purjolök	leeks
pytt i panna	chunks of meat, sausages, fried potatoes served with a fried egg and pickled beetroot
rådjur	venison
rapphöna	partridge
ren	reindeer
ripa	ptarmigan
ris	rice
rotmos	mashed turnips
saltgurka	pickled gherkins
skaldjurssoppa	seafood soup
stekt potatis	fried potatoes
stekt strömming med potatismos	fried herring with mashed potatoes
surkål	sauerkraut
tonfisk	tuna fish
vinbär: svarta, röda, vita	currants: black, red, white
vinbärsgelé	currant jelly
vispgrädde	whipping cream

Health

ESSENTIAL INFORMATION

- It is preferable to purchase a medical insurance policy through the travel agent, a broker or a motoring organization.
- Take your own first aid kit with you.
- If you fall ill, you will be charged for each visit to a hospital clinic and there is also a prescription charge.
- For finding your own way to a doctor, dentist, or drugstore see p. 237, 239.
- If you need a doctor look for the following words in the telephone directory or on signs:
  SJUKHUS (hospital)
  AKUTMOTTAGNING (emergency ward of a hospital)
  DISTRIKTSLAKARE (district medical officer)
- In case of an emergency, dial 90 000 (applicable for all three emergency services).

What's the matter?

I have a pain . . .	Jag har ont . . .
	ya har oont . . .
in my ankle	i min vrist
	ee min vrist
in my arm	i min arm
	ee min arm
in my back	i min rygg
	ee min reeg
in my belly/tummy	i min buk
	ee min book
in my bowels	i min tarm
	ee min tarm
in my breast/chest	i mitt bröst
	ee mitt brerst

I have a pain . . .   **Jag har ont . . .**
ya har oont . . .

in my ear   **i mitt öra**
ee mitt *er*-ra

in my eyes   **i mina ögon**
ee m*ee*na *er*g-on

in my foot   **i min fot**
ee min foot

in my head   **i mitt huvud**
ee mitt h*oov*-od

in my heel   **i min häl**
ee min hail

in my jaw   **i min käke**
ee min sh*ai*ker

in my leg   **i mitt ben**
ee mitt bain

in my neck   **i min nacke**
ee min n*a*cker

in my penis   **i min penis**
ee min p*e*nis

in my shoulder   **i min axel**
ee min *a*k-sel

in my stomach/abdomen   **i min mage**
ee min m*a*hg-er

in my testicle   **i min testikel**
ee min test-*i*k-el

in my throat   **i min hals**
ee min hals

in my vagina   **i min vagina**
ee min vag-*ee*na

in my wrist   **i min handled**
ee min h*a*nd-laid

I have a pain here [*point*]   **Jag har ont här**
ya har oont hair

I have a toothache   **Jag har tandvärk**
ya har t*a*nd-vairk

I have broken . . .   **Jag har haft sönder . . .**
ya har haft s*er*n-der . . .

my dentures   **min tandprotes**
min t*a*nd-pro-tais

my glasses   **mina glasögon**
m*ee*na glass-ergon

I have lost . . . **Jag har tappat . . .**
ya har t*a*p-pat . . .

  my contact lenses **mina kontaktlinser**
m*ee*na kon-t*a*kt-linser

  a filling **en plomb**
en plomb

My child is ill **Mitt barn är sjukt**
mitt barn air shookt

He/she has pain in his/her . . . **Han/hon har ont i sin . . .**
han/hon har oont ee sin . . .

  ankle [*see list above*] **vrist**
vrist

How bad is it?

I'm ill **Jag är sjuk**
ya air shook

It's serious **Det är allvarligt**
det air al-var-ligt

It's not serious **Det är inte allvarligt**
det air *i*nter *a*l-var-ligt

It hurts (a lot) **Det gör (mycket) ont**
det yer (m*ee*-ket) oont

I've had it for . . . **Jag har haft det i . . .**
ya har haft det ee . . .

  one hour/one day **en timme/en dag**
en t*i*m-mer/en da

It's a . . . **Det är en . . .**
det air en . . .

  sharp pain **skarp smärta**
skarp sm*ai*rta

  dull ache **dov värk**
dov vairk

  nagging pain **molande smärta**
m*oo*l-ander sm*ai*rta

I feel . . . **Jag känner mig . . .**
ya shen-ner may . . .

  dizzy/sick **yr/sjuk**
eer/shook

  weak/feverish **svag/febrig**
svag/f*ay*-brig

Swedish

Already under treatment for something else?

I take . . . regularly [*show*]	**Jag tar regelbundet . . .** ya tar r*ai*g-el-b*oo*n-det . . .
this medicine	**den här medicinen** den hair medi-c*ee*-nen
these pills	**de här pillren** day hair p*i*ll-ren
I have . . .	**Jag har . . .** ya har . . .
a heart condition	**hjärtfel** y*ai*rt-fail
hemorrhoids	**hemorrojder** hemmo-r*oy*-der
rheumatism	**reumatism** ray-ooma-t*i*sm
I think I have . . .	**Jag tror jag har . . .** ya troor ya har . . .
food poisoning	**blivit matförgiftad** bl*ee*v-it m*a*t-fer-yeeft-ad
sunstroke	**fått solsting** fawtt s*oo*l-sting
I'm . . .	**Jag är . . .** ya air . . .
diabetic	**diabetiker** deeab*ai*t-eeker
asthmatic	**astmatiker** ast-m*a*-tik-er
pregnant	**gravid** gr*a*-veed
allergic to penicillin	**allergisk mot penicillin** al-*ai*rg-isk moot penicillin

Other essential expressions

Please can you help?	**Kan ni hjälpa till?** kan nee y*e*lpa til
A doctor, please	**En doktor, tack** en d*o*k-tor tak
A dentist, please	**En tandläkare, tack** en t*a*nd-laik-arer tak
I don't speak Swedish	**Jag talar inte svenska** ya t*a*-lar *i*nter sven-ska

What time does . . . arrive?	När kommer . . .
	nair kom-mer . . .
the doctor	**doktorn**
	doktorn
the dentist	**tandläkaren**
	tand-laik-aren

From the doctor: key sentences to understand

Take this . . .	**Ta de här . . .**
	ta det hair . . .
every day/hour	**varje dag/timme**
	var-yer da/tim-mer
four times a day	**fyra gånger om dagen**
	feera gong-er om dahg-en
Stay in bed	**Stanna i sängen**
	stan-na ee saing-en
Don't travel . . .	**Res inte . . .**
	rais inter . . .
for . . . days/weeks	**på . . . dagar/veckor**
	paw . . . dahg-ar/vaikor
You must go to the hospital	**Du måste till sjukhuset**
	doo mos-ter til shook-hoos-et

Problems: complaints, loss, theft

ESSENTIAL INFORMATION

- Problems with:
  camping facilities, see p. 246.
  household appliances, see p. 264.
  health, see p. 293.
  the car, see p. 303.
- If the worst comes to the worst, find a police station.
  To ask the way, see p. 236.
  Look for: **POLIS**

- If you lose your passport, report the loss to the nearest police station and go to the American embassy.
- In an emergency dial 90 000 if you require assistance from the police, fire brigade or ambulance. If dialling from a phone box, the call is free.

COMPLAINTS

I bought this . . .	**Jag köpte den här . . .** ya sherp-ter den hair . . .
today	**idag** ee-d*a*
yesterday	**igår** ee-g*o*r
on Monday	**i måndags** ee mon-dags
It's no good	**Den är inte bra** den air *i*nter bra
Look	**Titta** t*i*t-ta
Here [*point*]	**Här** hair
Can you . . .	**Kan ni . . .** kan nee . . .
change it?	**byta den?** b*ee*ta den
mend it?	**laga den?** l*a*-ga den
Here's the receipt	**Här är kvittot** hair air kv*i*t-tot
Can I have a refund?	**Kan jag få pengarna tillbaka?** kan ya faw p*e*ng-ar-na t*i*l-ba-ka

LOSS
[*See also 'Theft' below: the lists are interchangeable*]

I have lost . . .	**Jag har tappat . . .** ya har t*a*p-pat
my bag	**min väska** min v*ai*ska
my bracelet	**mitt armband** mitt arm-band

my camera	**min kamera**
	min ka-mera
my car keys	**mina bilnycklar**
	meena beel-neeklar
my car logbook	**mina bilpapper**
	meena beel-pap-per
my driver's license	**mitt körkort**
	mitt sher-kort
my insurance certificate	**mina försäkringshandlingar**
	meena fer-saik-rings-handling-ar

THEFT
[*See also 'Loss' above: the lists are interchangeable*]

Someone has stolen . . .	**Någon har stulit . . .**
	naw-gon har stool-it . . .
my car	**min bil**
	min beel
my money	**mina pengar**
	meena peng-ar
my purse	**min portmonnä**
	min port-mon-nay
my tickets	**mina biljetter**
	meena bil-yet-ter
my travelers' checks	**mina resecheckar**
	meena raiser-checkar
my wallet	**min plånbok**
	min plawn-book
my watch	**min klocka**
	min klocka
my luggage	**mitt bagage**
	mitt ba-gash

LIKELY REACTIONS: key words to understand

Wait	**Vänta**
	venta
When?	**När?**
	nair
Where?	**Var?**
	var
Name?	**Namn?**
	namn

Swedish

Address?	**Adress?**
	ah-dress
I can't help you	**Jag kan inte hjälpa dig**
	ya kan inter yelpa day
Nothing to do with me	**Det har inget med mig att göra**
	det har ing-et med may aht yer-ra

The post office

ESSENTIAL INFORMATION

- To find a post office, see p. 236.
- Key words to look for:
  POST
  POSTKONTOR
  or look out for this sign:
- For stamps look for the word **FRIMÄRKEN** (stamps) or **BREV** (letters).
- Stamps can be obtained at a stationer's or a tobacco shop, provided postcards are also sold there.
- Post offices are open 9 a.m. to 6 p.m. weekdays and 9 a.m. to 1 p.m. on Saturdays.
- Letter boxes are yellow.

WHAT TO SAY

To England, please	**Till England, tack**
	till eng-land tak
[Hand letters, cards or parcels over the counter]	
To Australia	**Til Australien**
	till ah-oost-ra-lee-en
To the United States	**Till Amerika**
[For other countries, see p. 318]	till amair-reeka
Airmail	**Flygpost**
	fleeg-posst
I'd like to send a telegram	**Jag vill skicka ett telegram**
	ya vill shik-ka ett tele-gram

Telephoning

ESSENTIAL INFORMATION

- Public phone boxes, **TELEFONKIOSK**, are painted grey or green, or they are in glass with red frames.
- Instructions on how to use the phone are printed in several languages. Foreign calls can be made from most boxes.
- For a call to the UK dial 00944, followed by the STD code (omitting the first 0) and then the subscriber's number. The code to the USA is 0091.
- For calls to countries which cannot be dialled direct go to a telegraph office, **TELEGRAF STATION** and write down the country, town and number you want on a piece of paper. Add **PERSONLIGT SAMTAL** if you want a person to person call or **MOTTAGAREN BETALAR** if you want to reverse charges.
- Post offices do not have telephone facilities.
- To ask the way to a public telephone, see p. 239.

WHAT TO SAY

I'd like this number . . .	**Jag vill ha det här numret . . .**
[*show number*]	ya vill ha det hair noom-ret . . .
in England	**i England**
	ee eng-land
in Canada	**i Kanada**
[*For other countries, see p. 319*]	ee kan-ah-da
Can you dial it for me, please?	**Kan ni slå numret åt mig?**
	kan nee slaw noom-ret awt may
May I speak to . . .?	**Kan jag få tala med . . .?**
	kan ya faw ta-la med . .
Extension . . .	**Anknytning . . .**
	ank-neet-ning
Do you speak English?	**Talar ni engelska?**
	ta-lar nee eng-el-ska
Thank you, I'll phone back	**Tack, jag ringer tillbaka**
	tak ya ring-er till-ba-ka

LIKELY REACTIONS

That's (4 crowns)	**Det blir (fyra kronor)**
	det bleer (feera kroon-or)

Swedish

Cabin number (3)	**Kiosk nummer (tre)**
[For numbers, see p. 313]	shee-*o*sk n*oo*m-mer tray
Don't hang up	**Häng inte upp**
	haing *i*nter oop
I'm trying to connect you	**Jag försöker anknyta dig**
	ya fer-s*e*rker ank-n*ee*ta day
You're through	**Du är anknuten**
	doo air *a*n-knooten
There's a delay	**Det är en försening**
	det air en fer-s*ai*ning
I'll try again	**Jag försöker igen**
	ya fer-s*e*rker ee-yen

Cashing checks and changing money

ESSENTIAL INFORMATION

- Finding your way to a bank or currency exchange, see p. 237.
- Look for these words or signs on buildings:
  BANK (bank)
  VÄXLINGSKONTOR (currency exchange)
- Banks are open from 9.30 a.m. to 3.00 p.m. on weekdays. In many large cities banks close at 6.00 p.m. All banks are closed on Saturdays and Sundays.
- Currency exchanges at frontier posts and airports are usually open outside regular banking hours.
- Have your passport ready.

WHAT TO SAY

I'd like to cash . . .	**Jag vill växla in . . .**
	ya vill v*ai*k-sla in . . .
this travelers' check	**den här resechecken**
	den hair r*a*iser-checken

these travelers' checks	**de här resecheckarna**
	day hair r*ai*ser-check-arna
this check	**den här checken**
	den hair ch*e*cken
I'd like to change this into crowns	**Jag vill växla det här till kronor**
	ya vill v*ai*k-sla det hair till kr*oo*nor

For excursions into neighboring countries

I'd like to change this . . .	**Jag vill växla de här . . .**
[*show banknotes*]	ya vill v*ai*k-sla day hair . . .
into Danish crowns	**till danska kronor**
	till d*a*n-ska kr*oo*n-or
into Norwegian crowns	**till norska kronor**
	till n*o*r-ska kr*oo*n-or

LIKELY REACTIONS

Passport, please	**Passet, tack**
	p*a*sset tak
Sign here	**Skriv under här**
	skreev *oo*n-der hair
Go to the cash desk	**Gå till kassan**
	gaw till k*a*s-san

Car travel

ESSENTIAL INFORMATION

- Finding a filling station or garage see p. 238.
  Is it a self-service station? Look out for
  TANKA SJÄLV
- Grades of gasoline:
  93 OKTAN (regular)
  96 OKTAN (normal)
  98 OKTAN (super)
  DIESEL OLJA (diesel)

Swedish

- 1 gallon is about 4½ litres (accurate enough up to 6 gallons.)
- In country areas, filling stations usually close at 6 p.m.
- Many filling stations also have automatic pumps. Watch for **NATT-ÖPPET SEDELAUTOMAT.**
- Filling stations are usually able to deal with minor mechanical problems. For major repairs you have to find a garage.
- In Sweden the driver and the passenger in the front seats must wear safety belts, and dipped headlights are obligatory at *all* times when driving.
- Drinking and driving see 'Ordering a drink' p. 283.

WHAT TO SAY
[*For numbers, see p. 313*]

(Nine) litres of . . .	**(Nio) liter . . .** (nee-oo) lee-*ta*ir . . .
(100) crowns of . . .	**(Hundra) kronor . . .** (hoond-ra) kroon-or . . .
Fill it up, please	**Full tank, tack** full tank tak
Will you check . . .	**Kan ni kontrollera . . .** kan nee kon-troll-*ai*ra . . .
the oil?	**oljan?** *oo*l-yan
the battery?	**batteriet?** bat-ter-*ree*-et
the radiator?	**kylarn?** sheel-arn
the tires?	**däcken?** d*ai*ken
I've run out of gasoline	**Jag är utan bensin** ya air *oo*t-an ben-s*ee*n
Can I borrow a can, please?	**Kan jag få låna en bensindunk?** kan ya faw l*aw*na en ben-s*ee*n-doonk
My car has broken down	**Min bil har gått sönder** min beel har got s*er*n-der
Can you help me, please?	**Kan ni hjälpa mig?** kan nee y*e*lpa may?
Do you do repairs?	**Gör ni reparationer?** yer nee ray-pa-ra-sh*oo*ner
I have a puncture	**Jag har punktering** ya har poonk-t*ai*ring

I have a broken windshield	**Jag har trasig vindruta**
	ya har tra*is*-eega v*i*nd-roota
I think the problem is here . . . [*point*]	**Jag tror problemet är här . . .**
	ya troor prob-l*ai*met air hair . . .
Can you . . .	**Kan ni . . .**
	kan nee . . .
repair the fault?	**reparera felet?**
	ray-pa-ra*ira* f*ai*let
come and look?	**komma och titta?**
	kom-ma ock t*i*t-ta
estimate the cost?	**kalkylera kostnaden?**
	kal-keel-*aira* kost-na-den
write it down?	**skriva ner det?**
	skr*ee*va nair det
How long will the repairs take?	**Hur lång tid tar reparationerna?**
	hoor long teed tar ray-pa-ra-shoon-erna
This is my insurance document	**Det här är mitt försäkringsbevis**
	det hair air mitt fer-s*ai*krings-bay-vees

RENTING A CAR

Can I rent a car?	**Kan jag få hyra en bil?**
	kan ya faw h*ee*ra en beel
I need a car . . .	**Jag behöver en bil . . .**
	ya bay-h*e*rver en beel . . .
for five people	**för fem personer**
	fer fem per-s*oo*ner
for a week	**för en vecka**
	fer en v*ai*ka
Can you write down . . .	**Kan ni skriva ner . . .**
	kan nee skr*ee*va nair . . .
the deposit to pay?	**deponeringssumman?**
	dep-on-*ai*rings-soom-man
the charge per kilometre?	**priset per kilometer?**
	pr*ee*s-et per kilo-m*ai*ter
the daily charge?	**priset per dag?**
	pr*ee*s-et per da
the cost of insurance?	**försäkringskostnaden?**
	fer-s*ai*k-rings-kost-naden
Can I leave it in (Malmö)?	**Kan jag lämna den i (Malmö)?**
	kan ya l*ai*m-na den ee m*a*l-mer
What documents do I need?	**Vilka dokument behöver jag?**
	vilka doc*oo*ment bay-h*e*rver ya?

Swedish

LIKELY REACTIONS

I don't do repairs	**Jag gör inte reparationer** ya yer *in*-ter ray-pa-ra-sh*oo*ner
Where is your car?	**Var är din bil?** var air din beel?
What make is it?	**Vilket märke är det?** *vi*lket m*ai*r-ker air det
Come back tomorrow/on Wednesday [*For days of the week, see p. 315*]	**Kom tillbaka imorgon/på onsdag** kom till-b*a*-ka *ee*-morron/paw *oo*ns-da
We don't rent cars	**Vi hyr inte ut bilar** vee heer *i*nter oot b*e*elar
Your driver's license, please	**Ert körkort, tack** airt sh*e*r-kort tak
The mileage is unlimited	**Milsträckan är obegränsad** m*ee*l-straik-an air *oo*bai-grainsad

Public transport

ESSENTIAL INFORMATION

- Finding the way to a bus station, a bus, a trolley stop, the railway station and a taxi stand, see p. 236.
- It is less usual to hail a taxi in the street: go instead to a taxi stand or telephone a taxi station.
- These are the different types of trains, graded according to speed:
  EXPRESSTÅG (stops at a few stations)
  SNÄLLTÅG (stops at many stations)
  LOKALTÅG (stops at all stations)
  PENDELTÅG (stops at all stations)
- There is generally a standard price ticket which entitles you to travel as far as you like. In Stockholm and Gothenburg you may purchase a 1 or 3 day tourist ticket which entitles you to travel as often as you like during the given period.
- Swedish State Railways (**SJ**) offers a 'low-price card' entitling the passenger to a reduction of 45% on all railway journeys within

Sweden (valid for 12 months on all routes except Fridays and Sundays).

- Three family members travelling together pay the low-price fare without having to buy the 'low-price card' and can also travel on Fridays and Sundays.
- Children aged between 6–16 pay half price and under 6 travel free of charge.
- The 'Nordic Railpass' – a 21 day or one month ticket entitles you to unlimited travel in Sweden and the rest of Scandinavia.
- Key words on signs:
  BILJETTER (tickets, ticket office)
  INGÅNG (entrance)
  UTGÅNG (exit)
  FÖRBJUDET (forbidden)
  PERRONG/PLATTFORM (platform)
  VÄNTSAL (waiting room)
  HITTEGODS (left luggage)
  SJ (initials of Swedish Railways)
  SL (initials of Stockholm Local Traffic)
  BUSSHÅLLPLATS (bus stop)
  TIDTABELL (timetable)

WHAT TO SAY

Where does the train for (Malmö) leave from?	**Var går tåget till (Malmö)?** var gor t*a*w-get till (m*a*l-mer)
At what time does the train for (Malmö) leave?	**När går tåget till (Malmö)?** nair gor t*a*w-get till (m*a*l-mer)
At what time does the train arrive in (Malmö)?	**När kommer tåget fram till (Malmö)?** nair k*o*m-mer t*a*w-get fram till (m*a*l-mer)
Is this the train for (Malmö)?	**Är det här tåget till (Malmö)?** air det hair t*a*w-get till (m*a*l-mer)
Where does the bus for (Arlanda) leave from?	**Var går bussen till (Arlanda)?** var gor b*oo*ssen till (*a*r-landa)
Is this the bus for (Arlanda)?	**Är det här bussen till (Arlanda)?** air det hair b*oo*ssen till (*a*r-landa)
Do I have to change?	**Måste jag byta?** mos-ter ya b*ee*-ta
Can I book a seat?	**Kan jag få en platsbiljett?** kan ya faw en pl*a*ts-bill-yet
A single	**En enkel** en *e*n-kel

Swedish

A return	**En tur och retur** en toor ock r*a*y-toor
First class	**Första klass** f*e*rsta klass
Second class	**Andra klass** *a*n-dra klass
One adult	**En vuxen** en v*oo*ksen
Two adults	**Två vuxna** tvaw v*oo*ks-na
and one child	**och ett barn** ock ett barn
and two children	**och två barn** ock tvaw barn
How much is it?	**Hur mycket kostar det?** hoor m*ee*-ket kostar det

LIKELY REACTIONS

Over there	**Där borta** dair borta
Here	**Här** hair
Platform (1)	**Plattform (ett)** pl*a*t-form (ett)
[*For times, see p. 315*] Change at (Helsingborg)	**Byt i (Helsingborg)** beet ee (h*e*l-sing-b*or*y)
This is your stop	**Det här är din station** det hair air din sta-sh*oo*n
There's only first class	**Det finns bara första klass** det finss b*a*-ra f*e*rsta klass
There's a supplement	**Där är ett tillägg** dair air ett t*i*ll-egg

Leisure

ESSENTIAL INFORMATION

- Finding the way to a place of entertainment, see p. 238, 239.
- For times of day, see p. 315.
- No smoking in cinemas, theatres or concert halls, and in some restaurants.
- Cinemas always show films in the original language with Swedish subtitles.
- It is customary to leave one's coat in the cloakroom in theatres and concert halls.

WHAT TO SAY

At what time does . . . open?	**När öppnar . . .** nair *e*rp-nar
the museum	**museet?** moo-say-et
At what time does . . . close?	**När stänger . . .** nair st*e*ng-er . . .
the skating rink	**skridskobanan?** skr*ee*-skoo-ban-an
At what time does . . . start?	**När börjar . . .** nair ber-yar . . .
the cabaret	**kabarén?** ca-ba-r*ai*n
the concert	**konserten?** kon-s*ai*rt-en
the film	**filmen?** f*i*lm-en
the match	**matchen?** m*a*tch-en
the play	**pjäsen?** pee-*ai*s-en
the race	**tävlingen?** t*ai*v-ling-en
How much is it . . .	**Hur mycket kostar det . . .** hoor m*ee*-ket k*o*star det
for an adult/child?	**för en vuxen?/ett barn?** fer en v*oo*ksen/ett barn

Stalls/dress circle	**Parkett/första raden**
[*State price, if there's a choice*]	par-kett/fersta ra-den
Do you have . . .	**Har ni . . .**
	har nee . . .
a program?	**ett program?**
	ett pro-gram
a guidebook?	**en guidebok?**
	en guide-book
I would like a lesson in . . .	**Jag skulle vilja ha en lektion i . . .**
	ya skool-ler vil-ya ha en laik-shoon ee . . .
skating	**skridskoåkning**
	skree-skoo-awk-ning
waterskiing	**vattenskidor**
	vat-ten-sheedor
sailing	**segling**
	saigling
Can I rent . . .	**Kan jag få hyra . . .**
	kan ya faw heera . . .
a boat?	**en båt?**
	en bawt
a fishing rod?	**ett metspö?**
	ett mait-sper
a windsurfing board?	**en vindsurfingbräda?**
	en veend-surfing-braida
a pair of skis?	**ett par skidor?**
	ett par sheedor
the necessary equipment?	**nödvändig utrustning?**
	nerd-vain-dig oot-roost-ning
How much is it . . .	**Hur mycket kostar det . . .**
	hoor mew-ker kostar det . . .
per day/per hour?	**per dag/per timme?**
	per da/per tim-mer
Do I need a license?	**Behöver jag licens?**
	bay-herver ya lee-sence

Asking if things are allowed

ESSENTIAL INFORMATION

- May one smoke here?
  May we smoke here?
  May I smoke here?   **Kan man röka här?**
  Can one smoke here?   kan man rerka hair
  Can we smoke here?
  Can I smoke here?
- All these English variations can be expressed in one way in Swedish. To save space, only the first English version (May one . . .?) is shown below.

WHAT TO SAY

Excuse me, please	**Ursäkta mig** yoo-shek-ta may
May one . . .	**Kan man . . .** kan man . . .
camp here?	**campa här?** kampa hair
come in?	**komma in?** kom-ma in
dance here?	**dansa här?** dan-sa hair
fish here?	**fiska här?** fiska hair
get a drink here?	**få en drink här?** faw en drink hair
get out this way?	**komma ut den här vägen?** kom-ma oot den hair vaig-en
leave one's things here?	**lämna sina saker här?** laim-na seena sak-er hair
look around?	**se sig omkring?** say sig om-kring
park here?	**parkera här?** park-aira hair
picnic here?	**ha picnic här?** ha picnic hair

Swedish

sit here?	**sitta här?** si*t*-ta hair
smoke here?	**röka här?** re*r*ka hair
swim here?	**simma här?** si*m*-ma hair
telephone here?	**ringa här?** ri*n*ga hair
wait here?	**vänta här?** ve*n*ta hair

LIKELY REACTIONS

Yes, certainly	**Ja, visst** ya veesst
Help yourself	**Var så god** var saw goo
I think so	**Jag tror det** ya troor det
Of course	**Naturligtvis** na-*toor*-lit-vees
Yes, but be careful	**Ja, men var försiktig** ya men var fer-si*k*-tig
No, certainly not	**Nej, naturligtvis inte** nay na-*toor*-lit-vees *i*nter
I don't think so	**Jag tror inte det** ya troor *i*nter det
Not normally	**Normalt inte** nor-m*a*lt *i*nter
Sorry	**Tyvärr** tee-v*a*ir

Reference

NUMBERS
Cardinal numbers

0	**noll**	noll
1	**ett**	ett
2	**två**	tvaw
3	**tre**	tray
4	**fyra**	f*ee*ra
5	**fem**	fem
6	**sex**	sex
7	**sju**	shoo
8	**åtta**	*o*t-ta
9	**nio**	n*ee*-oo
10	**tio**	t*ee*-oo
11	**elva**	*e*ll-va
12	**tolv**	tollv
13	**tretton**	tret-ton
14	**fjorton**	f-yor-ton
15	**femton**	fem-ton
16	**sexton**	s*e*x-ton
17	**sjutton**	sh*oo*-ton
18	**arton**	*a*r-ton
19	**nitton**	n*i*t-ton
20	**tjugo**	choo-go
21	**tjugoett**	choo-go-*e*tt
22	**tjugotvå**	choo-go-tv*aw*
23	**tjugotre**	choo-go-tr*ay*
24	**tjugofyra**	choo-go-f*ee*ra
25	**tjugofem**	choo-go-fem
26	**tjugosex**	choo-go-s*e*x
27	**tjugosju**	choo-go-sh*oo*
28	**tjugoåtta**	choo-go-*o*t-ta
29	**tjugonio**	choo-go-n*ee*-oo
30	**trettio**	tray-t*ee*-oo
31	**trettioett**	tray-tee-*e*tt
35	**trettiofem**	tray-tee-fem
40	**fyrtio**	fer-tee-oo
41	**fyrtioett**	fer-tee-*e*tt
50	**femtio**	fem-tee-oo

51	**femtioett**	fem-tee-*ett*
60	**sextio**	s*e*x-tee-oo
70	**sjuttio**	sh*oo*-tee-oo
80	**åttio**	*o*t-tee-oo
81	**åttioett**	ot-tee-*ett*
90	**nittio**	n*i*t-tee-oo
95	**nittiofem**	nit-tee-*fem*
100	**hundra**	h*oo*n-dra
101	**hundraett**	hoon-dra-*ett*
102	**hundratvå**	hoon-dra-tv*aw*
125	**hundratjugofem**	hoon-dra-choo-go-f*em*
150	**hundrafemtio**	hoon-dra-fem-tee-oo
175	**hundrasjuttiofem**	hoon-dra-shoo-tee-f*em*
200	**tvåhundra**	tv*aw*-hoon-dra
300	**trehundra**	tr*ay*-hoon-dra
400	**fyrahundra**	f*ee*ra-hoon-dra
500	**femhundra**	f*em*-hoon-dra
1000	**tusen**	t*oo*-sen
1100	**elvahundra**	*e*ll-va-hoon-dra
3000	**tretusen**	tr*ay*-too-sen
5000	**femtusen**	f*em*-too-sen
10,000	**tiotusen**	t*ee*-oo-too-sen
100,000	**hundratusen**	h*oo*n-dra-too-sen
1,000,000	**en miljon**	en mill-y*oo*n

Ordinal numbers

1st	**första**	f*e*rsta
2nd	**andra**	*a*n-dra
3rd	**tredje**	tr*ai*d-yer
4th	**fjärde**	f-y*ai*r-der
5th	**femte**	f*em*-ter
6th	**sjätte**	sh*e*t-ter
7th	**sjunde**	sh*oo*n-der
8th	**åttonde**	*o*t-ton-der
9th	**nionde**	n*ee*-on-der
10th	**tionde**	t*ee*-on-der
11th	**elfte**	*e*llf-ter
12th	**tolvte**	t*o*llv-ter

TIME

What time is it?	**Vad är klockan?**
	vad air klock-an
It's . . .	**Den är . . .**
	den air . . .
one o'clock	**ett**
	ett
two o'clock	**två**
	tvaw
three o'clock	**tre**
	tray
noon	**tolv på dagen**
	tollv paw dahg-en
midnight	**tolv på natten** or **midnatt**
	tollv paw naht-en meed-naht
It's . . .	**Den är . . .**
	den air . . .
five past five	**fem över fem**
	fem erver fem
ten to six	**tio i sex**
	tee-oo ee sex
twenty to six	**tjugo i sex**
	choo-go ee sex
five past five	**fem över fem**
	fem erver fem
twenty past five	**tjugo över fem**
	choo-go erver fem
At what time . . . (does the train leave)?	**När . . . (går tåget)?**
	nair . . . (gor taw-get)
At . . .	**Klockan . . .**
	klock-an . . .
13.00	**tretton nollnoll**
	tret-ton noll-noll
18.25	**arton och tjugofem**
	ar-ton ock choo-go-fem
23.50	**tjugotre och femtio**
	choo-go-tray ock fem-tee-oo

DAYS

Monday	**måndag** mon-da
Tuesday	**tisdag** tees-da
Wednesday	**onsdag** oons-da
Thursday	**torsdag** toors-da
Friday	**fredag** fray-da
Saturday	**lördag** ler-da
Sunday	**söndag** sern-da
last Monday	**förra måndagen** fer-ra mon-dahg-en
next Tuesday	**nästa tisdag** nais-ta tees-da
on Wednesday	**på onsdag** paw oons-da
until Friday	**till fredag** till fray-da
before Saturday	**före lördag** fer-er ler-da
after Sunday	**efter söndag** efter sern-da
the day before yesterday	**förrgår** fer-gor
two days ago	**för två dagar sedan** fer tvaw da-gar say-dan
yesterday	**igår** ee-gor
yesterday morning	**igår morse** ee-gor morsay
yesterday afternoon	**igår eftermiddag** ee-gor efter-mid-da
last night	**igår kväll** ee-gor kvaill
today	**idag** ee-da

this morning	**i morse** ee m*o*r-ser
this afternoon	**i eftermiddag** ee *e*fter-mid-da
tonight	**ikväll** ee-kv*ai*ll
tomorrow	**imorgon** ee-m*o*rron
tomorrow morning	**i morgon bitti** ee m*o*rron b*i*t-tee
tomorrow afternoon	**i morgon eftermiddag** ee m*o*rron *e*fter-mid-da
tomorrow evening	**i morgon kväll** ee m*o*rron kvaill
the day after tomorrow	**i övermorgon** ee *e*rver-morron

MONTHS AND DATES

January	**januari** yan-noo-*ah*-ree
February	**februari** feb-roo-*ah*-ree
March	**mars** marsh
April	**april** ah-pr*i*ll
May	**maj** my
June	**juni** y*o*onee
July	**juli** y*o*olee
August	**augusti** ah-g*oo*s-tee
September	**september** sept*e*mber
October	**oktober** ock-t*oo*ber
November	**november** nov*e*mber
December	**december** day-c*e*mber

last month	**förra månaden**	
	fer-ra maw-na-den	
this month	**den här månaden**	
	den hair maw-na-den	
next month	**nästa månad**	
	nais-ta maw-nad	
in spring	**på våren**	
	paw voren	
in summer	**på sommaren**	
	paw som-mar-en	
in autumn	**på hösten**	
	paw herst-en	
in winter	**på vintern**	
	paw vin-tern	
this year	**i år**	
	ee or	
last year	**förra året**	
	fer-ra or-et	
next year	**nästa år**	
	nais-ta or	
in 1985	**nittonhundraåttiofem**	
	nit-ton-hoon-dra-ot-tee-fem	
It's the 6th of March	**Det är den sjätte mars**	
	det air den shait-ter marsh	

Public holidays

● Shops, schools and offices are closed on the following dates:

January 1	**Nyårsdagen**	New Year's Day
. . .	**Trettondagen**	Epiphany
. . .	**Långfredagen**	Good Friday
. . .	**Påskdagen**	Easter Day
. . .	**Annandag påsk**	Easter Monday
May 1	**Första maj**	Labour Day
. . .	**Kristi Himmelfärdagen**	Ascension Day
. . .	**Pingstdagen**	Whit Sunday
. . .	**Annandag pingst**	Whit Monday
. . .	**Midsommardagen**	Midsummer's Day
. . .	**Alla helgons dag**	All Saints' Day
December 25	**Juldagen**	Christmas Day
December 26	**Annandag Jul**	Boxing Day

COUNTRIES AND NATIONALITIES
Countries

America	**Amerika**
	am*ai*r-reeka
Australia	**Australien**
	ah-oost-*ra*-lee-en
Austria	**Österrike**
	*e*rster-reeker
Belgium	**Belgien**
	b*e*ll-yen
Britain	**Storbrittanien**
	st*oo*r-brit-tan-ee-en
Canada	**Kanada**
	kan-ah-da
Czechoslovakia	**Tjeckoslovakien**
	checko-slov*a*-kee-en
Denmark	**Danmark**
	dan-mark
East Germany	**Östtyskland**
	*e*rst-teesk-land
Eire/Ireland	**Irland**
	*ee*r-land
England	**England**
	*e*ng-land
Finland	**Finland**
	f*i*n-land
France	**Frankrike**
	fr*a*nk-reeker
Greece	**Grekland**
	gr*ai*k-land
Iceland	**Island**
	*ee*s-land
India	**Indien**
	*i*ndee-en
Italy	**Italien**
	eet*a*-lee-en
Luxembourg	**Luxemburg**
	lux-em-b*oo*ry
The Netherlands	**Nederländerna**
	n*ai*der-lainder-na

New Zealand	**Nya Zeeland**
	nee-ah zailand
Pakistan	**Pakistan**
	pa-kee-stahn
Poland	**Polen**
	po-len
Portugal	**Portugal**
	porto-gal
Scotland	**Skottland**
	skot-land
South Africa	**Sydafrika**
	seed-af-ree-ka
Spain	**Spanien**
	span-yen
Switzerland	**Schweiz**
	shvaitz
Wales	**Wales**
	wales
West Germany	**Västtyskland**
	vest-tesk-land
Yugoslavia	**Jugoslavien**
	yugo-slav-ee-en
Norway	**Norge**
	nor-yer

Nationalities
[*Use the first alternative for men, the second for women*]

American	**amerikan/amerikanska**
	am-ree-kahn/am-ree-kahn-ska
Australian	**australiensare/australianska**
	ah-oost-ra-lee-en-sa-rer/ah-oost-ra-lee-en-see-ska
British	**britt/brittiska**
	britt/brittee-ska
Canadian	**canadensare/canadensiska**
	kan-ah-den-sa-rer/kan-ah-den-see-skah
Danish	**dansk/danska**
	dansk/dan-ska
English	**engelsman/engelska**
	eng-els-man/eng-el-ska

Finnish	**finsk/finska**
	finsk/*fi*n-ska
German	**tysk/tyska**
	teesk/*tee*-ska
Icelander	**isländare/isländska**
	ees-lainda-rer/*ees*-lain-ska
Norwegian	**norsk/norska**
	norsk/*no*r-ska
Scots	**skotte/skottska**
	sk*o*t-ter/sk*o*tt-ska
South African	**sydafrikan/sydafrikanska**
	seed-af-ree-k*a*hn/
	seed-af-ree-k*a*hn-ska
Swedish	**svensk/svenska**
	svensk/sv*e*n-ska
Yugoslavian	**jugoslav/jugoslaviska**
	yugo-sl*a*v/yugo-sl*a*v-ee-ska

Swedish

Do it yourself

Some notes on the language

This section does not deal with 'grammar' as such. The purpose here
is to explain some of the most obvious and elementary nuts and bolts
of the language, based on the principal phrases included in the book.
This information should enable you to produce numerous sentences
of your own making, although you will obviously still be fairly limited
in what you can say.

There is no pronunciation guide in the first part of the section,
partly because it would get in the way of the explanations and partly
because you have to do it yourself at this stage if you are serious –
work out the pronunciation from all the earlier examples in the
book.

THE

All nouns in Swedish belong to one of two genders: common or
neuter, irrespective of whether they refer to living beings or inanimate objects.

the	common	neuter	plural
the address	**adressen**		**adresserna**
the apple		**äpplet**	**äpplena**
the bill	**räkningen**		**räkningarna**
the cup of tea	**koppen te**		**kopparna te**
the glass of beer		**glaset öl**	**glasen öl**
the key	**nyckeln**		**nycklarna**
the luggage		**bagaget**	**bagaget**
the menu	**matsedeln**		**matsedlarna**
the newspaper	**tidningen**		**tidningarna**
the sandwich	**smörgåsen**		**smörgåsarna**
the suitcase	**resväskan**		**resväskorna**
the telephone directory	**telefon- katalogen**		**telefon- katalogerna**
the timetable	**tidtabellen**		**tidtabellerna**

Important things to remember

- There is no way of telling if a noun is common or neuter. You have to learn and remember its gender.
- *The* in Swedish is tagged on to the end of the word so that instead of *the apple* they say *apple the*. The most common endings are **-en** or **-n** after common nouns: **tidningen resväskan, nyckeln**, and **-et** or **-t** after neuter nouns: **äpplet**.
- Does it matter? Not unless you want to make a serious attempt to speak correctly and scratch beneath the surface of the language. You would be understood if you said **tidninget** or even **resväskat‗**, providing your pronunciation was good.
- The most common ending in the definite plural is **-na**, but first you must get the word right in the indefinite plural:
  newspapers **tidningar**
  the newspapers **tidningarna**
  suitcases **resväskor**
  the suitcases **resväskorna**
- For more about the indefinite plural see *A/an*, p. 324.
- In Swedish as in English 'luggage' has no plural.

Practice saying and writing these sentences in Swedish:

Have you got the key?	**Har ni nyckeln?**
Have you got the luggage?	**Har ni . . .?**
Have you got the telephone directory?	
Have you got the menu?	
I'd like the key	**Jag ska be att få nyckeln**
I'd like the luggage	**Jag ska be att få . . .**
I'd like the bill	
I'd like the keys	
Where is the key?	**Var är nyckeln?**
Where is the timetable?	**Var är . . .?**
Where is the address?	
Where is the suitcase?	
Where are the keys?	**Var är nycklarna?**
Where are the sandwiches?	**Var är . . .?**
Where are the apples?	
Where are the suitcases?	
Where is the luggage?	**Var är . . .?**
Where can I get the key?	**Var kan jag få tag på nyckeln?**
Where can I get the address?	**Var kan jag få tag på . . .?**
Where can I get the timetables?	

A/AN

a/an	common	neuter	plural
an address	en adress		adressen
an apple		ett äpple	äpplen
a bill	en räkning		räkningar
a cup of tea	en kopp te		koppar te
a glass of beer		ett glas öl	glas öl
a key	en nyckel		nycklar
a menu	en matsedel		matsedlar
a newspaper	en tidning		tidningar
a sandwich	en smörgås		smörgåsar
a suitcase	en resväska		resväskor
a telephone directory	en telefonkatalog		telefonkataloger
a timetable	en tidtabell		tidtabeller

Important things to remember

- *A* or *an* is **en** before a common noun and **ett** before a neuter singular noun.
- The indefinite plural is formed according to one of the five declensions.

	singular	indefinite plural	definite plural
a suitcase	en resväska	resväskor	resväskorna
a sandwich	en smörgås	smörgåsar	smörgåsarna
an address	en adress	adresser	adresserna
an apple	ett äpple	äpplen	äpplena
a glass	ett glas	glas	glasen

- The plural *some* or *any* is **några** in Swedish. The singular is **någon** (common nouns) or **något** (neuter nouns).

Practice saying and writing these sentences in Swedish:

Have you got a bill?	**Har ni en räkning?**
Have you got a menu?	
I'd like a telephone directory	**Jag ska be att få en . . .**
I'd like some sandwiches	**Jag ska be att få några . . .**

Where can I get some newspapers?	**Var kan jag få tag på några . . .?**
Where can I get a cup of tea?	
Is there a key?	**Finns det en nyckel?**
Is there a timetable?	**Finns det en . . .?**
Is there a telephone directory?	
Is there a menu?	
Are there any keys?	**Finns det några nycklar?**
Are there any newspapers?	**Finns det . . .?**
Are there any sandwiches?	

Now make up more sentences along the same lines. Then try these new phrases:

Jag vill ha . . . (I'll have . . .)
Jag behöver . . . (I need . . .)

I'll have a glass of beer	**Jag vill ha ett glas öl**
I'll have a cup of tea	**Jag vill ha . . .**
I'll have some apples	
I need a cup of tea	**Jag behöver en kopp te**
I need a key	**Jag behöver . . .**
I need some newspapers	**Jag behöver några tidningar**
I need some keys	**Jag behöver . . .**
I need some addresses	
I need some sandwiches	
I need some suitcases	**Jag behöver . . .**

SOME/ANY

In cases where *some* or *any* refer to things that can be counted, **några, någon,** or **något** are used. In cases where *some* refers to a part of a whole thing or an indefinite quantity, the word **lite** can be used.

the bread	**brödet**	**lite bröd**	some bread
the butter	**smöret**	**lite smör**	some butter
the cheese	**osten**	**lite ost**	some cheese
the coffee	**kaffet**	**lite kaffe**	some coffee
the ice cream	**glassen**	**lite glass**	some ice cream
the lemonade	**lemonaden**	**lite lemonad**	some lemonade
the pineapple	**ananasen**	**lite ananas**	some pineapple

Swedish

the sugar	**sockret**	**lite socker**	some sugar
the tea	**tet**	**lite té**	some tea
the water	**vattnet**	**lite vatten**	some water
the wine	**vinet**	**lite vin**	some wine

Practice saying and writing these sentences in Swedish:

Have you got some ice cream? **Har ni lite glass?**
Have you got some pineapple?
I'd like some butter   **Jag ska be att få lite smör**
I'd like some sugar
I'd like some bread
Where can I get some cheese? **Var kan jag få lite ost?**
Where can I get some ice
  cream?
Where can I get some water?
Is there any water?   **Finns det lite vatten?**
Is there any lemonade?
Is there any wine?
I'll have some beer   **Jag vill ha lite öl**
I'll have some tea
I'll have some coffee

THIS AND THAT

The following words can be used when pointing:
(this) **den här** (refers to a common noun)
      det här (refers to a neuter noun)
(that) **den där** (refers to a common noun)
      det där (refers to a neuter noun)

In order to correctly decide whether you should use **den** or **det**, you must first decide on the gender of the noun. However, don't worry too much about it, you will be understood even if you use the wrong one.

If you don't know the Swedish name for an object, just point and say:

Jag ska be att få den där	I'd like that
Jag vill ha den här	I'll have this
Jag behöver det här	I need this

HELPING OTHERS

You can help yourself with phrases such as:

I'd like . . . a sandwich	**Jag ska be att få . . . en smörgås**
Where can I get . . . a cup of tea?	**Var kan jag få . . . en kopp te?**
I'll have . . . a glass of beer	**Jag vill ha . . . ett glas öl**
I need . . . a bill	**Jag behöver . . . en räkning**

If you come across a compatriot having trouble making himself/herself understood, you should be able to speak to the Swedish person on his/her behalf. A pronunciation guide is provided from here on.

He'd like . . .	**Han ska be att få . . .** han ska bay aht faw . . .
She'd like . . .	**Hon ska be att få . . .** hon ska bay aht faw . . .
Where can he get . . .?	**Var kan han få tag på . . .?** var kan han faw tag paw . . .
Where can she get . . .?	**Var kan hon få tag på . . .?** var kan hon faw tag paw . . .
He'll have . . .	**Han vill ha . . .** han vill ha . . .
She'll have . . .	**Hon vill ha . . .** hon vill ha . . .
He needs . . .	**Han behöver . . .** han bay-herver . . .
She needs . . .	**Hon behöver . . .** hon bay-herver . . .

You can also help a couple or a group if they are having difficulties. The Swedish word for *they* is de.

They'd like . . .	**De ska be att få . . .** day ska bay aht faw . . .
Where can they get . . .?	**Var kan de få tag på . . .?** var kan day faw tag paw . . .
They'll have . . .	**De vill ha . . .** day vill ha . . .
They need . . .	**De behöver . . .** day bay-herver

What about the two of you? No problem. The word for *we* is **vi.**

We'd like . . .	**Vi ska be att få . . .** vee ska bay aht faw . . .
Where can we get . . .?	**Var kan vi få tag på . . .?** var kahn vee faw tag paw . . .
We'll have . . .	**Vi vill ha . . .** vee vill ha . . .
We need . . .	**Vi behöver . . .** vee bay-herver . . .

Try writing your own checklist for these four useful phrase-starters, like this:

Jag ska be att få . . .	**Vi vill ha . . .**
Han ska be att få . . .	**De vill ha . . .**
Hon ska be att få . . .	
Var kan jag få tag på . . .	**Var kan vi få tag på . . .**
Var kan han få tag på . . .	**Var kan de få tag på . . .**
Var kan hon få tag på . . .	

MORE PRACTICE

Here are some useful Swedish names of things. See how many different sentences you can make up, using the various points of information given earlier in this section.

		singular	plural
1	ashtray	**askkopp** (c)	**askkoppar**
2	bag	**väska** (c)	**väskor**
3	car	**bil** (c)	**bilar**
4	cigarette	**cigarrett** (c)	**cigaretter**
5	corkscrew	**korkskruv** (c)	**korkskruvar**
6	deckchair	**däckstol** (c)	**däckstolar**
7	drying-up cloth	**trasa** (c)	**trasor**
8	garage (repairs)	**bilverkstad** (c)	**bilverkstäder**
9	grapes	**vindruva** (c)	**vindruvor**
10	ice cream	**glass** (c)	**glassar**
11	melon	**melon** (c)	**meloner**
12	passport	**pass** (n)	**pass**
13	salad (lettuce)	**salladshuvud** (n)	**salladshuvuden**
14	shoe	**sko** (c)	**skor**

15	stamp	**frimärke** (*n*)	**frimärken**
16	station	**station** (*c*)	**stationer**
17	sunglasses	**solglasögon** (*n*)	**solglasögon**
18	telephone	**telefon** (*c*)	**telefoner**
19	ticket	**biljett** (*c*)	**biljetter**

Swedish Index

Conversion tables

Read the center column of these tables from right to left to convert from metric to U.S. measures and from left to right to convert from U.S. to metric, e.g., 5 litres = 10.57 pints; 5 pints = 2.37 litres.

pints		litres
2.11	1	0.47
4.23	2	0.95
6.34	3	1.42
8.46	4	1.89
10.57	5	2.37
12.68	6	2.84
14.80	7	3.31
16.91	8	3.78
19.03	9	4.26

gallons		litres
0.26	1	3.79
0.53	2	7.57
0.79	3	11.36
1.06	4	15.15
1.32	5	18.94
1.58	6	22.72
1.85	7	26.51
2.11	8	30.30
2.38	9	34.08

ounces		grams
0.04	1	28.35
0.07	2	56.70
0.11	3	85.05
0.14	4	113.40
0.18	5	141.75
0.21	6	170.10
0.25	7	198.45
0.28	8	226.80
0.32	9	255.15

pounds		kilos
2.20	1	0.45
4.41	2	0.91
6.61	3	1.36
8.82	4	1.81
11.02	5	2.27
13.23	6	2.72
15.43	7	3.18
17.64	8	3.63
19.84	9	4.08

inches		centimetres
0.39	1	2.54
0.79	2	5.08
1.18	3	7.62
1.58	4	10.16
1.95	5	12.70
2.36	6	15.24
2.76	7	17.78
3.15	8	20.32
3.54	9	22.86

yards		metres
1.09	1	0.91
2.19	2	1.83
3.28	3	2.74
4.37	4	3.66
5.47	5	4.57
6.56	6	5.49
7.66	7	6.40
8.65	8	7.32
9.84	9	8.23

miles		kilometres
0.62	1	1.61
1.24	2	3.22
1.86	3	4.83
2.49	4	6.44
3.11	5	8.05
3.73	6	9.66
4.35	7	11.27
4.97	8	12.87
5.59	9	14.48

A quick way to convert kilometres to miles: divide by 8 and multiply by 5. To convert miles to kilometres: divide by 5 and multiply by 8.

fahrenheit (°F)	centigrade (°C)	lbs/ sq in	k/ sq cm
212°	100° boiling point	18	1.3
100°	38°	20	1.4
98.4°	36.9° body temperature	22	1.5
86°	30°	25	1.7
77°	25°	29	2.0
68°	20°	32	2.3
59°	15°	35	2.5
50°	10°	36	2.5
41°	5°	39	2.7
32°	0° freezing point	40	2.8
14°	−10°	43	3.0
−4°	−20°	45	3.2
		46	3.2
		50	3.5
		60	4.2

To convert °C to °F, divide by 5, multiply by 9 and add 32.
To convert °F to °C, take away 32, divide by 9 and multiply by 5.

CLOTHING SIZES

Remember – always try on clothes before buying.
Clothing sizes are usually unreliable.

women's dresses and suits

Europe	38	40	42	44	46	48
UK	32	34	36	38	40	42
USA	10	12	14	16	18	20

men's suits and coats

Europe	46	48	50	52	54	56
UK and USA	36	38	40	42	44	46

men's shirts

Europe	36	37	38	39	41	42	43
UK and USA	14	14½	15	15½	16	16½	17

socks

Europe	38–39	39–40	40–41	41–42	42–43
UK and USA	9½	10	10½	11	11½

shoes

Europe	34	35½	36½	38	39	41	42	43	44	45
UK	2	3	4	5	6	7	8	9	10	11
USA	3½	4½	5½	6½	7½	8½	9½	10½	11½	12½

FOREIGN LANGUAGE BOOKS

Multilingual
The Insult Dictionary:
  How to Give 'Em Hell in 5 Nasty
  Languages
The Lover's Dictionary:
  How to be Amorous in 5 Delectable
  Languages
Multilingual Phrase Book
Let's Drive Europe Phrasebook
CD-ROM "Languages of the World":
  Multilingual Dictionary Database

Spanish
Vox Spanish and English Dictionaries
NTC's Dictionary of Spanish False Cognates
Nice 'n Easy Spanish Grammar
Spanish Verbs and Essentials of Grammar
Getting Started in Spanish
Spanish à la Cartoon
Guide to Spanish Idioms
Guide to Correspondence in Spanish
The Hispanic Way

French
NTC's New College French and English
  Dictionary
French Verbs and Essentials of Grammar
Real French
Getting Started in French
Guide to French Idioms
Guide to Correspondence in French
French à la Cartoon
Nice 'n Easy French Grammar
NTC's Dictionary of *Faux Amis*
NTC's Dictionary of Canadian French
Au courant: Expressions for Communicating in
  Everyday French

German
Schöffler-Weis German and English Dictionary
Klett German and English Dictionary
Getting Started in German
German Verbs and Essentials of Grammar
Guide to German Idioms
Street-wise German
Nice 'n Easy German Grammar
German à la Cartoon
NTC's Dictionary of German False Cognates

Italian
Zanichelli Super-Mini Italian and English
  Dictionary
Zanichelli New College Italian and English
  Dictionary
Getting Started in Italian
Italian Verbs and Essentials of Grammar

Greek
NTC's New College Greek and English
  Dictionary

Latin
Essentials of Latin Grammar

Hebrew
Everyday Hebrew

Chinese
Easy Chinese Phrasebook and Dictionary

Korean
Korean in Plain English

Polish
The Wiedza Powszechna Compact Polish and
  English Dictionary

Swedish
Swedish Verbs and Essentials of Grammar

Russian
Complete Handbook of Russian Verbs
Essentials of Russian Grammar
Business Russian
Basic Structure Practice in Russian

Japanese
Easy Kana Workbook
Easy Hiragana
Easy Katakana
101 Japanese Idioms
Japanese in Plain English
Everyday Japanese
Japanese for Children
Japanese Cultural Encounters
Nissan's Business Japanese

"Just Enough" Phrase Books
Chinese, Dutch, French, German, Greek,
  Hebrew, Hungarian, Italian, Japanese,
  Portuguese, Russian, Scandinavian,
  Serbo-Croat, Spanish

Audio and Video Language Programs
Just Listen 'n Learn Spanish, French,
  German, Italian, Greek, and Arabic
Just Listen 'n Learn...Spanish,
  French, German PLUS
Conversational...Spanish, French, German,
  Italian, Russian, Greek, Japanese, Thai,
  Portuguese in 7 Days
Practice & Improve Your...Spanish, French,
  Italian, and German
Practice & Improve Your...Spanish, French,
  Italian, and German PLUS
Improve Your...Spanish, French, Italian, and
  German: The P&I Method
VideoPassport French
VideoPassport Spanish
How to Pronounce...Spanish, French,
  German, Italian, Russian, Japanese
  Correctly

PASSPORT BOOKS
a division of *NTC Publishing Group*
Lincolnwood, Illinois USA